No More Tomorrows

No • More • Tomorrows

A Biographical Novel

BY

Alice La Bianca

ENTERTAINMENT, INC.
PUBLISHING DIVISION

ACKNOWLEDGMENTS

FIRST, to my eldest daughter, Cory, who encouraged me to complete the telling of my story when reliving the past became a painful burden. Her editing of my original manuscript was invaluable and any merit the final draft has, must go to her criticism and to her patience for putting up with my persistence.

My second daughter, Louise, further edited and suggested new material that I had overlooked. Her enjoyment of the reading gave me new incentives that encouraged me to publish my first attempt at such an overwhelming task.

To my son, Anthony, for his critique of what my motives were in telling the story at all, exposing myself to the criticism of whoever might read it. I had to search long and hard my reasons for wanting to put in print my personal memories. Giving a man and his family their true identity became the motivating force in my decision to expose my own mistakes and weaknesses.

To my daughter, Maurine, who quietly approved, inspiring me to continue, insisting that I keep the title that had given me motivation in the beginning.

And to my brother, Dana, a far more eloquent writer than I, who insisted in the beginning, when I asked him to write it for me, that I was the only one who could tell the story.

To my beloved sister-in-law, Emma, and her husband, Pete, who filled in the gaps on history of the family and the business.

There are many more who reminded me of events I had long since forgotten—my sister, Edith, and my lifelong friends, Ann and Howard and Roxie.

We are scattered now, I and my children, leaving California and living in remote sections of the country, but we are together in spirit, never forgetting the early, happy years before tragedy struck.

Alice LaBianca
1974-1989

FOR THE LA BIANCAS

AUTHOR'S NOTE

THE events in this story are told as I remember them—honestly, without intent to judge or malign—mostly fact, some fiction. The characters are depicted from my perspective alone. The conclusions are mine and subject to individual interpretation.

A.L.B.

CONTENTS

PHOTOGRAPHS

Page

PHOTOGRAPHS (continued)   Page

PART VII

EPILOGUE

All photographs are from the author's private collection, unless
otherwise stated.

All you I have loved who are no more,
My lovely ladies and gentlemen,
I love you still as I did before,
And I pray we may meet again,
Though I don't know how that may be or where,
In another time and another space,
What name or number we may bear,
Or even what form or face,
But whatever I have for a heart will leap,
And we will turn and know and touch,
For, O my lovelies, love runs deep.
And I have loved you much.

James Dillet Freeman

Printed by permission of the author

No More Tomorrows

PROLOGUE

"Our Father, Who art in Heaven;
Hallowed be Thy name..."

I fought back the tears as Loren sang. I had wanted him to officiate at Cory's wedding, but he had no church except the Senior Citizen's Building on the corner—not as elaborate a place for a wedding as the Newport Beach Presbyterian Church. Cory and John had insisted that he sing, at least, and his heart and soul poured into every note.

"For Thine is the Kingdom,
And the Power, and the Glory;
Forever and ever . . . Amen."

As his voice held on in prayer, my throat filled and I could feel the tears coming. "Leno is here," I told myself. "He wouldn't miss his daughter's wedding."

The bridesmaids were coming down the aisle and I had to stand to face the procession. First came Maurine, Bill's daughter—beautiful, brilliant Maurine. She was serious for her twelve years. Her big, blue eyes and long blonde hair framed under the yellow, frothy hat reminded me of my last doll, as a child, come alive. She looked like her father—an impish smile, restrained, as she walked slowly toward me.

Behind her came Louise, looking all grown up at nearly fifteen. She couldn't hold back her warm, friendly smile. Her hair was long and brown and flowed casually. Her brown eyes were full of excitement. She had a regal air and noble stature, I thought, and I swallowed hard as my throat felt full again.

"I mustn't cry," I told myself, and as the "Wedding March" started and Cory appeared with all her mature beauty, Leno's hand seemed to take mine as he whispered, "That's our little girl."

Cory looked the same as she had when she was two years

1

old—round, elf-like face, big brown eyes, beautiful smile—with an air of anticipation and enthusiasm which permeated everything around her with excitement. As a child, she was like no other, and now as a woman of twenty-two, she was a combination of Italian exuberance and Anglo-Saxon restraint. Her face glowed, her eyes shown; her smile was infectious and her step apprehensive.

She was on Anthony's arm. "Our son—so like you, Leno. Watching him now is like seeing you again at nineteen—all of his thoughts and feelings revealed in his eyes."

My mind wandered... back to August 9, 1969 when my only problem was finding a new place to entertain Bob and June in Newport Beach. I had discovered Mark Davidson, the best jazz pianist I ever heard, playing at the Chef's Inn in Corona del Mar. His renditions of "MacArthur Park", "Sunny", "When Johnny Comes Marching Home Again", and "Autumn Leaves" were incredible. The evening passed quickly as we enjoyed his artistry, but I had to leave before the bar closed or I wouldn't make it to church in the morning.

"Mark, you were great! Thanks for a fantastic evening." Then to Bob as I left, "I'll see you and June tomorrow at Mother's."

Arriving home around midnight, I found Anthony diligently working on his movie, "The Vampire Slayers," setting it to music with the tape recorder. Louise and Maurine were asleep upstairs and I went to bed remembering that I hadn't missed a single Sunday at church for a year, a record for me. I drifted into fitful slumber and awakened when Cory came in around three a.m. I heard the stereo playing loudly downstairs. "Are you going to stay up all night?" I called down to Anthony.

"I've got to get this done," was his only reply.

I relaxed, knowing all the children were safely home again, but my sleep was intermittent and when I awakened at seven a.m., I wondered why I didn't resign as treasurer of Newport Unity Church.

I heard Anthony going to bed and realized he had been up all night. I arose reluctantly and showered and dressed without enthusiasm.

"Praise God that good is everywhere,
Praise to the love we all may share,
The life that thrills in you and me,
Praise to the Truth that sets us free,"

sang the congregation, ending the morning church service. By the time I had exchanged heart-warming conversation with my friends and our minister, Loren Flickinger, I knew why I still came to church. Listening to his sermons and inspirational solos and being with him for even short

2

periods of time, lifted my spirits and gave me renewed faith in whatever it was that life was all about.

As I arrived home to change into more suitable beach attire, Cory was on her way out with John, her current steady beau.

"Aunt Edith called," she said. "She didn't leave a message."

That seemed strange since Edith lived sixty miles away and didn't make long distance phone calls without good reason.

"Maybe something's happened to Pop," I thought sadly. "After all, he is ninety-nine years old." I couldn't face such an unhappy possibility and decided to call her when I got to Mother's.

Anthony had gone swimming with Dirk, Louise had gone sailing with Jan, and I dropped Maurine off at the Orange County Fairgrounds to go horseback riding. I was free to spend the afternoon at Mother's oceanfront home with Bob and June.

When I walked in the door and Mother came toward me, I knew something was wrong. She started to speak and tears filled her eyes as she embraced me lovingly.

"Did something happen to Pop?" I asked.

"No, honey, it's your father. He died in his sleep last night."

Dad was in perfect health and his sixty-eighth birthday was only two days away. I hadn't seen him for a year and when Edith invited me to dinner to celebrate his birthday, I had told her I couldn't make it. I hated to drive to Los Angeles, especially on Sunday, and had suggested they all come to Newport Beach, but Dad didn't want to leave his animals all day.

"I can't believe it," I cried. "What happened?"

Mother continued in a broken voice. "According to Edith May, your dad fell asleep on the couch last night, as usual. When Alice Ruth came out this morning when breakfast was ready and tried to awaken him, he didn't respond. She called the fire department, but they couldn't revive him."

Bob comforted me in his quiet way and I took a walk along the beach, remembering how Dad loved the ocean; how frightened I had been when he carried me into the surf on his shoulders, before I learned to brave it by myself. I had tried for several years to get him to move down to Newport Beach, but when he retired four years ago he stayed in Los Angeles with Alice Ruth, his wife of thirty-nine years, and his dogs and his cats and his pigeons. Now he was gone! Just like that—I would never see him again.

I remembered his saying once, "When my time comes, don't spend any money on a funeral. Just put me in Dana's old army foot locker and dig a hole in the back yard."

"At least, he went quietly with no pain or suffering," I convinced myself. "That's a lot to be thankful for."

As we sat on the patio listening to the roar of the surf and drinking bourbon and Scotch, we mellowed. Relaxing and reminiscing seemed to ease the pain. We called Dana in New York. He would be out for the funeral, but I wished he was with us now.

Dana and I were especially close as children. Time hadn't changed that, although he had been living in New York for several years. Bob was a dear brother, too, and a close friend, but we had different fathers, so he didn't share my loss in exactly the same way.

By the time Bob and June dropped me off around ten o'clock, I was used to the idea of Dad being gone, but every time I thought of him, my eyes filled with tears.

As I entered the house, Cory came running toward me.

"Thank goodness you're home. I just had the strangest phone call. It sounded like Sue, but I couldn't be sure. She said Dad had been shot, then hung up."

"Did you call their house?" I asked in disbelief.

"I called and there was no answer," Cory continued.

"Let's call Emma," I suggested. "It's probably just a crank call."

There was no answer at Emma's house, either. "Why isn't anybody ever home when you need them?" I thought.

Just then, Anthony came in and when we told him what was going on, he suggested we call the Hollywood police station.

By this time, I was trembling, trying to keep a positive attitude, afraid of the worst.

"This is Tony LaBianca," I heard Anthony saying. "Someone just called us to say that my father had been shot. He lives at 3301 Waverly Drive. Can you give me any information?"

Anthony's face turned white as he listened.

"Can you call me as soon as you get the report? My number is area code 714, 645-5823. Thank you." He turned to face me.

"There has been a report of a homicide in that area, but that was all he could tell me. It may be hours before he can let us know."

He turned away and went quickly up the stairs to his room. I was stunned. I put my arms around Cory, who was now crying uncontrollably. The commotion had awakened Louise and Maurine who had come downstairs and now stood there as shocked as I. "It must be a mistake," I said, trying to believe my own words. "Let's all go back to bed and as soon as I hear anything, I'll call you. We may not know anything until morning."

The three girls went into Cory's room and closed the door.

4

I called Loren.

"Alice, I'm so sorry. We can't understand these things, but you must have faith that whatever has happened is all a part of God's perfect plan," I heard him saying.

I thanked him for his thoughts, wondering if I could believe his words if Leno were actually gone. I felt the tears coming as I took down from the closet shelf a box of souvenirs and letters that I hadn't looked at for over twenty years.

August 10, 1945
Straubing, Germany

My darling Alice,

Gee, honey, the war news is so great tonight that it's almost impossible to believe. The Russians have started an offensive in Manchuria and there is talk of a possible Jap surrender in the making. But then I know it's too good to be true. Life just isn't that way. Of late, my life, and probably yours too, has been just one disappointment after another. It's hard for me to believe that all of a sudden, everything we have hoped and prayed for, for so long, will finally come true.

When the war ended over here, I reluctantly adjusted my mind to at least another year of war in the Pacific. I even took it for granted that I might be in the Pacific a great part of the time myself. But now with this spectacular news, I don't know what to expect. If only we knew what the future had in store for us!

If the Japs decide not to quit, and fight on for several more years, we'll just have to keep going on, like we have in the past, until our dreams and hopes are eventually realized.

I've tried hard these past few months to remember your saying that "everything happens for the best," but I also try to be prepared for the worst. That keeps me from being hurt too badly if things don't always turn out just right.

You can't realize how much I wish we could be together again... talking and laughing. Think of me often and love me forever.......

PART I

In the Days of Our Youth

"I am youth, I am joy, I am freedom"
"Peter Pan" by Sir James M. Barrie

1

IN 1939 Benjamin Franklin High School looked like a hospital. All of the old regal buildings were white, and Greek pillars bordered the steps leading up to the auditorium. The two-storied structures were connected by long, covered hallways and sprawled over several acres fringed with green lawn. Nestled in the foothills of Highland Park, a suburb of Los Angeles, California, Franklin was a few short blocks and down the hill from where we lived on North Avenue Fifty-three.

I eagerly awaited my first day at high school, having graduated from Luther Burbank Junior High where I had organized the "Lamb Dab" Sub-Deb Club, the envy of every girl who didn't belong. The Lamb Dabs had acquired their name by scrambling the initials of the six original members. My brother, Dana, and I composed their theme song to the tune of "Deep in a Dream."

THE LAMB DAB SUB-DEB CLUB SONG

Sing:

> Here comes personality, fame and romance,
> Sit up and take notice, boys, here is your chance;
> A club full of fun, when each romance is won,
> We're the Lamb Dab Sub-Deb Club.
> We know the Three D's, a club about town,
> When we get together, it's turned upside down.
> At night it's fun and laughter, until the morning after;
> We're the Lamb Dab Sub-Deb Club.

Speak:

> First comes Berta, the girl that makes them fall;
> Succeeded by Lorraine, whose eyes are on them all;

Next in line is Marianna, the girl with the golden hair;
Followed by Beverly, who has an important air.
Then there is Alice, the girl with the dimpled smile,
Whose pep and personality make your time seem
    worthwhile;
Last, but not least, is Dolores, the one with the
    delicate air;
Now, don't you think each one would make half
    of a perfect pair?

Sing:

We are the characters in our little song,
Take us to heart, boys, but don't get us wrong;
We're all out for fun, with our happiness won,
We're the Lamb Dab Sub-Deb Club.

My junior high school "class prophecy" predicted I was destined for outstanding achievement and I was anxious to get started. The members in our counterpart boys' club, the "Three D's," were one year behind us in school. Our social life at Franklin depended heavily on our finding replacements.

My morning classes weren't too exciting, except for the boy I met in Latin—Bill Waddell. He promptly introduced himself and we became, almost at once, good friends. He was outgoing and full of honest humor. Tall, thin, with a ready smile, he exuded charm to all around him.

His desk was across the aisle from mine, so we became well acquainted in the weeks that followed. Our Latin teacher, Mrs. Griffin, was one of my favorites. I do believe Bill and I were her pets as she seemed to enjoy our playful spirit. She called on members of the class to read the lesson in Latin, allowing them to continue until they made a mistake. Soon Bill and I were competing for length of reading time, which pleased the other members of the class since it saved them the embarrassment of making errors. Of course, we studied together at lunch time and over the telephone in the evening, and that gave us a definite advantage.

Miss Fraser's English class after lunch was quite a different story. Barbara Pierce, who joined the Lamb Dabs after its formation, was blonde, witty, fastidious and a match-maker. She was on the look-out for boyfriends for all of us when she spotted across the room a dark, handsome boy talking to his tall, good-looking, red-haired buddy. Miss Fraser also noticed their chummy discourse and called for silence in the classroom. The dark-haired boy retorted, under his breath, "Talk about the Gestapo!"

Miss Fraser's head snapped and her face became distorted. "Who said that?" she questioned with fire in her eyes.

"I did," he answered boldly.

She frantically searched her attendance records and her head began to shake nervously. She shrieked at him, "What is your name?"

"Lino LaBianca," he announced with pride. "Spelled L I N O, and you say it as in 'Lee-no.'"

All eyes in the room were upon this boy who had the nerve to speak to a teacher with such defiance. He was obviously enjoying her outrage, as a faint grin turned the corners of his small mouth.

"It's just that I believe in free speech," he continued.

At this point, Miss Fraser was so unnerved she dared not allow this confrontation to continue. Our country was on the brink of war with a dictator who challenged the free speech of the world and had marched into Poland only the week before. She wasn't prepared to discuss the merits of the Bill of Rights. She managed to control her voice, but her head was still shaking.

"Please take your books and move to the table at the rear of the room," she said.

Lino grinned and proudly walked to his isolated location where he was to remain for the rest of the semester. The classroom laughed quietly.

He placed his chair in such manner that when I looked up from my table, I gazed directly into his big, beautiful, brown eyes. He immediately stroked his chin, feigned a smile and looked down. But not before our eyes had met.

> June 3, 1945
> Cardiff, Wales

My darling Alice,

Well, hon, the days are beginning to drag already, here in Cardiff. I wish I were back in Germany with the Company, where I would have, at least, a little work to keep me busy.

Last night as I lay in bed, my thoughts drifted back to our first days together. I dread to think how empty my life would have been if I had never met you... I'll never forget how much I looked forward to Miss Fraser's English class (in spite of Fraser) just because you were there. I would look at you from my "special"

11

table in the back of the room, and sometimes I would catch your eyes. I remember it embarrassed me an awful lot, but I loved it...

In the weeks that followed, I learned that Lino was quiet, shy and equipped with a subtle humor. He had a great capacity for getting himself innocently into all kinds of trouble. He and his buddy, Howard Bumpass, made Miss Fraser's dull English class an exciting adventure that I eagerly awaited each day. Howard's friends had nicknamed him "Bumpy." He was a likeable boy with a sardonic sense of humor. He cajoled Lino into situations which were difficult for him to avoid. They were both more mature for their ages than the other boys in school and tried hard to be "suave" and "debonair." They talked about their "Bugatti" and "Duesenberg" and almost had me believing them.

Barbara liked Bumpy, but they never became more than just good friends and both were instrumental in my getting better acquainted with Lino. Barbara had met Lino's sister, Emma, in one of her classes and learned more about Lino from her, which she related to me.

"He's Italian and his father owns the Gateway Markets in Cypress Park. He has two older sisters. Stella has already graduated from Franklin and works in her father's office. I met his other sister, Emma, in my gym class. She's in the B-11."

"It's just as easy to fall for someone who has money," I quipped.

"Lino went to Nightingale Junior High," she continued, warning, "He is also a good friend of Bill Waddell's."

I became envious of Barbara's friendship with Emma and arranged for her to introduce us at lunch. Emma was quite the opposite of Lino and protective of her little brother. They bore a slight resemblance, although Emma's hair was a lighter brown and she didn't have her brother's magnificent, penetrating eyes or restrained personality. She was out-going, talkative, friendly, and laughed a lot; a great gal. I liked her instantly.

She did let me know, however, that Lino was taken. They lived next door to the Ragones who had a daughter, Angie. She had been picked out as Lino's future bride for a long time.

That did it! I decided to plan a Lamb Dab party. It seemed a good time to let Lino know that I was around and definitely interested in him.

I couldn't invite Angie Ragone because her parents didn't allow her to go to parties or out with boys at all. Angie was a beautiful girl, jet black hair and pale blue eyes; sweet, too. I felt sorry for her because she was forbidden to go out with her friends. My parents were divorced and Mother allowed me the freedom of having parties at our house and dates with boys.

"I have faith in your good judgment," Mother had said on my first date at twelve years old. "And I trust you."

She and my Uncle Tom had educated me at an early age as to the problems of dating. "They may not come back a second time, but they'll respect you. That's what is important. Don't ever lose your self-respect," Mother had cautioned. I couldn't understand parents who didn't trust their children and allow them to learn and develop in a normal, healthy way.

We decided to have the party before Christmas vacation. I invited Lino, Bumpy and Bill Waddell. Berta brought Al Foxcroft, her steady beau who had dropped Beverly last summer. Beverly immediately resigned from the Lamb Dabs, our first casualty. Marianna and Dolores invited two new recruits.

The party was a disaster for me. Bill thought I had invited him for myself and wouldn't leave my side all evening. When we paired off for the scavenger hunt, Bill, Lino and Bumpy ended up on my team. Lino made few overtures toward conversation with me and the evening became painful and disappointing. One thing did become apparent, however. Bumpy was very much smitten with Angie and Lino gave him his blessings. That was the highlight of the party as far as I was concerned.

But the year 1939 came to a close with my thoughts turbulent. How could I get a real, honest-to-goodness date with this charming, magnanimous Italian boy, whose quiet shyness had won my heart.

Angie and Lino

Lino gets a pie in the face from
Masi, Bumpy, Roxie and Harry

2

WITH the new year came more frustration. I only saw Lino in my English class, and in spite of my deliberate attempts to be in the places I thought he might be, I seldom had a chance to talk to him.

Our house on North Avenue Fifty-three was an active one. My younger brother, Dana, and I were close in age and camaraderie. We were both sensitive, dramatic and creative. We had been effective in drama in junior high and I was looking forward to his arrival at Franklin in the fall.

Our older sister, Edith May, myself and Dana were the progeny of Jane McCallum Forline and Carl Skolfield. The Skolfields were a proud New England family, dating back to the Mayflower, who had come west in the early 1900s.

The cruel Portland, Maine winters brought the family first to Phoenix, Arizona, where an uninsured fire destroyed their home and all their precious family heirlooms. California beckoned as a land of opportunity and they settled at 4610 South Gramercy Place in the southwest part of Los Angeles when the open countryside was visible as far as the eye could see. We spent much of our childhood and youth in that house with our grandparents, Mildred and George Skolfield, our "Nana" and "Pop."

Our dad was the eldest of five boys, and he and his brothers, Stuart, Tom, Herbert and George, each only one year apart, kept Nana and her mother, Grammy, busy making all of their clothes on the Singer treadle sewing machine that still graced the front bedroom.

Mother had a very different history, albeit an illustrious one. Her mother, May McCallum, died when Mother was only six, making her childhood an unstable one. Her father, Dr. Hamilton Forline, was beside himself with grief, being left with a ten-year-old son, Jack, and three little girls, Katherine, eight, Mother, and three-year-old Marjorie. The children were separated and alternately reared by their father, Grandmother Forline, Grandmother McCallum and Aunt Pearl McCallum.

Mother's father, whom we called "Foxy Grandpa" at his request, traced his ancestry back to Alexander Hamilton. Dr. Forline had been famous in Western Springs, Illinois, having perfected the supra-dural injection method in treatment of spinal cord diseases. He brought his family to California in 1904 to be near May's sister and mother, Pearl and Emily McCallum, who were all that was left of the illustrious McCallums, the first white family to settle in Palm Springs.

Foxy Grandpa was the last of a breed of doctors who cared for their patients on a personal basis, never taking money if they couldn't afford to pay and being at their bedside whenever called. He married a young girl, Elizabeth, fifteen years after May's death, and they had a son, Hamilton. Foxy Grandpa died suddenly, alone, penniless, in 1935 and Mother never got over the grief of losing him.

Elizabeth and Hamilton lived with us when I started to Franklin, sharing expenses and allowing us to have a better house. I don't remember ever living with my father, as he and Mother were divorced by the time I was three.

Mother married Earl Dixon in 1929, having a little girl, Elizabeth Jane, who was now nine years old. Mother's marriage to Mr. Dixon was an unhappy one and ended in divorce after three years. Mother married again in 1935, believing "the third time's a charm"—this time to Robert Taylor, who was a far cry from the movie idol. They had a son, Robert McCallum Taylor, who was now a year and a half old and as cute as a bug's ear.

Edith had moved to Nana's the year before, when living with Robert Taylor became unbearable. He had since been asked by Mother to leave. So, there we were, renting a big, old, sturdy house with stone pillars framing the large front porch: Mother, myself and Dana, little Jane and Bobbie, Elizabeth and Hamilton.

Most of the household chores and caring for Bobbie fell on my shoulders as Mother was in delicate health. I was scrubbing the kitchen floor one afternoon, feeling a little sorry for myself. I didn't see enough of Lino at school, Bill had been out sick all week and classes were dull. The phone rang.

"Hi," Barbara said rather glumly. "You know you said that Bill hadn't been at school for a couple of days? Well, I just got off the phone with his mother. She said that he collapsed last Saturday and is completely paralyzed."

I was stunned. "Do they know what's wrong with him? Where is he? Can we go see him?" I asked all in one breath.

"Well, calm down first, Alice," Barbara advised. "They don't know what's wrong with him, but it isn't polio. He's in the White Memorial Hospital. I have his mother's phone number, if you want to call her."

Nana   Pop

Their home circa 1920

I and my father

My mother

As I hung up the phone, my eyes filled with tears. Poor Bill! He was such a great guy. Maybe he would die. I had never lost anyone close to me and couldn't handle the thought of death. More than two hours passed before I could control myself enough to call Mrs. Waddell.

"Bill has told me so much about you, Alice," she said in a warm, friendly voice with a slight mid-western accent.

"How bad is he, Mrs. Waddell?" I asked. "Do they know what's wrong with him yet?"

"No, he really has the doctors baffled. It's apparently not contagious, though, so you can go see him at the hospital. If you come to my house, I'll take you over with me."

"All right," I answered. "Barbara would like to go, too. We'll come tomorrow about one-thirty."

She gave me their address in Cypress Park and Barbara and I went together on the streetcar the following day, Saturday.

Mrs. Waddell was a congenial woman who immediately put us at ease. She talked steadily about Bill, his childhood and companions.

When we arrived at the hospital, she was still talking and as we walked into Bill's room, she finally stopped, sensing our uneasiness. Bill was lying flat on his back, unable to move his head from one side to the other, grinning from ear to ear.

"Hi! How're you doing?" I asked, trying to be cheerful.

"I'm fine. Of course, I can't move, but the nurses feed me and give me lots of attention. How's everything at school?"

"Latin has been pretty dull without you," I answered. "I have to do most of the reading out loud."

"I've really got the doctors stumped," he went on cheerfully. "They've ruled out polio, otherwise you wouldn't be allowed in to see me." He was obviously enjoying the doctors' dilemma.

"How did it happen?" I asked.

"When I woke up last Saturday morning, I felt sick to my stomach. I jumped out of bed, heading for the bathroom and my legs gave out from under me. I vomited all over the floor and couldn't get up. I called for Mom, who came running, followed by Dad. They got me back onto the bed and called the doctor. And here I am. I feel pretty good now. I should be out of here in a few days."

As Bill told his story, he laughed at himself, showing no signs of discouragement. I thought he was being overly optimistic and two weeks later he was still paralyzed and in the hospital when Barbara and I delivered the table purchased by the Latin class. It was made to sit on his bed and could be adjusted for reading, writing and eating. The members of the class had inscribed their names with notes in Latin on the table.

I had inscribed "Te Amo" and signed my name. In Latin this means "I love you." Bill's immediate response to my inscription was heart-warming, but I wondered if I hadn't gone too far.

He was admiring our gift and attempting to translate the many other Latin notes when Lino and Bumpy arrived. Bill was delighted to see them and my heart skipped a beat as I saw Lino, who was obviously touched at seeing Bill so helpless. Bill noticed his distress and kept the conversation lighthearted.

We were laughing and having fun translating the notes, some of which were quite amusing, when we came to mine. Bill smiled and looked at me with endearment, Bumpy grinned and looked at Lino and Lino and I both lowered our eyes. My face felt warm and must have been red. I wanted to run from the room, but I looked up quickly and laughed. Lino laughed, too, but rather unhappily, I thought; or hoped.

We all left the hospital together. Barbara and Bumpy continued to kid me about the inscription, but Lino didn't say a word.

Bill began to improve and when he regained the use of his arms, he went home where I visited him frequently. The doctors decided he must have had polio, since they couldn't determine any other cause for his illness.

Mrs. Waddell spoiled my visits with Bill, always referring to me as his girlfriend and insisting that we were in love with each other. She attributed his remarkable recovery to my persistent attention.

One day when Lino's name was mentioned, she commented in her inimitable way that his mother's face looked like the map of Italy. Suddenly, I didn't like Mrs. Waddell anymore.

To engage Lino in conversation at school became increasingly difficult. He seemed to be avoiding me. I decided to plan another party.

3

VALENTINE'S Day was coming up and roller skating would be fun, I thought. The Hollywood Rollerdrome was an exciting place, located on a sound stage of the old Warner Brothers Studio on Sunset Boulevard. It was frequented by many celebrities and you never knew whom you might see. I had skated with Jackie Cooper there in 1938, but skating with Lino seemed much more exciting. All I needed was the opportunity to invite him.

Barbara and I devised a plan. She gave Lino and Bumpy a map to Bill's house in their Latin class on Thursday with the note, "Why don't you go over to see Bill? Alice and I are going on Saturday."

We hadn't been at Bill's very long on Saturday when the two of them showed up. Lino was his usual bashful self and Barbara and Bumpy kept the conversation going.

"Old 'Flash' LaBianca, here, is the hottest contender we have this year in the shot put," Bumpy laughed. "The Franklin Press had a big write-up on him in yesterday's paper."

Lino's face turned red. "Knock it off, Bumpy," he said. "Bill isn't interested in hearing about that."

"Sure I am," Bill retorted. "Listen, I was going to be a hot contender for the 220, but someone up there had a different plan. What do they say about him?"

Howard whipped out his paper and began to read from the sports page. "LaBianca looks very impressive in the shot put and, as he is only in the A-10, he will undoubtedly be our best man in this event for the next two years."

"That's great, Flash," laughed Bill. "When did they start calling you Flash?"

"Old Bumpy got tired of being the only one in the gang who had a nickname, I guess," Lino answered.

"It goes over great with the girls," laughed Bumpy.

I smiled and agreed that Flash was a suitable pseudonym, but I never called him Flash. I wasn't impressed with what moved the "other" girls. We said goodbye to Bill and to make Lino jealous, I guess, I said, "Goodbye, honey," and kissed Bill on the cheek.

We all walked out together and Barbara told them about the up-coming skating party. "It sounds fun," said Bumpy, "but my Duesenberg is in the garage."

"Maybe we could get Masi or Roxie to go. They have a car," suggested Lino. "They're really good friends of mine. Do all the girls have dates?"

"I don't know," I answered. "I have one, don't I?"

Lino's face turned red again. He lowered his eyes, stroked his chin and asked, "You're going with me, aren't you?"

"That was the idea," I quipped.

Masi Lucarelli was two years older and his younger brother, Roxie, was a year older than Lino. They had all grown up together in Cypress Park, along with Bumpy, and were inseparable. Masi was tall and blond, with a charm and personality that were appealing. Roxie was shorter, cuter and equally likeable.

They brought their own dates, and Barbara and I went with Lino and Bumpy in Masi's 1935 Ford. There were "inside jokes" all evening between the boys, and Barbara and I had a few of our own. The other girls had rounded up their dates and cars and we met them at the Rollerdrome.

It was Saturday night and crowded. The organ music filled the air and a large lighted sign at one end of the huge sound stage announced numbers: men's singles, women's singles, couples only, everybody skate, figure skating, waltzing only and, of course, the highlight of the evening —the Grand March. Couples followed a leader around the stage, separating, then joining hands to form an arch for the couples to skate under as they came together again, ending in a single line that became "crack the whip." It was great fun and Lino was everything I expected.

He was so handsome with his dark eyes and dark hair; about five foot-eleven with a fabulous physique. He dressed with impeccable taste and had a fastidiousness I had never seen in a boy. But it was more than his physical prowess I admired. I loved his quiet shyness, which camouflaged an inner magnetism. He didn't say much, but he didn't have to. His eyes and mannerisms revealed more of his thoughts and feelings than any words could express; at least to me they did. I did most of the talking.

"Do you work at the stores?" I asked.

With a tone of bitterness, I thought, he said he had been a box boy since he was twelve years old. "My dad just doesn't understand that I want to do other things besides work after school and Saturdays. I wasn't able to go out for football because I had to work. Besides, he wouldn't sign the consent for me to play."

"Why do you have to work? Doesn't your father own the business?" I asked.

"Yes, but he wants me to learn everything from the bottom up. How long does it take to learn how to carry out boxes?"

I sensed the conversation was making him unhappy, so I changed the subject.

After skating, we went to the Sycamore Drive-In, next to Sycamore Grove, a small park on North Figueroa in Highland Park, which was to become one of our favorite places for hours of loving, planning and arguing. The hamburgers were fifteen cents, including shoestring potatoes, and the cokes were a nickel—but that was 1940 and before our world was turned upside down.

The evening passed all too quickly and it was time for Lino to walk me to my door. As he said goodnight, he paused, looked me in the eye, then dropped his gaze and said, "It's a habit of mine to kiss a girl on our first date." He kissed me softly on the lips and left quickly.

> February 1945
> Holland

...I received a sweet Valentine from you today... When I stop to think that it has been five years ago this month that I first took you out, it hardly seems possible... When we were together, there never seemed to be enough time...

Remember, honey?

...I remember all those dates which you mentioned in your letter, but I think you're wrong on the date of the skating party. It was on February seventeenth and not the fourteenth. I think I'm right. Let me know, for sure...

The date on the Sycamore Drive-In menu in my scrapbook is February 17, 1940.

4

I received the menu from the Hawaiian Cafe on North Figueroa Street, dated March 23, 1940, with "Highland Theatre" written on its face, the night we double-dated with Bumpy and Lorraine.

Poor Bumpy. He wanted to take Angie out, but knew her parents wouldn't let her go. I "fixed him up" with Lorraine Fouch, a pretty girl with black hair, dark brown eyes and a gift for sardonic witticisms, a match for Bumpy's humor, I thought. But she didn't appreciate Bumpy's jokes and let him know it every time he opened his mouth. The atmosphere wasn't too pleasant, but Lino and I didn't pay much attention.

"We have to move to a smaller house next week," I told him. "Hamilton and his mother have decided to go to Arizona. She's been offered a good job there in the State Capitol."

"I'll miss Hamilton," Lino answered. "If it hadn't been for him, I probably wouldn't have had enough nerve to ask you out tonight."

"Really? What did he have to do with it?" I asked.

"He calls to me through the fence when I pass his school. He kept asking me when I was going to ask you out again."

"So, I have Uncle Hamilton to thank for our date tonight," I teased.

"He's your uncle?" he asked, with surprise.

"Yes, he really is, but that's a long story."

Lorraine lived on North Avenue Fifty-four just down the hill from me, so we walked her home first. She didn't seem unhappy that the evening was finally coming to an end, although we left her laughing.

"She's carrying a torch for Pete Newquist," I told Bumpy as we walked up the steep hill to my house.

Bumpy waited by the curb for quite some time while Lino and I said good night.

"The last streetcar leaves at two a.m., Flash," he called out.

When we realized how late it was, Lino kissed me quickly, lingering, then he and Bumpy went running down the hill.

24

October 25, 1945
Germany

...Speaking of listening to the radio, this afternoon I heard "All the Things You Are," sung by Dick Haymes. What memories it brought back... I guess I'm what you might call a sentimentalist, but that can't be helped. And to top it all off, the very next song was "Cherokee." It wasn't my favorite arrangement by Charlie Barnett, but Glenn Miller's band played it almost as well. Do you remember the wonderful times we enjoyed when those songs were at their peak? There was your Christmas party, the skating party, the night you and I went to the Highland Theatre with Lorraine and Howard, our first beach party. Some people might say that those affairs weren't highly successful, but as far as I'm concerned, they were perfect. We were together and I was happy. I didn't know you too well at the time, but I did know you well enough to realize you were everything I had ever wanted in a girl. And you always will be, honey...

The following week we moved to 238 Joy Street. What a come-down it was for us and quite a jolt to my ego. How could I ever ask Lino over or have parties? Our new home was in the rear of another house with an alley on one side and in the back. Franklin was a mile away and we were a half-block from the "W" streetcar line on Monte Vista.

"We will have less rent to pay," Mother had said, "and have more money for clothes."

That sounded convincing at the time, but the living room and kitchen were so small. I could never have a Lamb Dab meeting there, especially with the two tiny bedrooms and one tiny bathroom connected without a hallway. Dana and Bobbie shared one bedroom and Jane and I the other. Mother had to sleep on the couch in the living room. We ate in the kitchen where we also did our laundry and sometimes it was pretty depressing.

On the first day of Easter vacation, I called Barbara and asked her if she wanted to take a bicycle ride to Cypress Park. I reminded her that it was about five miles, but that we could take our time and stop at Bill's on the way back.

"Why do you want to go way down there?" she asked. "As if I didn't know."

"Lino's working," I said. "I just need a little exercise."

We rode our bikes down Figueroa, past Sycamore Grove and the many large, Victorian houses built in the 1890s. They were deserted for the most part now and windows were broken, but the evidence of their elegant past was still visible. Two blocks beyond Florence Nightingale Junior High School at Cypress Avenue, we reached Avenue Twenty-six and Figueroa. Next to the Standard gas station on the corner stood store number three. "Gateway Ranch Markets," the neon sign read, imprinted over a white gate: "Open 24 Hours."

The produce was displayed in front of the store on the sidewalk. We walked past the check stands on the right and the liquor and delicatessen on the left to the turnstile and into the grocery department.

"This is a pretty nice store," I commented. It was crowded and looked almost brand new. We bought cold drinks and my heart was heavy as we left. I wondered where Lino was. It wasn't lunch time yet and he said he'd be working all week.

Barbara sensed my disappointment and said, "Let's see if we can find another Gateway."

"Where do we go from here?" I asked, not too enthusiastically.

"Up Cypress Avenue toward Division Street," she answered.

"Okay, but I'm getting hungry. If it's too far, I doubt if I can make it."

"Come on, Alice. You give up too easily. We can get a sandwich when we find the store."

We rode our bikes up Cypress Avenue along the "5" streetcar line and into the Italian neighborhood known as Cypress Park. The houses were small and unpretentious, but well cared for. I was getting hot and was angry at Lino for not being at number three, even though he had no idea I was looking for him on my bicycle.

We rode several blocks before we came upon another "Gateway Ranch Markets" sign over a smaller store. My heart skipped a beat as I saw Lino and Bumpy standing on the corner. They were quite surprised to see us.

"I thought you worked at store number three," I said sarcastically.

"I usually do," Lino answered good-naturedly, "but someone didn't show up today, so I was sent here. This is store number two."

"Where is store number one?" I asked, thinking he was handing me a line as Bumpy stood there grinning.

"It's about three blocks from here at Elm Street," he answered.

"How many stores do you have?" I asked. I was beginning to feel a little foolish and hating myself for doubting him. Why was I so jealous and mistrustful?

"Well, we have these three and the grocery department in store number five over on Main Street."

"What happened to number four?" I laughed.

"It's still in the planning stages. It will be on Verdugo Road about a mile from here," he answered proudly.

"Your father has been a busy man," I quipped.

"Oh, he has a wholesale grocery business, too. The retail stores are just a side-line," he answered.

"His old man runs Cypress Park," Bumpy remarked with a little bitterness, I thought. Then jokingly, "You better get back to work, Flash, or he'll have you emptying the garbage cans again."

"Well, don't work too hard," I said and as we rode off, Lino called after us, "See you later and take it easy."

I had forgotten all about being hungry.

December 15, 1944
Holland 9 p.m.

...There are so many things I want to do and time seems to be going by without my accomplishing anything. I get to thinking about finishing school and worrying whether I'll be too old to go back. Then I think about my athletic ambitions and worry some more. Lately, I've been wishing I could be back helping Dad with the business. I've got so darned many ideas, plans and ambitions about growing and expanding. And what good are they doing me over here? Just going to waste! I can't wait to get started doing something to make you and some of the "doubting Thomases" proud of me. I know I've never done anything that could vouch for my good intentions, but somehow I'm more sure than ever before that I could be a success at anything I tried. I don't mean to sound egotistical either, honey. It's just something that's been building up in me since I came into the army, especially from when I had to leave you.

I realize now that I didn't appreciate my opportunities when they were within my grasp. I know you have always had confidence in me, honey, and I promise you that someday you will be assured you were not wrong about me. Do you remember the bowling alley we've talked about and planned on building, "The Horseshoe"? Someday that's going to be a reality...

5

CANTUS

O Franklinensis Schola,
Semper florentissima!
O Franklinensis Schola,
Vivimus, vivamus!
Eris nobia ancora
O Franklinensis Schola,
Quantum te amamus!

MAY arrived and along with it our annual Latin banquet. As a first year Latin student, I participated as a slave and had to wait on the tables of the second and third year students, of which Lino was one. They sat on the floor and luckily I was assigned to Lino's table. All conversation had to be in Latin, so we didn't talk much, but there was much singing.

To the tune of *School Days*:

"Caesar, Caesar, good old book called Caesar,
I study it more than arithmetic,
But, Oh! in my mind it will not stick.
Indirect discourse makes me sad,
Temporal clauses! Oh, how bad!
All of these things and many more
Make Caesar a terrible bore!"

Afterwards, as we gathered together outside, Lino said, "My Duesenberg is in the garage. Can I walk you home?"

He hadn't seen our little house on the alley and the thought of it embarrassed me. Perhaps I could let him walk me to the front house, pretending to live there.

I confidently answered, "Sure," and as we walked together down North Avenue Fifty-four, we said good night to our friends one by one—Barbara at Buchanan Street, Lorraine just past Ash, and then waited with Bumpy for his streetcar on Monte Vista. We waved goodbye and headed toward Joy Street just beyond North Avenue Fifty. Lino quietly took my hand and I was sure this was heaven. His hand was warm and tender and firm. He was my master and I his slave for six blocks.

I was too excited to talk much, but Lino said he would be working at store number three all summer and perhaps I could come down and have lunch with him some time. I told him about my family; how I hadn't lived with my father since I was three and that my older sister lived with our grandmother so that I was the oldest one at home now and Mother needed me to help quite a bit. We talked about Howard and Angie.

"Her parents still won't let her go out with him. None of the Italian girls are allowed to go out unchaperoned. My older sister, Stella, is getting married in July. Pete comes over to see her, but they can't go out alone, even though they're engaged," he said.

"That's really old-fashioned," I mused thoughtfully. Then, "That reminds me, the Lamb Dabs are having a beach party on the last day of school. Can you go with me?"

"That would be great," he answered quietly.

By this time we had arrived at the front house on Joy Street and I said, "Well, this is it! It didn't take us long to get here, did it?"

"Maybe I can walk home with you after school now that track is over," he suggested.

The Franklin Press had reported, "The local B shot putters really went to town last week when four of them tossed the pellet over 45 feet. Those who performed this exceptional feat were Culvin Cardin, Howard Borschell, Lino LaBianca and Chubby Roussel."

"My streetcar goes right down Monte Vista and it really isn't out of the way," he went on. Then he drew me closer to him and kissed me gently on the lips. I put my arms around him and responded with warmth and affection. He was wearing a dark leather jacket, which he wore often and I grew to love. A leather jacket was not a sign of rowdyism in 1940.

"I'm going to be an actress, you know," I said suddenly.

He backed away slowly and the street light was just enough to catch his expression of disappointment.

"Really? That's a dumb thing to do. Why do you want to do that?" he asked.

"Edith, Dana and I have wanted to be in the theatre since we were old enough to talk. We have been called back in the finals for the Guy Bates Post Theatre scholarship auditions," I bragged, waiting for his reaction.

"What will happen if you win?" he asked quietly.

"We would attend the Theatre Arts school on a full-time basis. I guess I'd drop out of Franklin," I answered.

"Gee, Alice, I'm just getting to know you and I like you a lot. School wouldn't be the same without you." His words were what I wanted to hear, but there was a quiet anger in his voice I hadn't noticed before.

"This is what I've always wanted to do. We've never had the money for any training and this scholarship is an opportunity to really learn the theatre professionally," I argued.

"You're right. I'm just a guy and you could be a big star," he acquiesced sarcastically.

"Well, I probably won't win, anyway. There are five of us in the finals," I added.

We heard his streetcar coming, again, and he kissed me quickly and ran to catch it. Upon arriving home to an empty house, he sat down at the piano and set the following to music:

June 3, 1945
Cardiff, Wales

...I have too much leisure time to think about all the wonderful days we have spent together in the past. I love you so much, honey, that my heart honestly pains me when I think about those days. The hours we spent on the steps of that house on Monte Vista, after you moved to Joy Street, waiting for my streetcar. Those were wonderful hours, honey, and I'll always love you more for them. I could go on talking about our past together, but I'm sure you remember as well as I, and my writing would fill a book...

The Guy Bates Post Theatre finals were held in June and none of us won the scholarship. I've never been quite sure if I really tried my best to win.

6

I seldom walked home from school alone after the Latin banquet. Sometimes we stopped at "Oh Johnnies Cafe" on the corner of Figueroa and North Avenue Fifty for malts or Lino's favorite, a dish of pineapple. We talked longer each day, hating to say goodbye.

His parents didn't understand. They were from the "old school." He had no one else he could really confide in. He was due at work by four, but seldom left me before five. I finally admitted to him that I lived in the rear house and he couldn't believe that I thought it would matter to him. Occasionally, he managed to sneak out of his house on Sunday afternoon and we walked to Sycamore Grove. We walked in the rain and sunshine, talking and arguing. We carved our initials on the bridge that crossed over the Pasadena Freeway to the hills on the other side.

The Lamb Dabs had a beach party on the last day of school which was attended by the whole gang, except Howard and Angie. We swam all afternoon and had a warm bonfire and roasted weinies and marshmallows well into the night. We sat on the sand and talked about our future and truly felt our love was made in heaven.

"Pete and Stella want to go to Pasadena Civic next Saturday night. Would you like to chaperone them with me?" he asked, laughing.

"Some chaperones we'd make," I laughed, snuggling further into his warm embrace. Then, seriously, "Am I really going to meet the fabulous Peter Smaldino and Stella, at last?"

"Alice, you know how I feel about you. Of course, I want you to meet my sister and her future husband," he answered solemnly.

"According to Angie, Stella told her your father would never let you marry a girl who was not Italian," I said sadly.

"What does he have to say about it?" he answered angrily.

Saturday night they arrived in the family 1938 Buick sedan. Pete and Stella exuberated happiness and seemed pleased to meet me. Pete's smiling brown eyes and warm personality soon put me at ease. He was handsome with dark wavy hair, small features and six feet of dashing

32

self-importance. At nineteen, he was anxiously awaiting his forthcoming marriage to Stella who obviously regarded him as a prime catch.

"She's going to be the boss," he laughed affectionately.

Stella's countenance was one of strength and dignity. Her brown eyes revealed a certain sternness, although her smile softened her pretty face and minimized her arrogance. She referred to her father several times during the evening and was proud of his accomplishments. He was plainly the guiding force in her life and Pete fit comfortably into her filial adoration.

They talked freely of their wedding, which her father had planned and would pay for, although the Italian custom places this burden on the groom's family. They were expecting several hundred guests and everybody who was anybody in the Italian community would be there.

"Why don't you work for your future father-in-law?" I had to ask.

"I'm a welder, and a darned good one," Pete answered emphatically. "What do I know about the grocery business? I don't want to work for Dad. I want to be independent."

"You just don't want him bossing you around," retorted Stella, laughingly.

"I don't want any problems with him. He's a strong man and a genius. I couldn't live up to his expectations," he answered seriously.

Lino remained quiet and managed to change the subject. He handed me a small card which I read later. He had received a raise:

"Your salary will be $5.00 per week starting Sunday, June 23, 1940, for your regular fifteen hour week."

Pasadena Civic Auditorium was the Friday night hangout for Franklin and other high schools in the area. There was a huge dance floor and bandstand, and the spotlight was turned on various jitterbugs as they trucked, pecked and formed the Big Apple. That night Glenn Miller was there with his "Tuxedo Junction" and "In the Mood." Lino was too embarrassed to do much jitterbugging, but he was a smooth dancer and held me close, as if forever.

"Bob's Big Boy" in Glendale, a small drive-in with the best hamburgers in town for ten cents (fifteen cents for the deluxe "double-decker" cheeseburger), was the perfect place to end the evening, for those who had cars to get them there.

I wished Pete and Stella happiness in their marriage and Lino walked me to my door. He kissed me and lingered, then kissed me again. I felt loved and beautiful and secure.

Pete and Stella were married July seventh and on July tenth, I

Stella LaBianca
showing off her
engagement dress

Stella and Pete Smaldino
on their wedding day

received a card from Lake Arrowhead.

Busy People's Correspondence Card

A-21   Lake Arrowhead, California

DEAR	I SPEND MY TIME	DON'T
OLD THING	HIKING	FORGET ME
PAPA	FISHING	FORGET TO WRITE
MAMA	SWIMMING	LOVE ANYBODY ELSE ✗
WIFE ✗	BOATING	GET PINCHED
HUSBAND	HORSE BACK RIDING	WORK TOO HARD
FRIEND	DANCING	
SWEETIE	GOLFING	**THINGS ARE**
OLD STICK IN THE MUD	THINKING OF YOU	ROTTEN
BOYS	PETTING ✗	TOO GOOD TO BE TRUE
GIRLS	SIGHTSEEING	HAPPENING FAST
HOW GOES IT?	WORKING	KEEPING ME BUSY ✗
I AM	LOAFING	GREAT
BLUE	READING	
IN LOVE	SLEEPING	**THIS PLACE IS**
LONELY	MAKING WHOOPEE ✗	WARM
UNHAPPY	PLAYING TENNIS	COOL ✗
BROKE ✗	BASKING IN THE SUN	WONDERFUL
FINE	GOSSIPING	THE BUNK
HAVING A FINE TIME	PLAYING CARDS	IDEAL
(WISH YOU WERE	BUMMING AROUND	ALL WET
HERE)		**HOPE TO SEE YOU**
I NEED	**HOPE YOU ARE**	SOON ✗
SYMPATHY	WELL	LATER
YOU	BETTER	IN THE SWEET
MORE TIME	STAYING HOME NIGHTS ✗	BYE AND BYE
SLEEP	THINKING OF ME	**YOURS**
SOMEONE TO	KEEPING OUT OF	WITH LOVE ✗
LOVE ME ✗	MISCHIEF	ALWAYS
MONEY ✗	STILL TRUE TO ME	TILL THE COWS
KISSES		COME HOME

Time is Money—Check Items Desired

All kidding aside, I am having a swell time. I really wish you were here, so I could enjoy myself more thoroughly.

See you later and take it easy.

Love,
Lino

When I heard later from Emma that her girlfriend, Tish, had gone to Lake Arrowhead with them, I was upset with Lino for not telling me and my security vanished, but not for the last time. Tish and Lino had been paired off at Stella's wedding, but Lino had assured me it meant absolutely nothing to him. I wondered, feeling again the pangs of jealousy.

September 24, 1944

...Here it is Sunday afternoon and I'm lying under my pup-tent just thinking and dreaming of those what-seems-ages-ago Sundays we used to spend together.

I am sorry to hear that Pete S. is 1A and might have to go into the Army. I am mostly sorry for baby Louis and the expected new arrival. However, if Pete is drafted and nothing happens to him, I honestly think it will do both him and Stella a world of good. I have always thought they were too sure of each other and quibbled over the tiniest things. Being separated will definitely make them appreciate each other and the smaller things of life. We can vouch for that, can't we, honey?

However, in our case I think things were different. We would argue about some of the silliest things, but somehow, I think, we sensed that someday we would be apart for awhile, and knew we were lucky just being together.

We will be together someday soon and all these unpleasant days will be forgotten.....

7

LINO worked at store number three all summer and we met there often, sharing his lunch in one of the employee's cars in the parking lot, which didn't go unnoticed. We learned all there was to learn about each other, at least, at that particular time in our lives.

"I'd like to be a banker," he confided, "but I guess I'm stuck with the grocery business."

"It's a great opportunity for you if you like it," I answered. "People will always have to eat."

"I guess it's not being able to choose that's frustrating. Dad wants me to work for the wholesale business when I get out of school. 'State Wholesale Grocery Company, Inc.—a step up in the world from being a retail grocer only, cleaner and more prestigious,' my dad says."

Lino spoke with pride and a great deal of love, I thought. No matter what his secret ambitions were, I could see that he would always do whatever his father and mother wanted him to do. How envious I was that he had a complete family and parents whose children were so important to them.

Lino was still talking. "Dad thinks I'm a bum because I'm interested in other things. He got mad at me this morning because I hadn't mowed the lawn for three weeks. That's my job, too."

Our only real date that summer was walking to the Highland Park miniature golf course. There were eighteen holes and windmills, sand traps and waterfalls—par 61. Of course, Lino won, but the score was 72-to-71.

Walking home later I asked him where his name, Lino, came from. "My dad's father, of course. That's the Italian custom. They shortened it to 'Lino,' thank goodness. My father's brother has a son who is also named Lino. There were only two brothers, so there are only two Linos. Capeesh?"

"What does that mean?" I asked, laughing at the strange sound.

"'Do you understand?' That's what it means, dummy," he answered good-naturedly.

"What was your grandfather's name?"

"Do you think I would tell you that? I'm going to change the 'i' to an 'e' anyway, because no one pronounces it right," he answered angrily.

"Well, Alice isn't my first name, you know," I offered, realizing his unhappiness. "I was named after my grandmother, but never used her name. And I'm not going to tell you what it is, either," I laughed.

When school started again in the fall, Lino registered as "Leno." He never used his full, given name, which I didn't learn for two years, and then from someone else.

Bill Waddell had recovered enough to return to Franklin, although he had to take the tenth grade over again and was a year behind us. I had kept close contact with his convalescence which was slow and painstaking. He wore braces on both legs and used canes to walk with great difficulty. His perseverance and undaunted spirit had saved his life.

He was unaware of my close relationship with Leno and on the first day of school, going up the steps of the auditorium, I heard my name being called from an open window on the second floor.

"Hi, Alice! I made it!" Bill called with happy enthusiasm.

I waved up to him as Leno came walking toward me. Bill watched as Leno took my hand and kissed me on the cheek, and then suddenly disappeared from the window.

Before long, the word around school was that I had dropped Bill for Leno because of Bill's handicap; the beginning of a lifetime of misunderstandings with attempts at explanation only making matters worse.

On my sixteenth birthday in November Leno gave me a heart-shaped locket purchased from Hudson's Diamond Company for five dollars and thirty-six cents, including tax. He paid four dollars in cash and financed the balance of one dollar and thirty-six cents—the first time in his life he borrowed money, but not the last. He signed my birthday card, "Forget-Me-Not," and I never have.

I prepared a chicken dinner for Leno and myself, graciously serving it in a candle-lit setting in our little living room on Joy Street. He took me downtown on the streetcar to the Biltmore Theatre on Fifth and Olive, where we saw "Quiet Please" with Jane Wyatt and Donald Woods; a memorable comedy that kept us laughing. Still laughing on the streetcar going home, Leno broke the news to me.

"My dad bought a house last summer that's not in the Franklin school district. He's been redecorating it and I guess we'll be moving in next week."

"Can't you get special permission to continue at Franklin?" I asked, trying to ignore the emptiness in the pit of my stomach.

"My dad wants me to go to Marshall High. He wouldn't sign any request for me to stay at Franklin. We shouldn't go steady, anyway, Alice," I heard him saying. "We're too young and I won't be able to see much of you when we move. I really should go out with other girls, and there are plenty of boys who would like to take you out."

As we got off the streetcar and walked toward home, I couldn't believe this was happening. School without Leno? What did I care about going out with other boys? I was hurt and our beautiful evening ended with me in tears. A week later Leno moved to 3301 Waverly Drive and left Franklin and my life, I thought, forever. I was heartbroken.

I turned to the theatre once again as I always did when life, otherwise, didn't seem worth living. Kathryn Offill, the new drama teacher at Franklin, was doing "A Christmas Carol." Dana had started to Franklin in the fall and won the coveted role of Ebenezer Scrooge. The best girl's part was that of the fiancée of Scrooge's nephew, Nell, which I tried out for and won.

Phil Jackson, a handsome drama major, played the nephew and we had a love scene that called for a kiss in the second act. We gave an afternoon performance for the school which was such a huge success that the evening presentation for the parents played to a "standing room only" audience. Dana received a standing ovation for his portrayal of Scrooge and we were all sure he would be a famous actor one day, being labeled "Orson Skolfield" by the Franklin Press.

Leno surprised us back stage afterwards, being friendly but still showing complete independence. I asked him to go to the Sub-Deb Annual Christmas Ball at the Ambassador Hotel with me.

"Thanks a lot, but I can't make it," he answered coldly. I wondered why he had bothered to come to see the play at all and was hurt and humiliated by his attitude. I was determined to get even with him and called Masi Lucarelli.

"Our sub-deb club is going to a Christmas dance in two weeks. Would you like to go with me?" I asked.

Masi was surprised at the invitation and asked, "What about Leno?"

"We aren't going together anymore. I thought you knew. I guess he has another girlfriend," I answered.

"The dance sounds great, Alice. I would love to go." Then he called Leno to see if it was all right with him.

Leno said, "Sure you can take her," then called me. I had never heard him so angry. "Why did you have to pick one of my best friends to go out with?"

I tried to explain how I felt and how hurt I was by his independence, but the more I talked, the madder he got and for the first time since I had known him, he hung up on me.

The dance was uneventful and going to Van de Kamp's Drive-In afterwards only made me miss Leno more. It was one of our favorite places, and going with another boy brought back so many memories that the lump in my throat very nearly caused me to choke on my hamburger.

Masi was a fun escort, but when he put his arm around me, driving home, I avoided his attempts to kiss me, until the car went over a bump and his kiss landed on my nose. We both laughed.

> November 13, 1944
> Holland

...Yes, I remember your birthday last year, and also the one four years before that. You were living on Joy Street and we hadn't known each other long, but I knew that someday I would marry you. I gave you that heart-shaped locket, which wasn't worth much, I guess, but had a lot of meaning behind it.

Do you remember all the petty scraps we had at that time? We would sit around waiting for my streetcar to come to take me to work. I'd let ten or fifteen go by and as a result I'd be late every day. Mike David and Tony Distarce really thought of me as a "problem child." Sometimes I would make you phone them, saying you were Emma and that I was sick. Usually the only way I would ever leave was after some silly argument and then I'd storm off trying to show how independent I was. If I had only known at the time that I could never be independent again and that you were a part of me, no precious time would have been wasted on useless scraps.

Last night I saw a play at the theatre called "Three Cornered Moon." It was put on by GIs and was really corny, but it brought back the memory of a "character" I'd like to forget. What was his name, Phil or Fred Jackson? He really burned me up! I can still remember that scene in "A Christmas Carol" with him and you *very* plainly. I guess that one scene spoiled the whole thing for me. It was silly of me, I know, but I would probably feel the same way if we had it all to do over again......

8

IN January when the semester was nearly over, I was surprised to see Leno standing in the hall as I came out of class. He was talking to friends when our eyes met and he came over.

"Can I walk you home?" he asked.

I couldn't hide my delight at seeing him. "What are you doing here?"

"Let's walk and I'll tell you," he answered as he took my hand.

We hadn't gone far down Avenue Fifty-four when he said, "I'm coming back to Franklin next semester. I couldn't stand Marshall. The kids were such snobs, and besides, school wasn't much fun without you. I want to get back in time for track."

My whole world came alive again. "How are you going to get back and forth?" I asked. "It's a good ten miles, I imagine."

"Dad will drop me off at store number three and I'll take the streetcar from there. I've got it all figured out."

Leno came back to Franklin and Robert Taylor moved back into our house to "help out financially." His first move to get into our good graces was to buy me a car for twenty-five dollars—a 1928 Model A roadster that didn't have a top—and to teach me to drive it. After several frustrating attempts, ending in his losing his temper, he gave me the wheel at Alameda Street, a busy downtown thoroughfare. I drove on my own from the Union Depot to Washington Boulevard in extremely heavy Saturday afternoon traffic. I was nervous and scared beyond belief for the entire twelve blocks, having to stop and go frequently, shifting and braking and timing the clutch action without stalling the motor. I didn't need any more instruction after that harrowing experience and now considered myself a veteran driver.

Soon after, Leno suggested I pick him up and drive him to school every morning. He would pay for the gas. He told me to meet him at the bottom of the hill at Hyperion and Rowena by eight-thirty. This worked out well for a week or so until one evening, when I was struggling with my advanced algebra, Leno called.

"I'm at the San Fernando freight yards. I'm hopping a freight to San Francisco tonight and I called to say goodbye," he announced firmly.

"You're what?" I couldn't believe what he was saying. "What happened? What's wrong?" I asked frantically.

"I had a fight with my dad and I'm never going home again," he answered with conviction.

"It can't be that bad," I admonished, then, "You'd be leaving me, too."

"I know, Alice, but I can't take it anymore. He just won't understand!"

"Can I meet you somewhere?" I asked. "If you're leaving, I want to go with you."

"That's impossible, Alice, but if you want to meet me here to say goodbye..."

"Don't do anything until I get there. I'll leave right now and meet you at San Fernando Road and Division."

He was standing on the corner when I arrived and I had never seen him so angry. He climbed into the car and we found a quiet street to stop and talk. He put his arm around me and said, "I'm so glad you're here."

September 24, 1945
Germany

...You are the most important thing in my life and you should know that I won't allow the family to tell me what to do. When we moved to Waverly Drive my dad wanted me to go to Marshall High, so I went there to please him. But I couldn't stand it without you, so after a few weeks, I asked him about transferring back to Franklin. He wouldn't give me his consent so I forged his name to a "Notice of Change of Address." I know it wasn't the right thing to do, but it was just one of those things that had to be done. And I don't remember ever seeing my dad as mad as he was the night he found out about it...

Gradually, the story of what had happened unfolded as Leno started, "Apparently Dad saw you pick me up this morning and when we were driving home from work tonight, he started asking me about school," Leno confessed. "I had to lie to cover up and the more I lied, the madder he got. I began to realize that somehow he guessed I had gone back to Franklin. By the time we arrived home and started up the driveway, he was livid. He called me a liar and a cheat, and as we got out of the car, he asked me how I managed it without his consent. When I told him that I had forged his signature, I knew what was coming. He struck me hard across the face, nearly knocking me down. He said that I was no son of his and stormed into the house, leaving me stunned."

As Leno unburdened his heart, he mellowed, and continued thoughtfully. "He's never hit me before. I wanted to run as far away as possible and just headed for the freight yard."

I didn't know what to say. I kissed him and held him close, wanting to wash away the humiliation and despair that I knew he must be feeling. "If only we were older," I thought, "we could go away together." But we weren't, and we both knew it. "Your dad must be worried about you by now," I suggested. "Maybe you should go home and apologize. I'm sure he loves you very much."

Quietly, Leno continued. "He expects so much from me. I'm not like he is and I never will be. I try to do what he wants, but he's never satisfied." Then, "I guess you're right, honey, you always are. I better go home and face the music."

We drove slowly back to Waverly Drive. Leno kissed me softly on the lips and walked hesitatingly up the driveway. My heart was heavy as I drove home.

There was no further conversation between father and son that night, but the next morning a new understanding seemed to exist between them—unspoken, but nevertheless, unmistakably present. Leno stayed at Franklin and his father never again mentioned the incident.

9

LENO was a brilliant student. He never did his homework, while I diligently worked hours on mine. He crammed the night before exams and received "A"s, but I was lucky to get a "B" or a "C". We occasionally played hooky from school, and one morning Leno suggested we go to the beach. I had to be home by the time Jane and Bobbie got out of school.

"We can make it, let's go," he pleaded.

We decided that I should drive as Leno didn't have his driver's license yet and he didn't want to take the risk if we got stopped.

Our favorite way to the beach at Santa Monica was along Sunset Boulevard, a winding drive through the most affluent section of Los Angeles. The homes were elegant and palatial and the grounds magnificent. Our spirits were high and our joy was complete as we envisioned ourselves blissfully living our lives one day in these surroundings. Not being in school when we were supposed to be made our excursion more fun and the only damper to our exuberance was the reluctance of my Model A to keep up with the Cadillacs flying by.

A police car suddenly came up on my left and I pulled over, knowing we were in trouble. "May I see your driver's license?" the officer asked. After studying it, he looked in at Leno. "How old are you?"

"Fifteen," he answered quietly. I was glad he didn't choose this moment to be witty.

"Follow me," the officer commanded.

Behind the police car for almost ten miles, we wondered what kind of trouble we had gotten ourselves into. Leno worried about their notifying his father and I worried about being arrested. When we arrived at the Los Angeles Police Department, we waited outside a door marked "Truant Officer." Five minutes later we were ushered in and a middle-aged man in plain clothes greeted us. He stood up when we entered, shook our hands, gave us a quick once-over and said, "Playing hooky, eh?"

We looked at each other, laughed nervously, and nodded. He motioned for us to sit down, which we did with knees trembling.

"Where were you going?" he asked.

Leno answered, looking him in the eye. "To the beach."

"What grade are you in?"

We said together, "The A-11."

"Hmm." He looked at Leno. "You're only fifteen and in the eleventh grade?"

"Yes sir."

He asked our parents' names and addresses, writing them down.

"Here it comes," we thought. He looked through some files in his desk, and said, "The officer that brought you in said you are an excellent driver."

"Thank you," I answered.

"I don't think one day at the beach will hurt either one of you," he continued. "Anyone who is fifteen in the eleventh grade deserves a day off. Have a good time."

We did have a good time and when I arrived home in time for Jane and Bobbie, a letter was waiting from Mother who had gone to visit Aunt Pearl for two weeks. She was Mother's wealthy aunt who owned half of Palm Springs. Our great-grandfather's land had all ended up in her hands which bothered her enough for Mother to be invited to share her luxury occasionally.

JOHNNY LAMB, Tennis Instructor FRED EBBING, Swimming Instructor	P. O. Box 1468	TELEPHONE 6865	ANTHONY BURKE, Manager BETTY NUTHALL, Assistant Manager

PALM SPRINGS TENNIS CLUB
A PRIVATE ORGANIZATION FOR MEMBERS AND GUESTS ONLY
PALM SPRINGS, CALIFORNIA

Thursday, April 17, 1941

My "Little Woman,"

I address you in such manner, for that is what you must be if I am to stay down here a little longer as Aunt Pearl wants me to do. I enclose some three cent stamps so that when a check comes in, you can mail it down to me and I will mail it back and tell you what to do with it. When you mail it down address it to Mrs. Jane F. Taylor (in care of) Austin G. McManus, Palm Springs,

45

Uncle Austin and Aunt Pearl
in front of their home in Palm Springs

California, Post Office Box 520, Riverside County and be sure to tell me of any new developments that might put you in an embarrassing situation financially.

Please arrange everything with Mrs. Baird as I will probably come home next week sometime with Aunt Pearl.

I hope Dana can catch the 9:30 a.m. bus on Saturday morning of this week. He must get up early in the morning, take the streetcar about 8:15 to town, get a transfer, transfer to the "U" car going east on Fifth Street, get off at Los Angeles Street and walk back up to Sixth Street, where he can purchase a one way ticket for a dollar eighty-four to Palm Springs. Someone will meet him where the bus stops in Palm Springs. I am sure his dad will help him out on that as, after all, he will have a birthday soon.

It is perfectly beautiful down here now. As far as I am concerned, it is a "Little Bit of Heaven."

Next Monday is Aunt Pearl's birthday. Phone the Western Union (you can find it in the phone book) before you go to school Monday morning and tell them to send a singing telegram to Mrs. A.G. McManus and put it on the phone bill. (Monday, April 21st) Sign it from Alice, Dana, Jane and Bobbie.

Don't do too much. I don't want you to be too tired. I am depending on you to figure everything out as it comes along as I know you can. Love to all, love from all.

Mother

10

ANTONIO LaBianca.

I had heard so much about him. He was a hard man, who always had his way. Neither his family nor his business associates were a match for his genius nor his iron will. Leno would follow in his footsteps in his two prosperous companies and marry an Italian girl to have sons to carry on the LaBianca name. When Leno wanted to show me their home at 3301 Waverly Drive, I was terrified.

"My folks aren't there and it's such a beautiful place. I'll fix lunch for you and we'll be gone before anyone gets home," he said.

It sounded safe enough, since his mother had gone downtown shopping and his father never came home until evening.

I got my first real look at the house on the hill on a bright, blustery April afternoon. The entrance to the long, steep driveway was bordered by two white stucco pillars, each with a rustic wooden sign—one the street address, "3301," and the other, "Oak Terrace." We drove apprehensively into the rear yard which overlooked the fountain at Riverside Drive and Los Feliz Boulevard. Below, I could see the city of Glendale stretched out to the mountains. The back of the property was terraced down the hillside and planted with fruit trees and artichokes. Several steps led us down to a sizable barbecue with a massive brick chimney. A magnificent, sprawling mulberry tree shaded a lengthy picnic table, outside a large recreation room with a fireplace, bar and kitchen furnished with tables, chairs and a soft, cushioned, cozy couch where we relaxed and planned our future.

"When we have children, we'll remember how we felt," Leno said, "and be understanding of their problems."

"We'll make them mind, but let them know we love them," I answered.

Our love was complete, I thought. We wanted the same things for our lives—a beautiful home, children, and the love and security they would bring. We understood each other and felt a unity of purpose for our existence. From where we were sitting, we could view the fountain and city beyond. This was heaven and we were angels looking down on the teeming world below. Our dream ended abruptly when we realized how late it was getting and how hungry we were.

We went up the stairs and into the back door of the main house and more beauty—an immaculate kitchen and a bright breakfast room overlooking a manicured rose garden in full bloom. Looking through the many windows, I was completely overwhelmed at the beauty I saw and the love I felt for this boy and his home.

He showed me the formal dining room and large living room. Windows across the front of the house overlooked a porch, expansive green lawn, several giant fir trees and the Hyperion Reservoir. A fireplace at one end of the room added charm and warmth. A small, panelled den behind the living room and two bedrooms and a bath completed the west side of the house; decorated with impeccable taste—elegant without being ostentatious. The bedroom walls were delicately designed with patterns artistically scrolled.

Sunday, October 15, 1944
France 12 Noon

...this place is no Utopia. It rains quite persistently and there is lots of mud. We sleep in pup tents holding two men. The first night the ground was especially hard and cold. But we learned to improve our standard of living. I dug out a place in the ground for my hips and shoulders because they got pretty sore on the flat ground. I then hunted up some ferns, which made a rather nice mattress. I made blankets into a sleeping bag by doubling them up and pinning them together. Little by little, we are all learning new ways of becoming as comfortable as possible.

...every few nights that it doesn't rain too hard, we have movies. The movies are given in different areas each time so sometimes we have a five mile walk on our hands, but most of the time I feel it worth the walk... in the middle of the picture it began to rain. However, everyone stayed until it was over. So you see, we have quite a bit of recreation in our spare time...

Leno proudly displayed his home and ushered me into the kitchen to prepare our lunch. We had just sat down to a pineapple and cottage cheese salad, when we heard a car coming up the driveway.

"It's probably the gardener," Leno said. "You go out on the front porch and I'll try to get rid of him."

Antonio LaBianca

I ran outside and was admiring the beautiful view when the front door opened. I stepped toward it, expecting Leno. Instead, a handsome, fastidious man of obvious importance with dark hair, steel gray at the temples, and cold, dark, penetrating eyes appeared. There was no sign of welcome on his face and I stood frozen as I realized who he was. How ridiculous I felt, standing there, speechless, under his gaze. I had so much wanted to make a good first impression on this man I had learned to fear and respect. He spoke impatiently, with a slight accent.

"Well, come in. You don't have to stand out there."

Then he turned quickly and went back into the house. I couldn't move. How could I confront this man whom I had obviously embarrassed and at the same time angered? I didn't have long to wait. A car had started down the driveway. I heard footsteps coming around the house. It was Leno and he was upset.

"Come on," he said. "Let's get out of here."

I ran after him and jumped into the driver's seat of the Model A. As I drove down the steep driveway, I burst into tears.

"He made me feel so awful," I cried. "He looked at me as if I were a slut."

"Honey, don't cry. I honestly didn't think he would come home this early. He never does. He was really mad at me for taking you there alone. He never understands anything."

"Who does he think he is? I wanted him to like me and now he thinks I'm a tramp!" I continued, hysterically.

Leno couldn't control my outburst and made me stop the car.

"Honey, please stop this," he pleaded. "He isn't worth it! He doesn't think you're a tramp. He blames the whole thing on me. I'm the one he's disgusted with. He thinks I should be working all the time and not spending my time with girls." He put his arm around me and wiped away my tears. "I have to go to work now. Let's forget him and remember the fun we had while it lasted."

I felt reassurance in his strong embrace. By the time I dropped him off at store number three, it was time for me to go to work in the cashier's cage at the Franklin Theatre. It was quiet there in the early evening. I couldn't leave that afternoon's incident alone. I wanted to do something, but didn't know what.

I girded myself and placed a telephone call. A woman answered in broken English and I asked for Mr. LaBianca.

A stern voice said, "Hello."

"This is Alice Skolfield," I said nervously. "I'm the girl you found on your porch this afternoon."

No response.

"I wanted to tell you that we were just having lunch. Leno is so proud of his home. He wanted me to see it," I continued.

"Leno is too young to have girlfriends. He has to go to college," he answered angrily.

"Oh, I know," I said. "We both plan to go to college. I just didn't want you to be mad at Leno. There really wasn't anything wrong with my being there."

"Yes, all right. Thank you for calling," he said coldly and hung up.

So, that was the great Antonio LaBianca, I thought. He certainly isn't a very friendly man. No wonder Leno doesn't get along with him. I was proud of myself for having called him, although my heart was pounding and my hands trembling.

I felt angry and foolish at the same time. Would he ever accept me into the family? I hated him! Someday Leno wouldn't be under his thumb and we could live our own lives. But that day seemed so far away and I felt so rejected by his father. I would just have to be patient and if our love was meant to be, everything would work out for the best. And how that patience would be tested in the years to follow.

11

BOBBIE brought the mumps home to our house that spring. Never having had them as a child, they ravaged my system at sixteen—first on one side and then the other—confining me to my bed for six weeks. Since Leno was afraid of catching them, our only communication for what seemed like forever was through my bedroom window and on the telephone.

Leno had been inducted into "the" boys' social club of Franklin High as reported in the Franklin Press:

GASTRONOMICAL TORTURES ENDURED
BY NEW HI-HATTERS

There was laughter and rejoicing as eleven newly elected Hi-Hatters were brought into that organization last Monday evening at their semi-annual banquet.

The new members are Bruce Brady, Leno LaBianca, Jim Puryear, Dave Ward, Bob Aldrich, Elmer Black, Manuel Cruz, Darth Frank, Dick Overmier, Budd Kittleson, and Leland Zitko.

President Joe Kreuter and his cabinet are planning an extensive social season including a swimming meet at Oxy, a dance with the Girls' Council, and a swimming party with the Etiquette Club.

I lay in bed and cried as I read the Franklin Press article since I belonged to neither the Girls' Council nor the Etiquette Club.

As all things in life both good and bad do eventually come to an end, I finally recovered from the mumps and on my first day out, I chased the discus for Leno at Sycamore Grove. He had taken the lead in the Varsity shot put events and now wanted to excel in discus throwing. I had forced drama down his throat that semester, so helping him in his athletic endeavors seemed the least I could do.

Leno's best performance was in a short skit called "The Fool," perhaps because the character he portrayed came the closest to being like his own.

DRAMA I "THE FOOL" MAY 1941
by
CHANNING POLLOCK

Clare Jewett is 28. Smartly dressed, though in a fashion which suggests thought rather than expenditure; and pretty, in spite of a certain hardness. She is engaged to marry Daniel Gilchrist, assistant rector of a fashionable New York church. He has aroused the antagonism of his parishioners by preaching on social problems that are contrary to the rich men's ideas. At college Gilchrist was a football man, an ascetic; he is still in good condition. He is not the conventional reformer. He is humorous, honest and strong. As yet his exaltation is in his smile. His great gift is charm—and sympathy. It is Christmas eve. The scene is the chancel of the church.

CLARE
(Alice)
Got anything on your mind, Dan?
DANIEL
(Leno)
(Quickly) What do you—
CLARE
I mean anything special to do?
DANIEL
Oh!—No.
CLARE
Take me home.
DANIEL
(He beams.) I'm getting my Christmas present early! (Gets his hat.)
CLARE
Where's your coat?
DANIEL
Outside. That is—I lent it to a friend. Oh, I've got another—somewhere.

CLARE

But you can't go out without a coat. (Looks at wrist watch.) Anyway, I told the taxi man to come back at half past four. That's the worst of not having a car. Well, we may as well sit down! (He assists her, but his mind is afar.) What's the matter with you, Dan?

DANIEL

Nothing important.

CLARE

There will be if you insist on going around without an overcoat! (Looking at him narrowly.) You're too generous. (He is still afar.) I say, you're too generous! How are we going to be married if you go on giving things away?

DANIEL

(Laughs.) Is generosity a fault in a husband?

CLARE

That depends. Is it true you've been giving away—well—large sums of money?

DANIEL

Who told you that?

CLARE

A little bird. (He laughs.) And that you've refused to take part of your income?

DANIEL

Little bird tell you that?

CLARE

Yes.

DANIEL

Must have been a cuckoo!

CLARE

Is it true?

DANIEL

About the money? Yes.

CLARE

Why?

DANIEL

Well, there's the strike, and a good deal of unemployment, and I've got so much. Why—I've got you!

CLARE

(Rises.) Let's not talk about it now. (She turns left; hesitates; looks at her wrist watch; looks off left.) Yes; let's!—You're so changed. I hardly know you. We don't seem to want the same things anymore.

DANIEL

What do you want, Clare?

CLARE

I want to be happy.

DANIEL

That's exactly what I want.

CLARE

How can anybody be happy without money?

DANIEL

How can anybody be happy with it? Anyway, do you think people are? Happier than the people who just have enough?

CLARE

In our day and age there's nothing worse than poverty! There's nothing more degrading than having to scrimp, and save and do without, and keep up appearances! I've tried it—ever since my father died—and I know! I can't do it any longer, and I won't!

DANIEL

Clare! (She turns away and comes back somewhat calmer.) I don't want to quarrel with you, Dan. I just want you to be sensible... I love you, but I love the good things of life, too. I like to be warm and comfortable.

DANIEL

You can be sure of that.

CLARE

But that's only the beginning. I want good clothes, and furs, and my own car, and money to spend when I like. I want my own house, and my own servants, and a husband who amounts to something. I'm no different from other women of my class.

DANIEL

I hoped you were.

CLARE

A year or two ago people thought you were going to be a Bishop. Today you've made an enemy of every influential man in the church. All that may be very noble, but I'm not noble, and I don't pretend to be. I don't feel any call to sacrifice myself for others, and I don't think you have any right to ask it.

DANIEL

I do ask it, Clare.

CLARE

You mean you're going on like this?

DANIEL

I mean I can't give you expensive clothes, and servants, and a big house while all about us people are hungry.

CLARE

What do you propose to give?

DANIEL

A chance to help.

CLARE

To help wash the dishes, I suppose, in a three-room flat on a side street!

DANIEL

And to visit the sick, and befriend the friendless.

CLARE

A charming prospect!

DANIEL

It really is, Clare. You don't know how happy we can be with work, and our modest plenty. There's so much to do... and they won't let me do it here. We've got to get near the people in trouble, and we can't with a big house and all that. I don't think we shall come to a three-room flat. (He smiles.) We'll have five or six rooms, and our books, and each other.

CLARE

I can't believe you're serious. You've always been a dreamer, but I can't believe you're going through with this fantastic nonsense!

DANIEL

I've chosen a narrow path, dear, but I hoped it might be wide enough for us both.

CLARE

It isn't. With your means and opportunities, you're offering me what any bank clerk would give his wife. I thought you loved me, but you're utterly selfish, and I think a little mad. You've a right to throw away your own life, but you've no right to throw away mine. (She hands him his ring.) Our engagement is off. (A pause. She starts for the door, and then hesitates, looks at her wrist watch, waits for him to call her back. When he doesn't, she returns.) Don't you think you're making a terrible mistake?

DANIEL

(Looks up from the ring. Simply.) No.

(Clare turns again, this time quickly and with resolution, and exits left.)

THE END

October 2, 1945
Germany

...I hope you'll forgive me for not writing last night. The Sergeant Major was passing out some tickets to a stage play, "Rosalinda," so I thought I would go. The play was put on by the USO in Regensburg at 8 p.m., so we had to leave about 6:30. It was really a swell show and I'm sure glad I decided to go. It reminded me of all the fun we used to have in Offill's drama class. When I look back on some of those skits and plays, it still embarrasses me. Do you remember "The Fool"? We really had fun putting on "Dude Ranch", "Afterwards", "Little Foxes", and others, didn't we, hon? (Even if we did have a little trouble with Offill)...

Later that summer the Lamb Dabs rented a big old frame house at Manhattan Beach for two weeks and I reluctantly went down. Leno promised he would figure out a way to get there. My Model A had long since found its way to the junk yard and taking the streetcar from Los Feliz to Manhattan Beach was no easy task.

The Highland Park newspaper reported the following:

SUB DEB CLUB RETURNS FROM BEACH TRIP

Meeting at the home of Mida June Lawhorn, August 27, the Lamb Dab sub-deb club formulated plans for a party to be given soon. Colleen Vienna, social chairman, is in charge of the event.

Members of the club, all seniors at Franklin High School, recently vacationed at Manhattan Beach. Those spending the week there were Berta Axt, president; Barbara Hawkins, vice-president; Barbara Petersen, secretary; Mida June Lawhorn, treasurer; Colleen Vienna, social chairman; Barbara Pierce, publicity manager; Nadeane Rhea, historian; Helen Coupe, Alice Skolfield, Marianna Hillman, Beverly McBride, Lorraine Fouch and Dolores Williams. Chaperones were Mrs. Edith Williams and Mrs. Frances Rhea.

Climaxing their stay at the beach, the girls entertained with a party. Guests attending were Al Foxcroft, Frank Petta, Elmer Black, Leno LaBianca, Bob Hoyle, Jack Noel, Bill Rankin, Jack Johnson, all of Los Angeles, and Lee Theroux, Ed Gains, Manford Barnes, Frank Pantsee and Sandy Dick of Manhattan Beach.

January 22, 1945
Holland 7:30 p.m.

...You mentioned the wonderful times we have had together. It brought back old memories; the time you were staying at Manhattan Beach with your girlfriends. Remember, I was on my vacation and used to drive down to see you almost every day. I had to borrow somebody's car and usually there was some "minor" thing wrong with it: the battery would be dead (or dying fast); it wouldn't have any brakes, the tires would be all shot, etc. We would go swimming in the day; then lie around in the warm sun talking and planning our future. Gosh, honey, it was so much fun! At night, we would either go driving or just stroll along the shore listening to the breakers hit the sand, come rushing up to us; and then the sucking noise of the undertow as they rushed back to the sea. It was music to our ears. Usually, if we went driving something would go wrong with the car and I would get so darned mad. But then when it was all over, we would laugh about it and talk about the wonderful time we had...

12

LENO managed a few more days off during that summer and we always headed for the beach; usually Santa Monica because it was the closest and our gas money was scarce. Many a wallet Leno left as security for five gallons of gas.

Dana joined us on several occasions and on this particular one we had noticed that "Wuthering Heights" was playing at a small theatre in Hollywood. Dana and I had seen it for the first time in the summer of 1939 and were so impressed with its dramatics that we sought a repeat performance whenever possible. Heathcliff was my idea of the perfect lover; deeply and forever devoted to his Cathy. The superb performance of Laurence Olivier has remained in my heart to this writing as the most outstanding portrayal of a fictional character I have witnessed.

Leno hadn't seen the film. Dana and I were certain he had missed a significant and momentous experience in the theatre and planned to rectify that privation on the way back from the beach that evening.

As the sun was setting and we gathered our clothes together, one of Leno's shoes was nowhere to be found. We searched the sand, the trash barrels, the car and the shore line but found no trace of it. I was frantic! Leno couldn't go into the theatre without shoes and I was sure this would be the last time the movie would be shown anywhere.

"I'll think of something," he assured me and he did.

He wore one shoe and tore his undershirt to shreds to make bandages for his other foot and hobbled into the theatre. His performance was convincing as no one stopped to question his bandaged foot.

My fifth viewing of "Wuthering Heights" was more beautiful with Leno at my side and he had to admit afterwards that it was pretty great! I have since seen the movie some twenty-five times and memorized the entire screenplay, performing for family and friends all of the leading characters, sometimes simultaneously.

Two days later, we received the following invitation through the mail:

Alice and Dana:

You are invited to attend a birthday party to be given for Leno LaBianca. Refreshments will be served at his home and the rest of the evening will be spent at the Glendale Civic. The party will be over at 12:00 midnight.
If you are unable to attend, please call

OL 3355 before Tuesday, August 5, 1941.

Date: Saturday, August 9, 1941
Time: 6:30 p.m.
Place: 3301 Waverly Drive

PART II

Confrontation with Change

"Life is a series of surprises, and would not be
worth taking or keeping if it were not."
Ralph Waldo Emerson

1

September 2, 1941
Los Angeles, California

Dear Alice,

THIS is the first time I have written you a letter and probably the last time, because I am not much of a writer. I can say things to you that sound silly when they are down on paper.

I really wrote to find out how you are, and am wondering if you are having a good time. I miss you very much and hope you come back to L.A. soon.

Oh, do you know what? We went to Sequoia National Park Sunday, and were planning to stay overnight, but the family didn't like it up there. So, we were going to find some place to stay on the highway, but the old man got a bug and drove all the way to L.A. that night.

Guess what? Howard got a 1937 Packard. (I'm sorry. Here's your chance!) I hope you have a swell time at the beach, and tell Dana not to work too hard. (I mean trying to get a sun tan!)

Take it easy,
L.A. LaBianca (Leno)

P.S. When are you coming back?

Love, LLB

Dana and I had gone to Emerald Bay, a private beach just south of Newport Beach, to spend a week with Aunt Pearl and Uncle Austin. We were treated royally, staying in a beautiful hillside home. Aunt Pearl traded the use of one of her Palm Springs "cottages" during the "season" for the use of a "beach cottage" when the summer heat became unbearable on the desert. Palm Springs was their home with Aunt Pearl's hundreds of acres of our great-grandfather's land, but she couldn't tolerate the desert when the one-hundred-and-ten degree weather arrived and she and Uncle Austin spent their summers on the coast when they weren't traveling to Europe or South America.

Dana and I spent the days on the beach, working on our tans, and the evenings frequenting the best restaurants on the coast—a lifestyle which was the exact opposite of our frugal existence on Joy Street. But after a week of their pompous indulgence, we were happy to get home to Joy Street and another year of Franklin High—my senior year.

To the tune of "On Wisconsin:"

On for Franklin
On for Franklin
Fight with might and main
Every man in his position,
Helping play the game. Rah! Rah! Rah!
On for Franklin
On for Franklin
Faith and courage gain.
That's the way, boys,
That's the play, boys,
Now score again.

To get to the ninth Annual Football Carnival held at the Los Angeles Coliseum we travelled on the "W" streetcar, transferring to the "V" downtown that took us directly to the Coliseum at Santa Barbara Street and South Figueroa. We sang and laughed all the way to the championship play-off between the north and south sides of the city. That year Franklin went into the game with the following record: Won—5, Lost—0, Tied—0, Percent—1,000! Having beaten Polytechnic, Marshall, Belmont, Lincoln and Wilson, Franklin was the Northern League champion.

Our team played their hearts out that day in the Coliseum and came away champions of the city! This great feat being accomplished primarily by Paul Roussel at fullback, Archie Wilson at right half, Loyal Tacy at left half, and Frank Petta at quarterback. Roussel, whom I had known since kindergarten and was affectionately called "Chubby," was later killed in action in the war; Wilson was picked up by the professionals and lost track of; Tacy married one of the Lamb Dabs, and Petta jilted one of them.

OFFICIAL PROGRAM

Los Angeles Coliseum
NOVEMBER 28, 1941 **9th ANNUAL FOOTBALL CARNIVAL**
PRICE 10c PARENT-TEACHERS ASSOCIATION MILK FUND

Archie Wilson
Captain, Franklin

FRANKLIN HIGH SCHOOL vs. ROOSEVELT HIGH SCHOOL

(North) SIXTH GAME — STARTING LINEUP **(South)**

NO.	NAME	POSITION	NAME	NO.
23	Schwenk	L.E.	Grbrovaz	56
33	Balchelor	L.T.	Klubnikin	29
2	Buliavac	L.G.	Kusada	54
21	Graham	C.	Basulto	45
22	Snegg	R.G.	Cohen	59
34	Shequen	R.T.	Eisenberg	41
13	Guglielmino	R.E.	Resnikoff	40
20	Petta	Q.	Leon	43
25	Tacy	L.H.	Pena	21
24	Wilson	R.H.	Regalado	17
27	Roussel	F.	Olivas	38

ROSTER

1 Toth	16 Coltey	26 Roberts	2 Cantor	40 Resnikoff	51 Infante
2 Buliavac, Bob	17 Hays	27 Roussel	9 Ayala	41 Eisenberg	52 Mawson
4 Cookmeyer	20 Petta	28 Walker	17 Regalado	42 Rhinehardt	53 Okabe
6 Kavser	21 Graham	30 Beal	21 Pena	43 Leon	54 Kusada
8 Hall	22 Snegg	31 Stansauk	29 Klubnikin	45 Basulto	56 Grbrovaz
10 Ward	23 Schwenk	32 Marty	31 Goldberg	46 Brajkovich	57 Valle
11 Buliavac, Ed	24 Wilson	33 Batchelor	37 Paulin	47 Varteresian	59 Cohen
13 Guglielmino	25 Tacy	34 Shequen	38 Olivas	48 Moldave	60 Kobzeff
14 Mathews		35 Glenn		49 Levergrant	

But in 1941 they were the greatest, and heroes to us all. How deeply hurt Leno was that he couldn't be part of that team. He had finished on top in the shot put in the spring, but track just wasn't football in his heart.

November 15, 1944
Holland 9 a.m.

...When you mentioned that it has been three years since Franklin had their championship football team, I was really shocked. I hadn't stopped to think about it lately and it didn't seem that long at all. We really had some good times that year, didn't we, honey? Also some very trying times, if you recall... But now that I can look back on them, they don't seem nearly as bad as they did at the time...

Sunday morning, ten days after the Franklin victory, Dana and I were still discussing the completed passes and ninety-nine yard field run by Archie Wilson on our way to Dad's house.

Dad lived in the southwest part of Los Angeles and to get there from Highland Park, we again took the "W" streetcar and transferred to the "7" on Main Street downtown. We got off at Century and Broadway and walked five blocks to 532 West Ninety-ninth Street. We were still talking about Archie's footwork as we walked through Dad's open front door.

He had the radio blaring and without saying "hello," he said, "Be quiet, I want to hear this."

"Japan suddenly opened war on the United States and Great Britain this morning," the announcer was saying. "A flotilla of planes bearing the "Rising Sun" of Japan on their wing tips appeared out of the south while most of the city was sleeping. The planes dove immediately to the attack on Pearl Harbor and Hickam Field, the giant air base lying nearby."

"Where's Pearl Harbor?" I asked.

"In Honolulu," Dad answered sharply. "Be quiet!"

"Three battleships have been struck as they lay at anchor in the naval base," the announcer continued. "The USS Oklahoma has reportedly been set afire. Latest reports are that the USS West Virginia has been sunk along with another warship, although there is no confirmation as yet. It has been reported that a direct torpedo bomb hit has been made on the Hickam Field barracks and that it's feared that three hundred and fifty men have been killed."

"How stupid this country has been," Dad remarked. "We've been sending all of our scrap iron to the Japanese for the past ten years and

Los Angeles Examiner

AN AMERICAN PAPER FOR THE AMERICAN PEOPLE • THE GREAT NEWSPAPER OF THE GREAT SOUTHWEST

Reg. U. S. Pat. Off.
Examiner Building, 1111 S. Broadway Examiner Telephone Richmond 1212

VOL. XXXVIII—NO. 362   CCC(®)   LOS ANGELES, MONDAY, DECEMBER 8, 1941   Complete Weather Reports on Page 2, Part II   Two Sections—Part I—FIVE CENTS

CALIFORNIA FORECAST
LOS ANGELES AND VICINITY—Fair and warm Monday and Tuesday, with slightly lower temperature Monday near the coast.
SAN FRANCISCO BAY REGION—Fair Monday and Tuesday with early morning fog.

TEMPERATURES

JAPS BLAST HAWAII

2 U. S. Warships, 2 Enemy Air Carriers Reported Sunk

Very Heavy Losses in Hawaii---F. D. R.

G-MEN SEIZE 4 JAPANESE IN LITTLE TOKYO

British, U. S. Navies Battle Nippon Fleet

IN THE NEWS

WELL, fellow Americans, we are in the war and we have got to win it.

There may have been some difference of opinion among good Americans about getting into the war, but there is no difference about how we should come out of it.

We must come out victorious and with the largest V in the alphabet.

We are not completely prepared for war.

We have not got a Swiss system of universal service that we will have to have some day, since the lands are full of robbers and seas of pirates.

But we will get better and stronger every day, and we will not have to get very good and very strong to knock the everlasting daylights out of Japan.

We may have some small reverses at first, but do not let that worry you—if it happens.

It is not who wins the first round but who wins the last one that counts for victory.

And there is no doubt about the victory, folks—none whatever.

The worst thing about the war with Japan is that it will *our efforts and prevent so* rendering the all out *Britain* that we were *do* and planning further to do.

But we will still manage to keep Britain going with our right hand while we poke

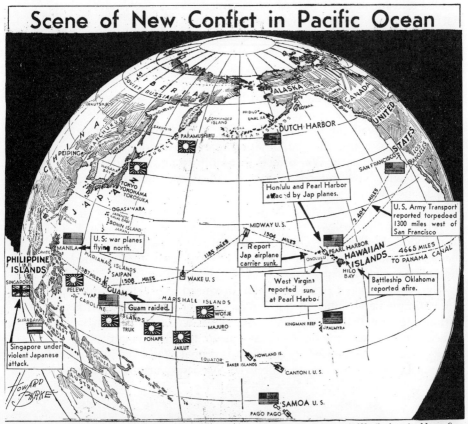

Scene of New Conflict in Pacific Ocean

Honolulu and Pearl Harbor attacked by Jap planes.

U. S. Army Transport reported torpedoed 1300 miles west of San Francisco

U. S. war planes flying north.

Report Jap airplane carrier sunk.

West Virginia reported sunk at Pearl Harbor.

Battleship Oklahoma reported afire.

Guam raided.

Singapore under violent Japanese attack.

SMASHING SAVAGELY, Japanese bombers yesterday opened total war on United States outposts in the Pacific. Double-headed arrow shows how Japanese islands encircle the Philippines. From several strongly fortified bases Japan can launch planes, closest being Formosa, only 230 miles from tip of Luzon. General Douglas MacArthur reported Japanese planes over Luzon and attacks on military bases.

they have built a war machine with it. Of course, this means all-out war," he continued. "I'll probably be drafted now."

"Oh, Dad, you're too old," I kidded. "What would they want with you?"

"What do you mean? I'm only forty. I'm in great shape. They need men like me. I'm registered with the draft board, you know."

Dad had always lived in his own little world of Saturday night poker games, semi-weekly bowling leagues and frequent lavish dinner parties aboard steamships from foreign lands. Wherever Dad went he was the "life of the party," always having a funny story to tell and doing so with lavish gestures and a colorful voice. His renditions of "Casey At The Bat" and "The Face On The Barroom Floor" had kept us entertained for years.

He was in charge of traffic at Sunkist, the California citrus growers cooperative, having worked his way up from office boy, and was often wined and dined by steamship and railroad officials.

He and Alice Ruth had been married ever since I could remember. She wasn't anything like Mother. She never had any children of her own and Dad was her whole life. She catered to his every whim.

Dad told me often, "I have never stopped loving your mother, but I just couldn't stand all those dirty diapers."

Dad, marching off to war? The possibility was absurd, I thought.

The possibility was real enough the next day at school when our classes were tuned into bulletins from all over the world:

"President Roosevelt expected to ask Congress to declare war on Japan today."

"British wait for Premier Churchill to implement promise to 'declare war within the hour' if Japan attacked America."

"The Secretary of War directs that all firms and manufacturing plants who have defense contracts will at once institute proper measures against sabotage."

When Radio Tokyo reported that Japanese naval ships had surrounded the island of Guam, a strategic American stronghold, and that an oil reservoir and hotel had been set afire, we were frightened. We didn't know what to expect next.

The Navy ordered San Diego Harbor closed to all ship movements almost immediately and an anti-submarine net was placed across the entrance to protect the huge fleet base. When we heard the harbor was mined, we were sure the Pacific coast was vulnerable to enemy attack.

Six thousand Japanese fishermen on Terminal Island, on the coast just north of Long Beach, were immobilized. Air-raid warning signals were moved into full wartime action and we were educated as to procedures in case of a blackout or enemy attack. Anti-aircraft artillery from Camp Haan, further north, was placed in position and ready for the enemy.

The blackout came. For several hours we waited in fear, then an all-clear warning was sounded and we relaxed once again. We learned later that Japanese submarines had been sighted off of the Southern California coast.

The Franklin Press had its comments regarding our first, frightening blackout via Campus News by Dana Skolfield:

Since December seventh, students at Franklin have never had an opportunity to run out of conversation. The days when a group of excited blondes gathered together to talk over last night's date or when a pack of "wolves" assembled to discuss the latest addition of feminine pulchritude to the campus—these days are gone forever.

The attack on Pearl Harbor started the ball rolling, for on Monday, December eighth, bits of conversation snatched from passing students were far from usual. Words such as "War!" and "Germany will follow..." and "Guam's lost"... filled the air. Now things are happening so rapidly that every day a new topic keeps tongues wagging and ears sharply tuned.

The main topic of last week was, "Where were you during the black-out?" Answers, interesting, exciting, dull and usual were offered. Katie McGregor was on her way to the beach. She and her friends had just started the car when suddenly a sound, first startling and then disappointing, reached their ears. The street-lights went out and there they were—all dressed up and no place to go...

Bebe Callus was in the theatre and was wondering whether he would have to sleep there for the duration or walk home in the dark...

Leno LaBianca was beginning to dust off his fiddle to see if he could recall the old musical days of recitals and such, but he didn't remember enough to play in the dark.

The following weeks brought daily announcements that were threatening our way of life. Canada, Australia, Costa Rica, the Netherlands, Mexico, Nicaragua and other South American countries declared war on Japan and Germany. All information concerning the strength, location and movement of forces outside the continental limits of the United States was rigidly censored, as well as almost everything

71

that was happening close to home.

Berlin blamed it all onto the "warmongering of the American President Roosevelt." This began the never-ending barrage of propaganda emanating from Germany, Italy and Japan, the "axis powers."

We had our own brand of propaganda that was to last throughout the nearly four years of hostilities, such as the Los Angeles Examiner editorial that appeared on December the eighth:

> Well, fellow Americans, we are in the war and we have got to win it. There may have been some differences of opinion among good Americans about getting into the war, but there is no difference about how we should come out of it. We must come out victorious and with the largest "V" in the alphabet.
>
> We are not completely prepared for war, but we will get better and stronger every day. We may have some small reverses at first, but do not let that worry you—if it happens. It is not who wins the first round but who wins the last one that counts for victory. And there is no doubt about the victory, folks—none whatever.
>
> The worst thing about the war with Japan is that it will divide our efforts and prevent us from rendering the all out aid to England that we were doing and planning further to do. But we will still manage to keep Britain going with our right hand while we poke Japan in the nose with our left.
>
> Japan has been wanting war for a long time. It has been swaggering around Asia, murdering a lot of unarmed Chinamen. Now it is going to get a war and a real one. Fortunately, we can manufacture ten ships to Japan's one, and ten aeroplanes to Japan's one. Naturally, we can fly the planes better and fight the ships better. And that means that as soon as we swing into action we will wash up the war. Before the war is over, we will have burned up all the paper houses in Japan and sunk most of their "scrap iron" battleships and put this bunch of Oriental marauders back on the right little, tight little, out of sight little island where they belong.
>
> Our main concern now is England. This attack by Japan upon us is largely to create a diversion. We must not be diverted anymore than is necessary for our own protection. The war is OUR war now—not only in Asia, but in Europe. We have got to win in both arenas. The European war, to be frank and factual, is not going to be so easy, but we can win it and will...

December 7, 1944
Holland

...Here it is, three years to the day that the war started for us. If we had thought at that time that it would last as long as it has already, we probably would have been very discouraged...

Day and night my mind is filled with memories and pictures of little things we used to do together. The sweet things you used to say and do for me, and which I took for granted. I long for the time when we will again have days like those in the past to live over again. Pray with me that that time is near...

2

I had met Leno's mother, Corina, and her aunt, Rose Bruno, affectionately called Zi Zi, at Leno's birthday party in August. They spent most of their time in the kitchen and I offered to help. Corina was a kind woman, anxious to please. She had an accent, but her speech and mannerisms were quiet and restrained, totally different from Italian women I had seen in the movies. She went out of her way to be friendly, but seemed uncomfortable. Her face was serious with dark brown eyes and a small mouth; her countenance, one of strength and compassion.

Zi Zi, on the other hand, was a jolly woman with a merry twinkle in her eye.

"You're Leno's girlfriend? Is that why you want to help?" she teased.

I was embarrassed, but pleased.

Zi Zi had no children of her own, but had an adopted son, Sammy, who was five years older than Leno and like a big brother to him. Leno had mentioned Sammy often because he had married a girl, Vernita, who wasn't Italian. There had been considerable objection from the family at first, but they all grew to love her, and Leno felt that had paved the way for us.

I had to face the family again at Christmas time. They were having their traditional Christmas Eve poker party at Zi Zi's and Leno wanted me to drop in with him on our way to the movies.

"Poker on Christmas Eve?" I asked. "That doesn't seem much like Christmas."

"We open our presents on Christmas Eve and then play poker all night, stopping only to go to midnight Mass. After Mass, we have a big feast. That's the way the family has done it for years," explained Leno. "We won't stay long. My dad will get mad if I don't, at least, make an appearance."

With apprehension, I entered Zi Zi's house—small but comfortably furnished—and sparkling with everything neatly in place. Noisy

Corina
LaBianca

laughter and conversation could be heard coming from the back of the house. Zi Zi and Emma met us at the front door and led us through the kitchen to a room with a large table, around which were seated several men, all speaking Italian noisily, obviously having a good time.

"You're the girl who wanted to help in the kitchen at Leno's birthday party," Zi Zi said cheerily.

She remembered me! That made me happy.

As we entered the room, Sammy shouted, "Hi, Leno!" and Leno introduced me. "So this is Alice. It's about time you brought her around to meet us," Sammy continued.

Then to his wife, who along with Emma, was the only female playing poker, "Vernita, this is Alice. Now you'll have someone to talk to that you can understand!"

Sammy was six feet, two inches tall and good-looking; Vernita was only five feet, two inches tall, blonde, pretty, good-humored and extremely friendly, putting me at ease.

I hadn't come face to face with Leno's father since our encounter on the front porch at Waverly Drive last spring. His eyes hadn't left his cards from the time we came in. Leno spoke up, "You remember my dad. Dad, this is Alice Skolfield."

Anthony looked up without a smile. "Oh, yes. How are you?" Then something to everyone in Italian, at which they all laughed. Their laughter was infectious and I laughed, too. I don't know why.

Vernita interjected, "They do that to me all the time. You'll get used to it."

Corina quietly smiled and tried to explain to me what he had said. Something to the effect that I kept turning up when he least expected me. As with all Italian jokes, I later found out, it wasn't funny in English, especially to me.

The men went back to their cards and Leno said, "We're going to the movies. Do you want to go, Emma?"

She laughed. "Are you kidding? I'm winning!"

We said goodnight and left, but not before I noticed that Anthony LaBianca didn't like me anymore at our second meeting than he had at our first.

"Your dad wasn't too happy to see me," I said after we were in the car, which happened to be his father's. "I'm an outsider and interfering with his precious traditions."

"Why do you care what he thinks? It's none of his business. He doesn't run my life," Leno answered emphatically.

Leno's relationship with me was a part of his rebellion, I thought. I felt uncertain and insecure. Was I just another way he had of defying his father?

December 31, 1945
Vienna, Austria

My darling Alice,

...I needn't tell you what night this is. The end of a terribly long and terribly painful year. You can't imagine how happy I am that it has finally come to a close.

Tonight doesn't seem like New Year's Eve at all. I went to the show with a new sergeant named Carlson and we saw "Nobody Lives Forever" with John Garfield and Geraldine Fitzgerald. I liked the show quite well because most of the story took place in L.A.

It's not even ten-thirty yet, but I don't think I'll sit up and see the new year in. There doesn't seem to be any sense in it without you. But next year we'll stay up all night at some real nice place, then drive to Santa Barbara for breakfast, like you wanted to the day of our graduation from Franklin...

3

MIKE Radogna was a close friend of Leno's and became a close friend of mine. I first met him at the Pasadena Civic on a Friday night when Leno had decided, again, we shouldn't go steady. Leno arrived with Mike and I had gone with Lorraine and Marianna.

Mike was handsome with black wavy hair, an easy personality and flashing smile. He was friendly and we danced together most of the evening. He told me about Dorothy.

"If you think Leno's old man is obstinate, you should meet mine. I work at my dad's grocery store in East L.A. That's where I met Dorothy," he confided. "I'm really crazy about her, but Dad goes into a rage whenever he sees me talking to her."

"I'd like to meet her sometime, if Leno ever asks me out again. Maybe we could double date," I suggested.

"Oh, he will, Alice," he answered. "You're all he ever talks about."

"Every six months or so, he gets independent with me. I've never been sure of him," I offered sadly.

"Well, he's had his eye on us all evening, but don't tell him I said so," he laughed.

"Why didn't you bring Dorothy tonight?" I asked.

"She's giving me a bad time right now. My dad has sold the store and bought one in Glendale. She knows how Dad feels about her and thinks he did it just to separate us. She may be right. She says it has to be Dad or her and I'm not ready for that choice," he answered thoughtfully.

"What is it with these Italian fathers? They look down on us girls because we have dates. Look at Angie! She and Howard see more of each other than Leno and I do, but they have to do it secretly. Since Bumpy got that Packard, they go to the beach more than they go to school!"

"Angie's father would kill Bumpy if he ever found out about them," Mike commented.

Before the evening was over, Leno had arranged a double date for us with Mike and Dorothy. Dorothy was a pretty girl and obviously adored

Mike, but she was discontented with their relationship. She had an unhappy home life and wanted to get married. Mike was only eighteen and wasn't prepared to make the break with his family. The four of us had some great times together that spring, but I disliked being put into the same frame of reference with her, as I was by Leno's friends and his family. We did have some similar problems, but that's where it ended.

Mike was graduating from Cathedral, a Catholic high school, at the same time Leno and I were graduating from Franklin. That is, we were hoping Leno was graduating. On June 2, 1942, his father received the following letter:

LOS ANGELES CITY HIGH SCHOOL DISTRICT

Benjamin Franklin High School

820 NORTH AVENUE 54
LOS ANGELES, CALIFORNIA

OFFICE OF THE PRINCIPAL

VIERLING KERSEY
SUPERINTENDENT OF SCHOOLS

June 2, 1942

Mr. Anthony LaBianca
3301 Waverly Drive
Los Angeles, California

Dear Sir:

Your son Leno has been transferred from a regular homeroom (Senior A) to a demote homeroom because of his low citizenship record. This means that he will be unable to participate in any of the Senior A activities including the commencement program.

However, if he does not loose any more merits from this date, he will be able to receive his diploma Friday afternoon after 2:30 p.m.

I am very sorry to have to inform you of this.

Very truly yours,

John R. Hoist

John R. Hoist
Counselor

H:V

THE LAMB DABS

Counter clock-wise, starting on right:
Jean Florey, Nadeane Rhea, Barbara Pierce, Lorraine Fouch, Alice Skolfield, Berta Axt,
Barbara Hawkins, Colleen Vienna, Marianna Hillman, Dolores Williams,
Mida June Lawhorn, Helen Coupe, Beverly Winnard

When a student received ten demerits, he was placed in the demote homeroom. When Leno arrived, Bumpy was already there, having played hooky once too often. The only time he could see Angie was during school hours and going to the beach was a lot more fun than holding hands between classes.

Leno received his demerits for three seemingly innocent incidents: (1) he spoke too frankly, (2) he trusted a friend and (3) he was too embarrassed to obey the teacher's request.

(1) Miss Greene was a short, chubby, elderly, narrow-minded, old-maid math teacher whom we all had to put up with throughout our high school careers. She referred to Leno and me as marshmallows—a term I never quite understood. I wasn't in Leno's algebra class, but the story I heard was this:

Miss Greene was expounding on the tragedy of the war and urging the students to save their old clothes to send to Britain and France to help the war orphans there.

Leno spoke up, quite honestly, "Why don't they send bundles to Italy and Germany? The children there are just as needy."

Miss Greene, her face a vivid red, in a rage, grabbed Leno out of his front-row seat, yelling and spitting, "Fascist! Nazi!" and dragged him to the boys' vice-principal's office.

Mr. Axe told Leno that his father would have to come to the school and explain the meaning of this outrageous statement made by his son.

Mr. LaBianca did come to Franklin. He was angry, but not at Leno this time.

"Thank God, this is a free country," he stated emphatically, catching Mr. Axe and Miss Greene off guard. "Isn't that what this war is all about?" He challenged them with fire in his eyes.

Then quietly, "My son was only thinking of the needy children in those countries because he knows of his cousins' plight in Italy. The children are not responsible for the acts of their leaders."

He managed to convince the school that neither Leno nor his family were enemy agents, but Leno received three demerits for being disrespectful to Miss Greene.

(2) As a Girl Guard, I was on duty in the halls of Franklin at noon to see that no one entered the building during the lunch hour. Leno was looking for me one day and had to pass Marianna, who was also a Girl Guard on duty, to get to my post.

"Go ahead, Leno, Alice is down the hall. I won't tell anyone," Marianna laughed good-naturedly.

She loved a good joke and reported Leno as being in the building without a pass. Marianna's little prank cost Leno three more demerits.

(3) Drama was a class Leno was in only because I wanted him to be. He found it painful at times, particularly the embarrassing requests that our drama teacher, Kathryn Offill, often made.

Kathryn was under five feet tall, a vivacious blonde, with energy that wouldn't end. Her handsome husband had recently enlisted in the Army Air Corps and she was six months pregnant. These two events had put her in an irritable, unreasonable mood most of the time. She wanted Leno to do an improvisation (skit without a script, impromptu) of a farmer calling his livestock to dinner.

"I'm not going to do that," Leno snapped.

She jumped up from her chair, unexpected by all of us, infuriated. "You're just too smart for this class," she retorted. We had never seen her like this.

Leno wouldn't let it pass. "I'm too smart to do the stupid things *you* expect us to do," he continued.

She grabbed him by the arm and virtually dragged him from the room. How this little pregnant woman could handle Leno, who towered over her, with such force we couldn't believe. But she got him down to Mr. Axe's office, which cost Leno four demerits and landed him in the demote homeroom.

February 18, 1945
Holland

...Yes, I remember Marianna turning me in for being in the hall once during the noon hour. Oh, well, she probably didn't mean any harm. I'm glad to hear she is getting married. I hope she and Ray will be very happy.

In one of your letters you mentioned my leaving you a couple of times in high school for several little "items." I'm not sure to what you refer, but I remember quite well that the few times we decided to call it quits had nothing whatsoever to do with any other girl. You know darned well you were the only girl who meant anything to me, even then. The reason we broke up a few times, as I remember it, was due to a silly feeling that most young boys have about being "tied down."

...Bumpy said in a recent letter that he might have to go overseas. That's a tough break now that the baby is almost due. In my answer to him I said that he and I always seemed to get the tough breaks, starting with our school days. Remember all the trouble we used to get into over the most trivial matters? We had some wonderful times at Franklin, honey, but we also had some *very trying* times. Remember?...

At six o'clock, June 25, 1942, at the Occidental College Hillside Theatre in Eagle Rock, Angie and I sang our hearts out with the rest of the class, while Leno and Bumpy watched and listened with the other spectators.

To the tune of "God Ever Glorious."

Franklin! All hail to thee,
Praises we sing;
Our love and our loyalty
To thee we bring.
Friendship has been thy gift
With laughter and tears;
With rainbow memories carried
Through the shining years.

My high school graduation

4

THE Sunday before graduation, Mother married Joe Geers, after knowing him only one week. Joe was good-looking and kind-hearted and reminded us of Melvyn Douglas. All of us, except Edith, called him "Dad," which pleased him as he had no children of his own. Mother was like an excited teenager as Edith and I went shopping with her to pick out her wedding outfit—a baby blue suit with a pale brown fur collar. And on her wedding day she did look beautiful, and happier than I had ever seen her.

Their simple ceremony in a small, quaint wedding chapel on Western Avenue in southwest Los Angeles turned into a gala family get-together.

Mother's lifelong friend, Ethel Barbour, had a reception afterwards at her home. Aunt Pearl and Uncle Austin made one of their rare appearances along with Mother's sister, Katherine and her daughter Babs. Joe's mother and step-father were there as well as all five of Mother's children and we had a grand time, singing around the piano to Aunt Katherine's lively tunes. Dana and I did several scenes from "Wuthering Heights," which convinced everyone we would be famous one day.

Leno was invited, but couldn't get away from work. He had advanced from being a grocery clerk to taking telephone orders at his father's wholesale grocery business. He worked Sundays and holidays, with hours more confining than ever. "It's just as well," I thought. "He isn't quite ready for exposure to my undisciplined family with its variety of personalities."

Of course, Mother told Aunt Pearl all about Leno and his father's successful business.

"It's amazing, Jane," Aunt Pearl commented. "A boy with all that family background being interested in your daughter. What does he think about your house on the alley?"

"That doesn't bother him a bit," Mother answered proudly. "He isn't interested in Alice's money."

Joe Geers and Mother
June 21, 1942

Top Row, from left to right: Austin, Edith, Pearl, Mother, Joe, Alice, Aunt Katherine, Dana. Front Row: Jane, Bobbie, cousin Babs, Aunt Pearl's Scotties.

"I'm going to buy you a nice house soon, Jane," Pearl continued, "when my taxes are all straightened out."

That was Aunt Pearl for you. She had been saying she would buy Mother a house for years, but she never did. She gave Mother and Joe a one hundred dollar check for a wedding present.

Shortly after graduation, we moved to a large two-story house on North Avenue Fifty-three, and Leno joined a Monday night league at the Highland Park bowling alley. I was quite upset, at first, since I hated being tied down to a bowling league. I went with him most of the time, but when he wanted to bowl on every one of our dates, trying to make a perfect score of three hundred, I became sick of the sport.

For graduation, Leno's father had given him a beige, 1941 Chevrolet coupe, but he owned it jointly with Emma. Her demands for the car didn't always coincide with Leno's, and as it turned out, Monday night was about the only time I saw him that summer, as he had the car reserved for bowling.

ALTITUDE 1,750 FT

Gilman
HOT SPRINGS *The San Jacinto Hot Mud Sulphur Springs*

THESE BATHS ARE UNEXCELLED
FOR RHEUMATISM IN ALL ITS
FORMS DISEASES OF BLOOD
STOMACH, KIDNEY, LIVER
AND NERVOUS COMPLAINTS

PHONE SAN JACINTO 8811

Gilman Hot Springs, Calif.

July 15, 1942

Dear Alice,

Well, you lucky kid, I finally found time to write you a letter. As you know, I am extremely busy up here tending to all the beautiful "girls." But seriously, I am sorry I couldn't write you sooner. Emma has been hanging around all the time, and I felt funny telling her I had to write a letter. (No offense meant.)

In case you want to know, I'll tell you what I have been doing. And in case you don't want to know, I'll tell you anyway.

We arrived here on Sunday about eleven a.m. We couldn't get a bungalow until three, so Emma and I went swimming. They have a fairly good pool, but I'll take the beach any old day. After swimming we unpacked and read the rest of the day. That night we just walked around; Emma and I, (no kidding) and looked the place over. Well, it seemed that we would have a wonderful time. Posters were all over the place advertising their activities, which included golf, tennis, swimming, hiking, horseback riding, fishing and hunting, archery, Ping-Pong, badminton, croquet, horseshoe pitching and bowling!

But Monday morning we were due for a big surprise. We discovered that from the great list of activities, the only ones which were functioning were golf (I can't play), tennis (we forgot our racquets), swimming (if they ever open the pool). It has been closed since Sunday (they say they are cleaning it). Then there is hiking (need I say more?), horseshoe pitching (Ha-Ha), and Ping-Pong (bring your own balls). You noticed the absence of bowling, didn't you? You're glad, too, aren't you? I guess I can get along without it for a week—maybe.

As the great philosopher LaBianca said, "When the likeable essentials are absent, one must divert his attention to less likeable ones." Pretty good, huh?

So I have been spending my time reading and sleeping. I've got to admit I have been eating quite a bit, too, but I guess that's not too odd.

As you can undoubtedly see, I am very bored with this place, and can hardly wait to get home. I miss you very much, Alice, and wish you were here. I think I might not mind the place then. I am going to try to get the folks to leave early, but I think it won't do any good, because they are enjoying themselves.

I will see you at the very latest on Sunday night or Monday morning. I think this is the longest letter I ever wrote, you lucky girl!...

That Monday Joe took us all to the beach. He promised that we would be home by six o'clock, in time for Leno to pick me up. When we were ten minutes late, I knew I had missed Leno and asked Joe if he would take me to the bowling alley.

"If he couldn't wait ten minutes for you, I don't think you should go chasing after him," he answered with authority.

A bitter argument ensued and I ran crying to my room. What right did he have to tell me what to do?

When Leno came by after bowling, Joe told him I couldn't see him as I was being punished for being disrespectful. I cried all night and the next morning I told Mother that I was leaving to go live with Nana.

"I can't stand living here with him bossing me around," I cried.

"You're seventeen, Alice, and can choose where you want to live,"

Mother said quietly; then tears filled her eyes. "Someday you may know what it is to have your daughter leave home. Just remember, I love you and want you to be happy, but you're breaking my heart."

I felt sad leaving Mother, but I wasn't used to having a man around and resented the authority she had given him. I had been free to come and go with Leno as I pleased all through high school, and didn't see why I had to be restricted now. I packed my few clothes, walked to the "W" streetcar line, transferred to the "9" and arrived at Nana's in the early afternoon. My sister, Edith, was happy to have me join her in the small, front bedroom of the modest, three-bedroom, brown frame house.

Edith was three years my senior. She had beautiful, black curly hair, expressive blue eyes and all the happy enthusiasm possible in one individual. She was shorter than I and always working on her figure. Edith had graduated from Manual Arts High School where our father had also gone, except that he had to leave at sixteen, before graduating, to get a job to help support the family. After six months at Woodbury Business College, Edith became a stenographer and was currently employed at Dunn and Bradstreet. Her weekends were occupied by a marine from Camp Pendleton, which was down the coast about fifty miles, and she didn't have any spare time to spend with me.

Almost as soon as I arrived at Nana's, I was sorry I had left Mother. I missed Dana, Jane and Bobbie and I would never see Leno now, I thought, living clear across town from him. But fate was on my side.

5

ANTHONY LaBianca's dream was coming true. His wholesale grocery business was flourishing, and that summer he moved into his new headquarters in the Vernon Central Manufacturing District, in the southeast part of the city. The large one-story concrete building was built on a spur of the Southern Pacific Railroad. The offices were expansive, covering about one-third of the building. The buying and advertising departments were off of the reception area in the front. The order and accounting departments were behind—three offices separated by glass partitions and large enough to accommodate future development of office machinery and computer equipment. Mr. LaBianca's office was behind the accounting department with a back door to the storage facility. The warehouse was equipped with modern fork-lift machinery manned by Italians and East Los Angeles Mexicans.

When Leno finished work there at nine p.m., Nana's house was not too far out of his way home, and he arrived there to take me out by ten o'clock on several occasions.

My father thought this a ridiculous hour for a young man to come calling and labeled me "bird brain" for "catering to Leno's every whim." In spite of this, Dad became quite fond of Leno. After all, they were both "Leos", with birthdays in August, only six days apart.

"The manager at Greenhagen's Market says Italians make good husbands," Dad commented whenever Leno's name was mentioned.

On August 8, 1942, I was invited to Mary LaBianca's sixteenth birthday party at 1231 Cypress Avenue in Cypress Park. Leno's cousins, Mary, Stella, Lino and Jane were the four children of Sam LaBianca, Anthony's brother. Sam resembled his brother, but his accent was a little thicker and sometimes I had difficulty understanding him. He was congenial, but like all Italian fathers I had met, was protective of his daughters, and only politely friendly toward outsiders such as myself.

His son, Lino, was twelve years old and handsome with dark, wavy hair and a cheerful personality—warm and friendly. He teased his older sisters, lovingly and constantly, and he and Leno were plainly great pals. His Italian name was undisturbing to him and my persistent quizzing revealed their grandfather's full name to be "Pasqualino."

"We had two choices," little Lino laughed. "Our names could either be shortened to Patsy or Lino. Lucky for us our parents didn't like the name of Patsy."

I never kidded Leno about his name, nor told him that his cousin had spilled the beans. Pasqualino was a part of Leno's heritage about which he had no sense of humor.

In the fall, Leno and I started to Los Angeles City College (LACC). I wanted to go into the drama department, but Leno was so upset with the idea, that I decided to major in accounting. He chose business administration and we had one class and all our free time together.

LACC was on Vermont Avenue just north of Clinton and the only college I could afford to attend. No tuition was required and my dad paid for my books and gave me an allowance of two dollars a week for carfare and lunches. I took the "9" streetcar from Nana's and transferred at Vernon and Vermont to the "V", which ended at the college—an hour-and-a-half trip for ten cents, while Leno took the bus from Hyperion and Rowena, which brought him directly to LACC.

College was not in Howard Bumpass' plans. Angie would be eighteen in November and he was counting the days. Her father, Paul, still forbade her to see him, but they rendezvoused in secret at Howard's house. Angie shortened her name to Ann and was dearly loved by Howard's family. His mother and father and younger brother, Walter, were just as warm and friendly as Paul was hostile, and were amused at Paul's attitude.

When Howard told his parents that he and Ann wanted to marry as soon as she was eighteen, they gave their blessing and assisted in the conspiracy. Howard needed their consent as he was only seventeen.

The wedding was arranged to take place at Howard's uncle's home several miles north of Los Angeles. Leno and I were asked to go along as their best man and maid of honor, but Leno didn't want to get involved. He purposely forgot to tell me until after Howard and Ann were safely married with his aunt and uncle as witnesses.

Paul was furious when he found out, and refused to speak to either one of them or allow them in his home. But Ann's mother, Mary, accepted their marriage happily, and secretly spent much time with her new son-in-law and daughter.

The war news was bad. Masi and Roxie Lucarelli had joined the

Navy, Mike Radogna had been drafted into the Army and Al Foxcroft and Elmer Black had joined the Coast Guard. Since the bombing of Pearl Harbor, a year before, the Japanese had taken possession of British and American strongholds in the Pacific, giving them dominion over three thousand miles of ocean, millions of square miles of land and millions of people. They had control of the Pacific from west to east between India and Hawaii and from north to south between Siberia and Australia, cornering 95 percent of the world's natural rubber and 70 percent of the world's tin.

General Douglas A. MacArthur had been appointed Supreme Commander of the Allied Forces in the Pacific and became the architect for the campaign to drive the Japanese from their strongholds in the Philippines and the islands north of Australia; as well as being placed in the position of defending Australia, itself.

President Roosevelt and Britain's Prime Minister, Winston Churchill, had reaffirmed a policy that the Atlantic war came first, no matter what the cost in the Far East. This policy left MacArthur with dangerously limited supplies and resources, allowing him to maintain only a line of strategic defense rather than one of offense.

In March, he had been ordered off of the Philippines and announced upon his arrival in Australia, "The President of the United States ordered me to break through the Japanese lines and proceed from Corregidor to Australia for the purpose, as I understand it, of reorganizing the American offensive against Japan, a primary object of which is the relief of the Philippines. I came through and I shall return."

"I shall return" became the battle cry of all the Allied armed forces who were now inching their way back through the conquered islands, one by one, constructing air bases, hoping eventually to reach Japan.

In Europe, Hitler was on the way to enclosing the entire Mediterranean and the Near East in a giant pincer where he planned to move eastward to join Japan.

In April the draft age for army recruits was established to be between eighteen and forty, which eliminated my father from the draft on the eve of his physical exam.

Our optimistic hopes for an early end to the war were fading fast. Rationing of auto tires, gasoline, sugar, coffee, meat, fats and oils, butter, cheese, processed foods and shoes had been in effect since the end of December, 1941, and the Office of Price Administration (OPA) had been established in January fixing price ceilings on all commodities except farm products. In April the War Manpower Commission (WMC) froze prices, wages, salaries and twenty-seven million workers in their jobs. Our future looked bleak.

On December sixteenth, the front page of the morning newspaper announced what Leno had called to tell me the night before. The headlines read:

$400,000 FIRE EATS UP L.A. FOOD

Canned goods and staple groceries valued at $250,000 yesterday were destroyed when fire swept through the State Wholesale Grocery Co., Inc., 4770 East 50th Street, Vernon.

Damage to the building was said by president Anthony LaBianca of the firm to run "well over $150,000."

The warehouse of the food company which supplies canned goods and other food items to 350 jobbers in Southern California was gutted by flames which started in an empty railroad box car in the rear of the establishment.

"The flames from the box car set the roof of the warehouse on fire and it was all lost in 20 minutes," said LaBianca.

LaBianca said it was impossible for any of the employees to

salvage any of the goods. The fire finally burned itself out about four hours later.

The 355 foot long concrete building was one of the largest food depots in the Los Angeles area. Fear that the large volume of canned foodstuffs destroyed by the fire would create another problem in the already critical food situation in the community was expressed by LaBianca. He said, however, that immediate steps would be taken to re-establish the property and continue business.

Anthony LaBianca did re-establish his property, but got permission to do so only on his written promise to lease the new building to the government for the duration of the national emergency.

His business was continued in a dreadful, old, dilapidated, warehouse and office building next to the Vernon stock yards, where my accounting career was soon to get underway.

6

WE saw 1943 in at Mike Lyman's restaurant in Hollywood with Howard and Ann. For two dollars a piece we had crab meat and avocado appetizer, matzo ball soup, California green salad, prime ribs of eastern beef, potatoes, vegetable, coffee and hot mince pie with brandy sauce.

In early January we finally got to see "The Drunkard." For ten years this famous melodrama and olio had been playing at the Theatre Mart on Clinton, close to LACC, and seats had to be reserved well in advance. We had the best table in the house on a Saturday night for two dollars and twenty-five cents, which included all the beer we could drink. Ours had to be root beer as none of us were twenty-one. Before we reached that coveted age, we would be seasoned beyond our years.

But in 1943, we could eat the Royal Dinner and dance at Lucca's restaurant at Fifth and Western for a dollar twenty-five and, of course, see Ken Murray's "Blackouts of 1943" with Marie Wilson and Daisy, the Wonder Dog, at the El Capitan Theatre in Hollywood. Damon Runyon said, "Blackouts of 1943 is one of the greatest vaudeville shows I have seen since the palmiest days of the old Palace and the big time. It is solid entertainment from start to finish."

When our first semester at LACC ended on January thirty-first, Leno decided to transfer to the University of Southern California (USC). We had both looked forward to the day we could attend this famous University, but the tuition was way beyond my father's budget at eight dollars a unit.

Once again we were separated and life at City College without Leno was unbearable. After two weeks of wandering around campus alone, I gave up my college career and went to work for the Bank of America. I was assigned to the industrial branch and trained as a machine bookkeeper for ninety dollars a month with an additional ten dollars for overtime. The debits and credits of the day's transactions had to be balanced by hand every night before we could go home. On only one

95

MIKE LYMAN'S

New Year's GREETINGS

1942

New Years Eve Dinner

SELECTION OF ENTREE INDICATES PRICE OF DINNER

To Start the
New Year Right
May We Suggest the
Following Wine and
Liquor Courses—

APPETIZERS

Fresh Seafood Cocktail   Fruit Cocktail   Louisiana Shrimp Louis
Fresh Crabmeat and Avocado, 1000 Island Dressing
Nova Scotia Smoked Salmon   One-half Grapefruit   Marinated Herring
Gefuelte Fish   Chopped Liver   Chilled Tomato Juice

SOUP

Cream of Celery aux Croutons   Consomme or Beef, Vermicelli
Jellied Consomme   Chicken with Noodles   Cold Tomato Bouillon
Matzo Ball Soup   Cold Borscht with Sour Cream   Kreplach Soup

COCKTAILS
Lyman's Martini

Lyman's Manhattan

California Green Salad, Special French Dressing

Choice of

California Sherry .25

California Port .25

Roast Young Oregon Tom Turkey, Dressing and
Cranberry Sauce 2.00

Roast Long Island Duckling, Dressing and Apple Sauce 2.00

SPECIAL
SELECTED
DELICIOUS
NORTHERN
CALIFORNIA
WINES

Roast Prime Ribs of Eastern Beef,
au Jus 2.00

New York Cut Sirloin Steak 3.00

Filet Mignon 3.00

            ½
     Bottle Bottle Glass
Claret   1.10 .60 .25
Burgundy 1.10 .60 .25

SPECIAL
SELECTED
DELICIOUS
NORTHERN
CALIFORNIA
WINES

Potatoes   Fresh Vegetable

Choice of
Hot Apple Pie, Vanilla Sauce
Hot Mince Pie, Brandy Sauce
Old Fashion Pumpkin Pie
English Plum Pudding, Brandy Sauce
Tangerine Sherbet
Vanilla or Chocolate Ice Cream
Frozen Tom and Jerry Ice Cream

            ½
     Bottle Bottle Glass
Sauterne 1.10 .60 .25

AFTER DINNER
CORDIALS

Coffee

occasion did we have to stay late. A check had fallen behind one of the monstrous bookkeeping machines and wasn't found until after ten o'clock.

I left Nana's before dawn on the "9" streetcar, transferring to the "V" again; except going east instead of north. By seven in the evening I arrived home, a depressing place in those days.

My two uncles, Tom and Stuart, both still lived at home. Although they were in their forties, they had never married, primarily because their finances wouldn't allow it. Tom had gotten a job at North American Aviation when the war started, the only steady job he had had for ten years. Now he was looking for a wife, but hadn't had any luck. Evenings were spent in the small, crowded living room around the radio listening to war news every hour on the hour, Lux Radio Theatre, Fibber McGee and Molly, One Man's Family, Red Skelton, and Jack Benny. I retired early to avoid the frequent political arguments.

Edith discovered her marine was married; his wife back home in the east somewhere. She was so upset she decided she needed a change and left Nana's to share an apartment with a girlfriend.

Leno was no longer working at State Wholesale; store number three being more convenient to USC. Since he was also bowling five nights a week, I seldom saw him.

My girlfriends were getting married: Barbara Petersen and Loyal Tacy had been married in December, and Helen Coupe and Elmer Black were making plans for a May wedding along with Berta Axt and Al Foxcroft. I was eighteen and a half and feeling like an old maid.

My depression increased. I couldn't sit on Nana's front porch waiting for Leno's calls for the rest of my life. I decided to write to Aunt Pearl. She had invited me to live with her in Palm Springs many times. In a few days, my answer came:

Dear Mildred Alice:

Thank you for your very nice letter. Your Aunt Pearl and I don't think this would be a good time for you to come down. We are under a lot of expense now and it's almost property tax time again. We send our love to your mother.

With love,

Uncle Austin

Love to your mother! Don't they know Mother followed her husband, Joe, to Neosho, Missouri when he was drafted into the Army and sent there? Expenses! Property taxes! I doubted if Aunt Pearl had even seen my letter! But what could I do about it?

I missed Mother and Jane and Bobbie so much. I tried double-dating with Edith and some of her friends. I became more depressed. There was no one in the world like Leno and no one could ever take his place. Why was he so wrapped up in bowling? What was the attraction?

When Mother left for Missouri, Dana moved in with Dad on Ninety-ninth Street and was commuting to Franklin. He had to take the "7" streetcar on Main Street and transfer to the "W" at Eleventh and Broadway, which took him to North Avenue Fifty-four and Monte Vista—an hour-and-a-half on the streetcar. Since he was graduating in June, it seemed worthwhile.

Weekly dances were held at the Ebell clubhouse on North Avenue Fifty-seven in Highland Park and one Friday night Dana talked me into going. Most of the crowd was from Franklin and I knew many of them.

"Could that be Bill Waddell?" I asked myself as he approached to ask me to dance. It was Bill, beaming from ear to ear.

He managed to dance rather well, although both legs were still supported by braces. He was graduating in June and his courage was inspiring. We enjoyed each other's company on several ensuing Friday nights.

Mrs. Waddell did most of her shopping at Gateway and when she announced one day, within Leno's range of hearing, that Bill and I had met once again and the old spark was still there, I received a dozen red roses with the following note: "Better late than never. Love, Leno."

From then on, my Friday nights were spent watching Leno bowl in the Mixed-Double League at the Highland Park bowling alley.

Joan Brown was an older woman—twenty-one with a husband overseas. I remembered her from Franklin. She was athletic, attractive and of questionable reputation. She bowled on Leno's team on Friday nights and after seeing them together, I was sure that I knew where he had been spending his time the last couple of months.

November 12, 1945
Germany

My darling Alice,

I received a couple of letters from you today but I can't say that I was happy to get them. You sounded very hurt because you had heard (from very reliable sources, no doubt) that Joan Brown used

98

to visit me at store number three. Honey, I don't know where you got your information, but if I thought anyone was deliberately trying to cause friction and distrust between us—well, I can't say just what I would do. It isn't very comforting to know, though, that you believe anything and everything you hear about me when I am over here unable to defend myself. Anyway, if you care to listen, I'd like to straighten you out on a few things.

While I was working at store number three, I do remember having seen Joan Brown in the place several times. I even remember talking to her once or twice in the delicatessen, where she bought whiskey, as I recall. And I remember this because at the time it seemed quite odd to me that she should be shopping at Gateway. But if she came there to visit me, this is the first time I knew anything about it. It was certainly none of my doing. And if you think that old bag ever attracted me, well, you're just mighty mistaken. Honestly, hon, you must have a terribly low opinion of me.

You probably think that the letters which I have been writing you for the past fourteen months are just a lot of baloney. Believe me when I say I've meant every word about loving you, missing you, needing you, wanting you, and being true to you.

I don't know what I can do to convince you that I'll love you until the day I die. Someday soon maybe I can prove it to you, but right now I've got to be satisfied with telling you... and hoping that you will believe me. You mean more to me than my very life...

7

I had been working at the Bank of America three months and just received a forty dollar raise and promotion to general ledger bookkeeper when Emma called.

"How would you like to come to work at State Wholesale?" she asked. "We need a receptionist and switchboard operator. I'll train you. How about it, Alice?"

She didn't have to ask twice. They would pay me one hundred and twenty-five dollars a month and there would be no overtime.

Two weeks later I took the "V" streetcar again—this time to the end of the line in Vernon, then walked two blocks to State Wholesale's wartime location.

The offices were on the mezzanine, through the warehouse and up the winding, metal staircase. They were small; three rooms—one large room for two order clerks, switchboard operator, comptometer operator, accounts receivable and payable bookkeepers, the office manager, Lenore Nicassio and Emma, who was her dad's secretary. The second room housed the buyer, Frank Mumolo, and Nella Mae Ness, his assistant and advertising clerk, and the third was Mr. LaBianca's office.

I was starting at the bottom. I opened the mail and distributed it, I ran the switchboard, I listed all incoming checks by customer name and sometimes helped Emma with the bank deposit. I learned how to operate the ten-key adding machine, without looking at the keys, and how to correct an error on the tape. Statements were supposed to go out every Monday night and I had to see that they did, running envelopes for over three hundred customers through the postage meter.

I became accustomed to Anthony LaBianca's stern "good morning," and his total grasp of everyone's job. He knew what we all did, and why.

His American Legion post was participating in a gala picnic celebration, honoring "I Am An American Day" on May the ninth. He had served in the American Army during World War I and organized an Italian post of the American Legion when the war ended and was an active participant at the picnic.

This was not a "hot dog" affair. The women arrived with fried zucchini, asparagus and artichokes as appetizers to their spaghetti and ravioli. Their tomato sauce was home made and seasoned to perfection.

All of Leno's family was there, including a new prospective member, Peter J. De Santis. His father, John, had worked as a truck driver in the produce department at Gateway for several years, and he and his wife, Jenny, were pleased when Pete asked Anthony's permission to call on Emma. Apparently, Emma was pleased as well, and he was now her steady beau.

I liked Pete. He was friendly and sure of himself. He knew where he was going and never doubted his ability to get there. He was nineteen and the eldest in a family of five, having two brothers and two sisters. He was used to taking charge and being looked up to by his family for decisions and plans. This gave him a good-natured air of self-confidence and authority. Emma could handle this as she, too, had developed amiable self-assurance.

They were both fun to be with and since Emma couldn't go out with Pete unchaperoned, Leno and I joined them on many fun occasions.

Pete soon joined the work force at Gateway, being trained as a butcher, while Leno still worked in the delicatessen. Sunday nights were busy and chaotic at store number three. Help was increasingly difficult to find, so the four of us helped man the cash registers. With five minutes of instruction, I was checking droves of people out through the check stand, collecting rationing stamps for most items, as well as cash. We needed separate stamps for sugar, coffee, butter, meat and canned goods. Animated confusion existed for nearly four hours as the long lines continued without let-up. We worked until they stopped coming, usually about ten p.m. Then we headed for Hollywood and movies about the war.

Pete had been honorably discharged from the Navy due to a punctured eardrum, but Leno would be eighteen in about three months. We looked forward to our future with trepidation and prayed for the war to end soon.

The accounts receivable bookkeeper at State Wholesale left to join her husband in some remote part of the country, and although I had only been there three weeks, I advanced to the position. I learned the ten-key posting machine on which I entered shipments for the prior day, as well as payments made. This involved two statements: one for cash and one for rationing stamps. The procedure divided the statement for stamps into five parts: coffee, sugar, fats and oils, meats and processed foods (canned fruits and vegetables). Each invoice had to be extended for cash and points on the comptometer and then posted to over three hundred individual statements. Most customers had one delivery a week, so about sixty statements were involved each day for posting and balancing. A similar procedure was followed for the accounts payable. It had been several months since the accounts payable had been posted and balanced, but I soon had that all caught up and offered to help the comptometer operator extend the invoices. Then I started looking for ways to improve the procedures. I had to look long and hard.

I hadn't been at State Wholesale long when Emma invited me to drive home with her and stay overnight. This was my second view of "Oak Terrace." The house looked the same as we drove up the steep driveway, but most of the fir trees were gone. "Dad had to cut them down," Emma explained. "Two of them developed some kind of disease and the others were keeping the lawn from growing," she laughed.

Corina welcomed me with a smile and Emma took me to her room. She knew I had been there once before, but showed me around as if for the first time. Leno used the den for his bedroom and awkwardly showed me his pictures and trophies.

Corina explained that she had spent the whole afternoon preparing the sauce from "scratch," but she didn't start cooking the spaghetti until Anthony arrived, after seven.

Leno and his father discussed business in the living room, while I helped Emma and Corina in the kitchen. When the spaghetti was cooked to perfection, Corina announced that dinner was ready. Dinner was a formal affair. Anthony sat at the head of the table in the large breakfast room and served the spaghetti. The atmosphere was warm and friendly; the sternness and chill from the office disappeared. As Corina sat down at the table, Anthony spoke to her in Italian and they all laughed. She jumped up to bring in the salt and pepper.

"Dad has a bet going with Mother," Emma told me laughingly. "He agreed to give her one dollar every time there is nothing missing from the table."

"I haven't had to pay her anything, yet," Anthony added.

"If I set the table perfectly, will you pay me?" I asked.

"I'll pay anyone who can set this table without forgetting something," he chided.

I tried many times, but Anthony always managed to point out something I had missed. As my visits became more frequent, Anthony and I found many subjects to discuss. We talked about the office. Every suggestion I had for improvement was shown by him to be unnecessary for a reason I hadn't thought of. He had set up the procedures and knew their importance. His system of "internal control" was instinctive.

We talked about politics and the war. He said the Russians and the Chinese would be our enemies when the war ended. I didn't believe it. We argued. We got excited and raised our voices, each trying to outdo the other. He said people in this country didn't know what hardship was. I resented that.

"You have opportunity here. We had no resources in Italy, no way to better ourselves. Our town was poor," he explained. There was no bitterness in his voice, only compassion for his people, as he told his story good-naturedly, laughing at himself and his experiences. He brought new ideas and understanding to my thinking. This country and all it meant to those who had lived where there was no hope, only back-breaking toil, hunger and death, took on a new significance for one lucky enough to be born here. Anthony and I became great friends and my love for his son deepened.

Corina introduced me to many new Italian dishes and Catholic traditions. We always had fish on Fridays and Saints' days. I learned there were many other kinds of pasta than spaghetti. Corina made her own tomato sauce every fall when the tomatoes were best, seasoned with home-grown herbs. I was introduced to mortadella, provolone, salami, Gorgonzola cheese, garbanzos, Italian peppers, veal and eggplant parmigiana and Italian wine—Dago red.

Meal time at Oak Terrace was an adventure, a time of friendly arguing and laughing. From the time the pasta was served until the fruit and nuts were enjoyed, we exchanged ideas and cultures, and I felt so lucky to be there.

Pete and Emma's engagement party on August first at the Garibaldini Hall on Castelar Street just off North Broadway was attended by nearly three hundred, mostly from the Italian community. We wore long dresses and the boys wore dark suits and ties. We danced and ate sandwiches of barbecued Italian sausage. I met friends of Anthony's and Corina's that had come here from the same small town in Italy. Most of them were prosperous and some held important positions in business and government. I was proud to be a part of this group of people—the finest I had ever met. And they loved their families—their brothers and sisters, their children and grandchildren. Their lives were dedicated to one another. They had their differences and they expressed them vehemently, but that didn't interfere with their camaraderie.

I was still remembering the fun of the party on August eleventh when Leno called to tell me that their house had been broken into while they were all sleeping.

"The scary part about it was that none of us woke up. We didn't even know anyone was here, until we went into the living room this morning and found our pants and Emma and Mom's purses lined up on the living room floor. All our money was taken."

"How did they get into the house?" I asked.

"Apparently through the kitchen window. It was locked, but they broke it open. Imagine, while we were all asleep." He spoke in disbelief.

"It's dark and lonely up there at night," I said. "It's a good thing you *didn't* wake up. You might have been hurt."

"It's lucky for *them* we didn't wake up. My Dad and I would have killed them!"

8

AS Emma and Pete's wedding drew near, Leno became more serious and attentive toward me. Bouquets and corsages arrived at unexpected intervals with poetic verses. One, in Leno's handwriting:

Lingering Love,
Luscious, Lovely lady,
Longingly,
Lonesome-for-you,
Leno

I was spending two or three nights a week with Emma, taking an active part in her excited anticipation. I was to be a bridesmaid and Leno an usher. I began to feel secure in my position with the family. They were my family now, I thought. I loved them dearly, although Pete told me on one occasion that as for him, he didn't want to "mix the blood."

One evening, just as I was getting out of the tub, Nana called me to the phone. It was Leno and he was obviously upset.

"They took little Lino to the hospital tonight, Alice. They think he has polio."

"Oh, no," I cried, "how bad is it?"

Polio was a very real threat to all of our lives in 1943. Every time anyone had a high fever, polio was feared. Lino looked the picture of health only the day before.

"He was pretty sick, but in high spirits," Leno continued. "He told us not to worry, that he would be okay." His voice broke. "They put him in an iron lung, Alice, but he kept smiling and never stopped. He was kidding us all for being so serious."

Since the age of twelve, I had been a student of Unity School of Christianity, centered in Lee's Summit, Missouri. Their literature taught the following:

To them that love God, all things work together for good... God is omnipotent, and man is his image and likeness, and has dominion over all things... Whoever you are, wherever you may be, you are the channel through which divine action takes place.

I prayed all night: "There is no power but God. Lino is a child of God, filled and surrounded by the perfect peace of God. God is with him and God is love."

Lino passed away sometime during the night and his father, Sam, was devastated, losing his only son so suddenly.

The traditional Catholic Rosary was held for Lino the night before the funeral, which I didn't attend. The casket had to be closed because of the communicable disease that had taken Lino's life. I met Leno Saturday morning at Stella's house to go with the family to the funeral.

Stella and Pete lived in the family's former home on Elm Street in Cypress Park with their one-year old son, Louis. Stella had lost her first-born at birth; a girl whom they named Angela. Pete had escaped the draft as he was a welding instructor at the San Pedro shipyards, which was essential to the war effort.

They greeted me with warmth amid much confusion, but everyone was self-controlled under Anthony's supervision. Strength and courage were the order of the day, although a sense of great sadness pervaded the scene.

Almost as soon as I arrived, I became ill. Corina made me lie down immediately. "The funeral is upsetting her," she told the rest of the family. Perhaps that was it, I thought. I had never attended a funeral before, nor lost anyone close to me.

"I'll be all right when it's time to go," I reassured her, trying to absorb some of her courage.

But I wasn't. I kept getting worse. By the time the black limousines arrived, I couldn't get up without feeling dizzy.

"You can stay here with Louis, Alice," Stella said. "It's better for you not to go."

I agreed, and as soon as the cars disappeared around the corner at Cypress Avenue, I began to feel better. "Why can't I be strong like they are?" I asked myself. "They have lost someone close to them, and I'm falling apart."

I realized how much I was affected by what happened to others. Their sorrow was mine. I couldn't face the reality of what had happened to Lino. My prayers had not been answered. Or had they? I remembered another Unity quote:

Trust in the good that underlies all appearances. Trust and accept that perfect answer to prayer, especially when it challenges your personal wishes. God's way transcends human understanding.

Emma's wedding party
Pete is behind Emma on right

9

EMMA'S wedding day arrived October twenty-fourth, and all members of the wedding party congregated in the living room at Oak Terrace. We were an impressive group, as we headed down the steep driveway and into the limousines at nine a.m. Sunday morning.

Jane LaBianca and Sammy Bruno, Jr. led the procession—she the flower girl and he the ring bearer. Emma was resplendent on her father's arm, carrying ten yards of satin train. Her maid of honor, Tish, followed, with Leno and myself right behind. "How could I have been jealous of Tish," I thought, as I walked triumphantly on Leno's arm.

The rest of the wedding party were Pete's cousins, his brother Mike, and his sister, Mary. Pete's other brother, Johnny, was in the army stationed in Texas and unable to attend. His younger sister, Rina, was too old to be a flower girl and too young to be a bridesmaid.

We headed for St. Peter's Italian Church on North Broadway. The church was small and ancient, but this gathering brought it to life. Their reception held that evening at Roger Young Auditorium on Washington Boulevard was attended by nearly five hundred. Victor Monteleone, a long-time friend of the family, took charge of the evening's events. The eight piece Italian orchestra played "I Love You Truly" as Pete and Emma danced alone on the dance floor. Anthony and Corina soon joined them, as did Pete's parents, John and Jenny DeSantis. Then Pete's best man and Tish, Leno and I, and the rest of the wedding party, one couple at a time, participated. The evening was filled with dancing and eating until the Grand March to the wedding cake was announced. I remembered the Grand March at the Rollerdrome on my first date with Leno, as we all came together in the same manner.

"It has taken me nearly four years to get to this point with Leno and his family," I thought. "I wonder where the next four years will lead us?"

Underneath the fun and exuberance of the reception was a lingering dread of what we knew was to come. The war dragged on with very little good news.

Mike Radogna
US Infantry

Farewell dinner at Casa Manana
with Ann and Howard
June 6, 1943

Last January at the final press conference of President Roosevelt's meeting in Casablanca with Churchill, Roosevelt had announced, "...The elimination of German, Japanese and Italian war power means the unconditional surrender by Germany, Italy and Japan. It does not mean the destruction of the population of Germany, Italy and Japan, but it does mean the destruction of the philosophies in those countries which are based on conquest and the subjugation of other people...."

This was the first official reference to the ultimate Allied objective. Roosevelt had made it clear there would be no bargaining with the enemy which extended the possibility of an early victory.

A long and bitter struggle in Russia for Stalingrad ended the defeat of Hitler's Sixth Army there, but the Russians suffered heavy losses. By February they had taken the offensive against the Germans and regained much of their conquered territory, but were demanding a second front. In August Roosevelt and Churchill met again, this time in Quebec, to discuss military strategy. A landing in France by the Allies was imminent, but we didn't know when.

The Allies had been victorious in North Africa and invaded Southern Italy, where General Mark Clark's Fifth Army was engaged in pushing through the mud, dirt and slush toward Rome.

Bumpy enlisted in the Army Air Corps in June and we had a farewell dinner before his departure at the Casa Mañana, a restaurant and dance hall in west L.A., another great place to hear and dance to the "big bands." Ann followed him to Texas when he had finished his basic training, and they were both still there together.

General MacArthur's Pacific Command had recaptured Guadalcanal by February and moved north to secure the north Solomon Islands. The Aleutian Islands had been cleared of Japanese by August and the threat to Alaska and the west coast was dissipated. Sea battles raged, but we were making slow progress when Leno received his induction papers into the Army in November.

He was to report to Fort MacArthur in San Pedro on December the second. I couldn't believe it was happening. We had been in the war for two years and we seemed as far from victory now as we had when it started. We decided to become engaged before Leno had to leave, for who knew how long.

The Italian custom, which I wanted to follow, was for my family to give the engagement party and Leno's family to give the wedding; although we didn't plan to get married until the war was over.

When I discussed the idea with my father, he wouldn't agree to paying for a big engagement party, but Alice Ruth consented to preparing dinner for Anthony and Corina, Stella and Pete, Emma and Pete and Edith and Dana in their little house on West Ninety-ninth Street. I was embarrassed at having them there and the party was not my idea of a dream come true, but when Leno put that diamond ring on my finger, I forgot the location and size of our party.

I had spent my last dime on a sixty-five dollar cameo ring, which I presented to Leno as the family looked on. My father was on his best behavior and he and Anthony had fun all evening laughing and kidding each other with their Italian jokes. Alice Ruth's dinner was scrumptious, as usual, and I was sure my future was secure, at last.

December second came all too soon and when we said goodbye to Leno at the Pacific Electric station, I thought I would die. All that kept me sane was the hope that he would be stationed somewhere close and the war would, somehow, end soon.

December 2, 1944
Holland

...Do you remember this day just one year ago? Boy, it was one of the saddest days of my life and I'm not kidding. I can remember you and Mom and Emma down at the P.E. station with me. I didn't feel too bad until I kissed you goodbye and turned to leave. I hope you don't think I'm silly when I say I had a lump in my throat as big as an apple.

Remember my first few days at Fort MacArthur? I used to phone you every night and I was terribly lonesome for you, even then. I guess I knew that I would probably have to leave you and go overseas someday. But I didn't realize how very much I would miss you. Of course, I loved you, but a person just doesn't know what it means to be away from his loved one until he actually leaves...

PART III

Sudden Departure

"Courage is the first of human qualities because it is
the quality which guarantees all the others."
Winston Churchill

1

524 M.P. Bat., Co. C.
365-45th Place
Oakland, 9, California
December 8, 1943

Dearest Alice,

WELL, here I am in Oakland. We arrived about 1:30 p.m. The reason we got here so late was that we sat in the train for quite some time after I left you in the depot. I arrived here "safe and sound" physically, but as for finding out what I am going to do or be, everything is mixed up and I don't know whether I'm coming or going.

Right now we are stationed at a small M.P. post, but it is rumored that we are going to Tanforan, a few miles south of San Francisco for our basic training. I am not sure we are going there, honey; for all I know, we might go to New York!

The food and barracks here are all right, but I just can't get used to not having you near me. I really wish we could be married so that you could come up here and be with me. That would be like heaven to me. How about you?

Write as soon as possible to the address at the top of this letter, and if I am not here, they will forward the letters to my new location.

Well, so long, honey; see you soon.

Lovingly,
Leno

December 9, 1943
Oakland, California

Dearest Alice,

How are you, honey? I am fine and everything is all right, but I still miss you terribly. I guess I have to expect a little of that, as anyone with good sense would miss you if they knew you.

As I write to you, the wind is howling! There was a big forest fire last night a few miles away and the wind was blowing so hard they couldn't get it under control for several hours.

I am going to try to get in the Quartermaster Corps, honey. I asked my dad to speak to that Colonel he knows in San Francisco. I hope you don't think that I'm lazy, but I can see already that you need a pull for anything you do in the Army.

Well, I better get going, honey, as we are now going to "retreat." That means standing at attention and saluting while the flag ("colors" in Army talk) is lowered. You better send me your zone number so that my letters will get to you sooner. Don't forget to write *soon* and *often*, honey.

Your loving fiance,
Leno

December 10, 1943
Oakland, California

Darling Alice,

Here's that man again. (Or am I bragging?) Well, I am still in Oakland as you can see, and as far as I know now, I will be here for the duration. The C.O. (Commanding Officer) called about eight of the new boys into his office today and I was one of them. He asked me some questions about the Business Administration I took in college and then dismissed me. As far as I know, he is going to keep some of us here and send the rest to Tanforan for basic training. Well, whatever happens, happens for the best, I guess.

How have you been, honey? How are your father, stepmother, grandmother, grandfather and the rest? How about sending me your picture, honey? I would very much like to have it up here.

We got another shot in the arm about an hour ago. It hasn't

116

started hurting yet, but I guess it will anytime now. I will miss you hitting it, Alice, but I will get another one next week and maybe you will be able to hit that one.

I have got to go to "chow" now, honey. Write soon, and miss me a lot.

Always thinking of you,
Leno

P.S. Please excuse my short letters, but I am saving a few words for every day. Don't let that stop you from writing long ones, though.

LLB

December 11, 1943

Dearest Alice,

Well, another day without you, and another day wasted. I guess this training will make a man of me, but I would rather stay a boy with you.

We went on a ten-mile hike today, and, boy, am I tired! We have been drilling, marching, and handling the rifle the last few days, and we are beginning to look like soldiers. When we got back from the hike, our sergeant said he would take us to the show at Camp Knight, a few miles away, if we learned our eleven general orders. I learned mine fast and the show was great.

It still looks as if I will be stationed here permanently. I won't mind it so much if we get married and you come up here to live. But that would be too much to expect from you because you would be alone quite a bit and I wouldn't like that much. It still makes me happy to think about it, though.

I had better leave you, honey. I love you *very, very* much.

Lovingly,
Leno

December 13, 1943

Hello honey,

I guess you get tired of hearing from this old Buck Private, but whether you like it or not, I am going to write you for the duration and six months, unless, of course, you are with me.

It really was quite a treat talking to you on the phone yesterday. I hope you don't mind my reversing the charges, but I just didn't have any money. There have been so many things to buy up here with extra clothing, milk (they serve coffee and you buy your own milk if you want it), and lost equipment. I know you're not worrying about it, but I will send you that money plus the eleven dollars I owe you as soon as I get paid; which will be soon, I hope.

We got our first real pass last night, a five-hour one. I went into town with a fellow named Jacobs. He is as bad as I am. All he talks about is L.A. and his girl and folks. We went to a show and saw "Shanghai" with Charles Boyer and Loretta Young. I had seen all the other pictures in town.

Well, I guess that's about all for now; we have to go out and drill. Remember me always; I will be thinking of you.

Your loving boyfriend,
Leno

December 14, 1943

Dearest Alice,

I received the letter you wrote on Wednesday and Friday and was really pleased to hear from you. It also makes me wish you were here next to me saying all those nice things.

Today they woke us up a little early to tell us we were going to the rifle range. We "fell out" and they stuffed us into our "taxi" (army truck), which holds about twenty-five men with some sitting on the floor. We drove over the Oakland and Golden Gate bridges to some camp about twenty-five miles away that had a rifle range. Our place is too small for that. We used .22s and shot at moving targets which were supposed to represent different types of bombers; such as level bombers, dive bombers, etc. I did fairly well, and all in all, it was rather interesting. We got back to camp about one, just in time for "chow," which consisted of roast beef, mashed potatoes and gravy, pork and beans and a real nice salad. Then we drilled for an hour or so. Our sergeant really worked us over, but I like drilling best of all. After a little session on "military courtesy," it was time for "chow" again.

I wrote everything above this line before supper. After supper, at mail call, I received another wonderful letter from you, honey, and the first letter from my mother and father. My mother wrote it in Italian and she sounded rather sad, which made me feel blue. I guess you are right about my thinking of you and home so much, but it is *very* hard not to think of you. Don't worry about me, though, honey, because I'm usually all right and I will gradually become accustomed to it.

I am *very* happy to hear that you and the folks are coming up Christmas. I hope I can get off, but if not, you can come on the post.

> With love and kisses,
> Leno

> December 15, 1943

Hello honey,

Well, I have been in Oakland one week today. It seems like it has been a year, though, without you.

Today we got up at seven; which is our usual time. Pretty soft, huh? We had our exercises for half an hour, then went into breakfast. After "chow" we have another half hour to wash up, shave, make our beds, sweep out the barracks, etc.

After cleaning up today, we fell out for "drill." Instead of giving us our usual "close order drill," though, they stuffed us into our army "taxies" and took us up into the hills to hike. We went up steep hills and down deep gullies, and I was really sweating when it was all over, but I took a shower when we got back and felt swell.

Gee, honey, I can get a seven or eight hour pass every night now, since I'm not on duty yet. If I were an M.P. here I would only get two or three nights a week off. I don't take the passes unless I want to go to a show or have shopping to do in town. I sure wish you were here so I could go out with you every night. Write and tell me about everything you have been doing, Alice.

Hoping to see you soon,
Your loving boyfriend,
Leno

December 17, 1943

Dearest Alice,

In case you don't remember the date, I phoned you at the office today and it sure sounded good to hear your voice. I didn't mean to worry you about my going overseas, honey, but I know this outfit is leaving pretty soon, and I don't plan on being with them if I can help it. I have no idea where they are going. It could be England, Italy or anywhere. I hope you don't think me cowardly for saying things like that, but I have so much to live for in you that I plan on living for a *long, long* time...

We went on that hike I was talking about on the phone today, and it was the toughest yet. Gee, in time I will be a real tough "hombre."

Say, honey, I am not hinting or anything, but you asked me what I needed. Well, I need: 1 garrison cap, 1 garrison belt, 1 pair of civilian shoes, 1 radio, stationery, a shoe shine kit, etc., etc., etc. Think you can supply me? Ha! Ha!

Well, I have to go to "retreat" now. Love and kisses.

Your one and only, I hope,
Leno

Sunday,
December 19, 1943

Hello honey,

Received your letter of the twelfth yesterday. The reason I didn't write then was because we worked until 9 p.m. cleaning the barracks for Sunday, and I was just too tuckered out. You see, we had gone on a *nice* hike in the afternoon, too.

What did you mean by that crack: "Am I doing all I can to end this war?" I would gladly give my left arm to end this terrible war and to come home to you.

I just can't wait to see you Christmas, honey. I feel just like a kid waiting for Santa Claus to climb down the chimney on Christmas Eve.

This morning they let us sleep till eight which was quite a treat. They said we were supposed to report to the Orderly Room right away. Two other fellows and I had to clean and mop up the shower room. It wasn't a very tough job, but Sunday is supposed to be our day off. That doesn't necessarily mean that we get a pass, but we are not supposed to do any work unless we are on K.P. duty. It will be just my luck to get K.P. on Christmas day. Anyway, we finally finished the job and went into breakfast.

I decided to wash my dirty clothes which I had never done before, but I was running out of underwear, handkerchiefs and towels, and it was a necessity. I had to use Lux chips because that's all they had in the P.X. (Post Exchange, our store). I let them soak for awhile, then scrubbed them. They didn't come out too bad, but what can I do to make them cleaner? I will make you a swell wife when I get out of the Army. After washing, I went into dinner. We had chicken; what do you think of that? I am now writing letters to you and the rest of my family. Naturally, I wrote your letter first, though.

Loads of love
Leno

P.S. I hope you don't mind waiting for your Christmas gift. My financial situation is not the best.

December 22, 1943

Dearest Alice,

Just two more days until Christmas! I can hardly wait to see you. By the time you receive this letter you will probably have been up here and gone back to Los Angeles again. But I will have seen you and that means everything in the world to me.

Today, they woke us up about 6 a.m. and sent us on a nice hike. This time they made us carry a "full field pack" for the first time. A "full field pack" consists of everything but the kitchen sink. Then we drilled and marched some more and everything seemed to go wrong. If the "sarge" said left face, everybody turned to the right. It was just one of those bad days. In the afternoon we practiced the different firing positions: lying down, sitting, squatting, kneeling and standing. This gets boring but I guess it is necessary.

I received a letter from Mike Radogna today and he is getting a furlough, after which he thinks he is going over. I sure hope not.

Well, honey, I had better leave you now, sending all my love and best wishes.

Your loyal boyfriend,
Leno

2

WE left for Oakland in Stella and Pete's 1941 Chevrolet coupe. The inland route was the quickest and Highway 99 took us straight up the San Joaquin Valley. I had only made the trip once before, reluctantly, with Mother and a friend in 1940 to visit her cousin in San Mateo. I hated to leave Leno, even then, and had a miserable time. Now I eagerly anticipated our reunion. He had been gone only three weeks, but it seemed like three years.

We stayed over night in Fresno at the El Rancho Motel and arrived in Oakland early Christmas Eve. Finding Company "C" of the 524th Military Police Battalion was not an easy task. We had quite a tour of Oakland before we arrived at the group of wooden buildings that looked like an old school.

The 524th had been formed in June of 1941 in Boulder City, Nevada, from a group of officers and noncoms (men with stripes on their sleeves) from infantry units at Fort Lewis, Washington. They were trained in military courtesy, traffic control, anti-sabotage, mob control and a thousand and one other subjects which were considered essential.

At the end of July the battalion was moved by motor convoy to the Presidio of San Francisco, California where another six weeks were spent in more training. They again climbed aboard trucks and journeyed through Northern California and Oregon to Vancouver barracks in Washington, where maneuvers gave them their first taste of practical Military Police work; particularly in respect to traffic control between there and Fort Lewis. When maneuvers were finished, they returned to Nevada and were taught everything from Judo to first aid. They learned the Articles of War and The Soldiers Handbook backward and forward. They marched for hours on end and had tactical combat problems in the field. They read maps, studied them, drew them and dreamed about them at night. They practiced at breaking up mobs and apprehending saboteurs, guarding Boulder Dam for diversion.

123

When Pearl Harbor was attacked, they were sent to Fort Mason in San Francisco Port of Embarkation to police the waterfronts and load troops, supplies, vehicles, tanks and weapons onto ships which they guarded. People of Japanese ancestry needed to be removed from the west coast area and the 524th got the job of posting notices and escorting them on trains to internment camps; practically living with them.

With that job completed, Company "C" moved across the bay to Oakland and settled at 365-45th Street. Their job was broad in scope, encompassing such duties as seeing that army traffic flowed smoothly through their area and keeping resident and transient troops under control.

One platoon went to Stockton, California to handle motor convoys, and another platoon to Sacramento, California for escorting convoys and guarding aircraft—all heading for the Port of Embarkation. Their men were detailed to duty on all the important passenger trains up and down the west coast. Visiting celebrities, who came their way, were insured safe visits to their area.

Their Captain O'Melveny basked in the glory of having a first class organization with the best dressed and best disciplined soldiers in the State. While in Oakland they worked hard and played hard; many of their men marrying. Lieutenant O'Neil replaced Captain O'Melveny who was called to a new job with the Western Defense Command.

In November and December of 1943 new faces again appeared when brand new rookies arrived from reception centers, including one Leno LaBianca, from Fort MacArthur. In a few short weeks, the new recruits had to catch up with the Company's prior two-year's training.

Leno's face beamed quietly when he approached us in the reception area at 365-45th Street. He was lucky that weekend. He had passes to leave the Post. We all had dinner and danced at the Lido Club in San Francisco on Christmas Eve; foregoing the annual poker party, as Leno had to report back by midnight.

Christmas morning we headed for Golden Gate Park and Anthony directed us to a ten-foot pine that became our Christmas tree. We spread our packages underneath its branches and opened them one by one. We cherished each moment, knowing our time together would soon be over.

The day after Christmas we picked Leno up early and headed for a bay north of Oakland where oysters were known to abound. The raw oysters were fresh out of the bay and everyone enjoyed their succulence but me. I remembered my initiation into the Good Form Club at Franklin when I was blind-folded and fed a slippery, fishy-tasting object that I was later told was a raw oyster. I couldn't understand how they could all

Our Christmas Tree

Dad remembering the
"Good old army days"

Opening presents

be relishing them so much. Pete set the record, downing an even dozen, as I looked on in disgust.

Our happy time soon ended and by four o'clock, we had to leave Leno standing at the sign with the crossed pistols, trying very hard to look like a soldier.

I was fine until we headed south. Pete and Anthony were in the front seat and I was sandwiched between Corina and Stella in the back. We were all silent, our hearts heavy. I tried without success to hold back the tears I felt coming.

The American counter-offensive was getting underway in the Pacific, but the anticipated landing by the Allies in France was still a long way off. I couldn't bear the thought of being separated from Leno for what seemed was going to be forever.

The silence continued through my sobs as Stella took my hand and held it securely.

> Christmas Eve
> December 24, 1944
> Holland 7 p.m.

...I haven't written you for several days, honey, but honestly it's been impossible since I haven't been working in the office, but you have been constantly in my thoughts. Sometimes I don't know what would become of me if I didn't have so many wonderful memories of you and our past together to keep me going.

Here it is Christmas Eve and we're still thousands of miles apart. I certainly remember where we were last year at this time: Oakland, California. And was I glad to see you! You and I, Mom and Dad, and Pete and Stella went to Frisco for dinner. Come to think of it, we even had a little scrap about something or other that night, didn't we? "What fools these mortals be." Oh well, things just wouldn't seem right if we didn't have a little scrap now and then, would they, hon? ...

3

December 26, 1943
Oakland, California
5:55 p.m. (W.S.T.)

Dearest Alice,

YOU just left Oakland about a half hour ago and already I miss you terribly. I can't tell you how much your presence means to me. When you are near me I am happy and life seems to be a peek into heaven, but when you are gone, life is just an empty bubble of dreams and memories.

Well, honey, all good things must come to an end and this was no exception. I really enjoyed myself very, very much; how about you? Of course, I would have liked it much better if we could have been alone just for a little while. Well, if everything turns out right, we will be together always. I guess I had better leave you now, honey. There are so many things to straighten up around this place.

Lots of love,
Leno

December 28, 1943
1:00 p.m.

Dearest Alice,

I just received your letter from Madera, California. I had a few moments to spare and could not resist the temptation to sit right down and write to you. Just reading your letter made me wish that you were back here with me so I could convince you that you have nothing to worry about in regards to losing me, and that I love you very, very much.

As for the war's ending a year from now, you heard what Eisenhower said. He said the war would be over in Europe before 1944 ends. Isn't that encouraging news?

By the way, what do you mean by saying if everything turns out o.k. we would get married in 1950? I remember when we made the agreement and it was romantic and all that, but if you are not my wife years before that, I certainly would be a stupid fool!

Honey, I think I will ask the Sergeant about getting into the A.S.T.P. (Army Special Training Program) now that you have been up here. Wish me luck.

Be a good girl and remember that I am always thinking of you and love you more every day.

Your loving boyfriend,Leno

December 31, 1943
6:45 p.m.

Dearest Alice,

How are you, honey? I would like to wish you a very happy New Year. Gee, Alice, I wish you were here to usher in the New Year with me. This is the first New Year's eve we haven't been together for three years, isn't it? I guess there are lots of other people in the same boat this year. Possibly next year the world will be at peace and we will be together again, honey.

Today they issued our "full field packs" to keep. This includes one blanket, half of a "pup" tent, toilet articles, raincoat, shovel, steel helmet, "mess" kit, etc. All in all, it's quite a load. We will have to carry it with us on all hikes from now on.

The fellows are playing poker in here and no one is allowed to go out tonight, so I guess I will play for a little while.

I got paid this morning, so send me the telephone bill I have run up and I will send the money. They only paid me thirty-five dollars this month. I guess they took out for insurance.

Well, honey, write soon and miss me a lot.

Your loving boyfriend,
Leno

P.S. I didn't write yesterday because we went on a night hike and didn't get back until 11:30. It started raining like heck on the way back and we didn't have our raincoats. "Sarge" said it was good for us.

January 2, 1944
9:30 p.m.

Dearest Alice,

I'm pretty tired tonight as I drew K.P. duty today. They woke me up at 6 a.m. and put me right to work. I washed out garbage cans, emptied rubbish pans, swept and mopped the kitchen floor, washed pots and pans, then peeled spuds for the remainder of the time. I got out of there about 7:30 p.m. I am not exaggerating either. It wasn't too bad, though, because it reminded me of working for Gateway.

The people are yelping for a victorious year in 1944. Well, I hope it will be one. I would like nothing better than to be living in a small cottage by the sea with you, and I wouldn't care what city or state it was in either. You probably think this is a crazy letter, but that's the way I feel after talking to you on the phone.

I was talking to you about the A.S.T.P., wasn't I? I told you that this sergeant said I probably was ineligible because I went to college. Well, this afternoon I decided to find out for sure. (I have never gone after anything like I am this, except you, of course.) Well, I found this book on qualifications for A.S.T.P. and in my eyes I was qualified; so I took this book right into the orderly room and showed it to the sergeant. He said, "I could be wrong," and that he would keep the book and read it over. He is really swell though, and has helped me in every way he can.

Well, I better leave you now, honey. I have to write to my uncle in Washington. I received some cigarettes and candy from him and gave the cigarettes away.

With all my love,
Leno

Try as he would, Leno never got out of the 524th Military Police Battalion. There was no way they were going to let him go.

Leno was a very special kind of person. His appearance was impeccable, even though his army uniform didn't fit him properly. He had a commanding stature, a well-developed physique and a striking countenance. His eyes looked straight into yours with conviction and caring. His intelligence far exceeded that of the average recruit and he was a gentleman. He was the epitome of what the 524th wanted to represent them.

January 4, 1944
8:30 p.m.

Dearest Alice,

Still miss me? I hope so, because I miss you terribly. When they play old songs we used to dance to, I think of you and all the good times we have had together. Sometimes we argued or just stayed home and talked, but I was satisfied because we were together. People don't realize how happy they are until something happens that changes their general routine of life, and then they would give anything to get back to that routine. Oh well, such is life.

As soon as I find out exactly where I am going to be, I want to be married. What do you think, honey?

Today we went out on the rifle range for the first time and I fired the Army M-1 rifle. It fires a .30 caliber cartridge and kicks quite a bit until you get used to it. We fired at targets 200 yards distant. I did pretty well, considering. We just fired for practice today, but tomorrow we fire for record.

I phoned you tonight and the operator said there would be several hours delay. I can't understand it. The holidays are over. I have to be up early tomorrow so I don't think I will be awake when she calls back. I wanted to talk to you so much.

Well, honey, all my love and love me always.

Leno

January 11, 1944
11:30 a.m.

Hello honey,

I just got up about ten minutes ago. It sure feels good sleeping late for a change. I guess the reason I slept so soundly was because I heard your sweet voice over the phone last night.

As I told you, they sent me on town duty this week. I had to wear an M.P. arm band and billy club. We walked into a movie and watched the show for a half hour or so. Nothing happened until about 11:30 and then we had to break up a fight in the middle of the street. It isn't the best type of work in the world, but I guess there are lots of things we don't want to do in this life.

Enclosed you will find a twenty dollar bill. Take out whatever you think is necessary for the phone calls and put the rest aside for our future.

Well, honey, will write again tonight. Lots and lots of love,

Your faithful boyfriend,
Leno

January 15, 1944
Oakland, California

Dearest Alice,

Received your letter of the 13th. You know, the sermon. Kidding aside though, I like to have you write that way once in a while.

You made a remark about your joining the Army. I not only do not want you to do such a thing, I know you would be sorry. Enough said.

Honey, I just couldn't wait to hear your voice tonight. I was so lonesome for you on our three-day bivouac. It got pretty darned cold at night and I would have given anything to have your warm body cuddled up, next to mine. Well, it won't be long before we are married.

Honey, you don't realize how much I appreciate your turning to the Catholic Church. I really think that it is the nicest thing anyone could do. I also am very happy that you are interested in the religion; something, I believe, that neither one of us expected to happen. What's the deal? Are you and Father Michael getting chummy?

Here it is Saturday night and I don't even feel like going out. I will stay in and probably play poker or gin rummy or some other "interesting" game.

> All my love to you, honey,
> Leno

As soon as Leno had mentioned he wanted to get married so I could join him in Oakland, I began to get prepared. I wanted to please his mother and father and I knew if I didn't join the Catholic Church, we couldn't have a Catholic wedding.

Father Michael Cecere, 19 years old and fresh out of the seminary, was the new pastor at St. Peter's Italian Church. He was handsome and shy and got the job of teaching me my Catechism. Emma and all of Leno's family adored his quiet reverence and I was an excellent student under his guidance.

My father and grandmother were quite surprised at my decision, but accepted it without complaint because they were so fond of the LaBiancas.

> January 19, 1944
> Oakland, California

Dearest Alice,

I hope you are not sore at me, honey, for asking for some money, but I really did want a camera. I have a little money left, but I will need that from now till payday. I thought that it might make you happy if I took pictures of myself and friends while working or drilling.

How are you doing with Father Michael? When do you plan on taking First Communion and Confirmation? Alice, do you think your folks will be mad at the idea? I certainly hope they won't be.

I go on Interior Guard for the first time tonight from 11 p.m. till 3 a.m. I will walk around the building with a rifle, supposedly protecting the place. I imagine it gets rather tiresome.

I received the pictures you took at Christmas time. The ones of you are swell, but some of the ones of me are awful! I didn't realize I looked so lousy in my uniform.

I had better go now. I will see you in L.A., I hope.

Always, always yours,
Leno

January 20, 1944
9 p.m.

Dearest Alice,

How are you, honey? I asked the sergeant how he was coming along with my request to get into the A.S.T.P. tonight. He said again that he had been pretty busy getting things in order before we leave and hadn't had the time to work on it. He said he was sure I was qualified but he didn't have the proper forms. He said if I could get them from the University of California, it would save him some time. Sounds a little better, doesn't it? If I can get in, we will be married and everything will be swell!

We had a little excitement around here for a change. There's a fellow that came up here from MacArthur with us that hadn't taken a shower since we arrived. Now, this was beginning to tell on him and we knew he was in the room with our eyes shut. We got the mess sergeant's permission, practically an order, to give him a GI bath. You should have seen him wriggle and kick when we picked him up and told him what we were going to do. He had a knife in his hand and came close to stabbing us with it. We finally subdued him and scrubbed him with a GI brush until he looked like a lobster. The whole Company was standing around laughing. Even the First Sergeant was there! I guess it was kind of a mean trick, but we live awfully close together in these barracks, and that's the way things are done in this d___ army.

I don't think I mentioned the fact that I was given a small leather shaving kit for making "sharpshooter" in the rifle. It really isn't bad and I didn't expect it.

Honey, I love you more than these silly words on this sheet of paper can express. Love me always and always, please.

Your faithful boyfriend and
husband-to-be,
Leno

P.S. What do you do with my letters? If you keep them, do you think they will sound silly in future years? Or do they sound silly to you already?

LLB

January 24, 1944

Dearest Alice,

You are going to have a heck of a time reading this letter. Please excuse my writing as you can see I am writing left-handed. It is very hard on the nerves, but I don't mind doing it for you. All I do in the hospital is think of you. I have it soft here, but it gets very boring. I never leave the room because I have this pack on my hand all the time. Don't worry about the nurses, as I have an old lady that takes care of me. But you would not have to worry, anyway, because I love you and you alone and would never do anything to hurt you.

Better leave now; all the love in the universe to my charming wife to be.

Your faithful lover,
Leno

January 26, 1944

Dearest Alice,

How are you, honey? I am not in the best of mental moods. I just heard from one of our boys who is also in the hospital that we are going to Fort Ord Sunday morning. I think it is official news, honey, but I will have phoned you by the time this letter reaches you. Don't feel too bad about it. It is closer to you than my present spot and you can probably come up and see me. And don't think that just because I am going to Fort Ord that we are going overseas. It isn't true that everyone who goes there, goes overseas! Now be a good girl and everything will turn out for the best.

They are really giving me the works in this hospital. I had two blood tests today and a vaccination yesterday. I came in here for an infected thumb and they give me everything but the right thing. But it is usual Army Hospital procedure.

You asked if I received all your letters. I believe so, honey, although some days I don't get any and some days I get two or three. But that can't be helped, I guess. You also asked what I did with your letters. As much as I would like to keep them, and I honestly would, I just don't have the room for them. But I keep your sweet words engraved in my heart and don't think otherwise.

I think I had better go to sleep now. Honey, I just can't say how much I love you and miss you! I hope this damned war ends soon!

> All my love,
> Leno

> January 29, 1944
> 7:15 p.m.

Darling Alice,

Well, honey, I finally got out of the hospital today. I left about noon, and a jeep from our camp took me back. Just as soon as I arrived, they put me to work loading trucks with all sorts of junk. It was better than just lying around at the hospital, though. The Company is now on the alert, which means no one is allowed a pass. You should see all the old fellows go A.W.O.L. (Absent Without Leave). There is really quite an epidemic.

As far as I know, we will be in Fort Ord about two months taking "intensive training." All the while I am there I shall be trying to get into the A.S.T.P., if possible. Then, maybe there is some other way of working it out, such as getting transferred to a Los Angeles outfit or something. "Never say die!"

I am sorry the telephone bill at State Wholesale is so high, honey. To tell you the truth I didn't expect to pay for the calls at State. I thought my dad wouldn't mind my using the phone once in a while. If I did pay for the calls, I would probably have to write to him asking for money sooner or later, so what is the difference?

Well, we leave tomorrow morning. I will let you have my new address as soon as possible, honey.

All my love and passion, which I have stored up for you!

> Your husband-to-be
> Leno

January 30, 1944
Fort Ord, California
8:55 p.m.

Dearest Alice,

As you can see, honey, I arrived at Fort Ord. Although I am lonesome for you, I guess I can't complain too much about this camp. It is isolated, however, being about five or ten miles from a town, Monterey. The complete Fort, I am told, is about twenty miles in length. We are situated in a section four or five miles from the center of the camp called the East Garrison. We don't sleep in barracks, but live in small wooden buildings called hutments. Five men are assigned to each hutment. Instead of bunks, we sleep on army cots. I guess they are trying to make real soldiers out of us. The East Garrison is equipped with a Post Exchange, movie, cafeteria, etc. which will make life a little more pleasant, anyway. A corporal just opened the door and yelled "lights out!" I will finish the letter by candlelight.

I was lucky to be assigned to the same hutment as Jake and Clayton. These are the two fellows that I know best in our outfit.

Well, honey, I can't do too good a job of writing in this candlelight. I'll write sooner tomorrow night.

All the love that my body, mind, and soul can offer,

Your husband-to-be soon
Leno

February 4, 1944

Dearest Alice,

Here it is a Friday night. A year or two ago we would have been at the Civic "swinging out." Remember all the fun we used to have there and all the little jealous spats we had? Sometimes I would just glare at you for hours while you flirted with the other boys. You claimed later it was to make me jealous, but I don't know.

One of your last letters set me to thinking, honey. You said everything with me was "tomorrow." I guess that just about fits me to a "T", but that is going to be changed.

I went over to the Main Garrison which is about five miles

136

away to see Mike Radogna. It took me a long while to locate him, and almost too late. It seems he is leaving Fort Ord Sunday morning, heading for unknown destinations. He is confined to barracks as he is on the "alert." It was swell talking to someone I know so well so far from home.

Please excuse the scribbling as my hands are cold and I am using a flashlight for lighting purposes and it isn't too effective. I will phone you tomorrow—important!

All my love and deep devotion,
Leno

4

I sat in the big green chair in the living room at Oak Terrace, facing Anthony LaBianca as he read the evening paper. He had been quiet and stern all through dinner. Corina was thoughtful. I braced myself for the ordeal ahead. He studied his paper with complete concentration.

"Are you going to read the paper all evening?" I finally asked timidly.

He looked up at me with that cold penetration in his eyes I had learned to fear. "Do you have something you want to talk about?" he asked, daring me to answer.

"Leno wants to get married," I blurted out, and began to cry.

"That's foolish. He's too young. You were going to wait until after the war," he said with finality, although his eyes had softened.

"He's going overseas soon," I went on in between sobs. "He may not come back. We want to be together until he goes."

Corina sat down quietly on the footstool beside me.

"He's lonesome," she said angrily. "Mike Radogna just left and he misses him."

"It has nothing to do with Mike," I cried. "We love each other and want some time together before he has to leave. I would never forgive myself if something happened to him."

"And if something does happen," continued Corina, "who will want you then?"

"You can't get as much for a used horse as you can for a young fresh one," added Anthony.

"I don't care," I sobbed. "He's all that matters to me. I don't care about anyone else."

"He'll be changed when he gets out of the Army," Corina went on.

"You're not a Catholic," Anthony said emphatically.

"I'm studying with Father Michael. I can be baptized in a couple of weeks," I answered. The tears kept coming.

"How can he get away to be married? He's still in basic training," Anthony continued. "Don't you want a wedding like Emma's?"

"Of course we do. He said he can get a three day pass. If you will give us your blessing, I'm sure we can work out the details."

"If you want this so much, we won't stand in your way," he answered sadly.

"We only want what's best for you," Corina added. "We love you like our own daughter and don't want you to be sorry later."

"How could I be sorry?" I cried. "If it weren't for the war, we could wait. But it has changed everything and the separation is unbearable."

"After you're baptized, we'll go north to see Leno and make the wedding plans then," Anthony decided, almost to himself. "Now stop that crying and pull yourself together."

I laughed and blew my nose. I was thoroughly ashamed of my behavior, but it had done the trick; they had agreed to our wedding, if reluctantly.

CERTIFICATE OF BAPTISM
ST. PETER'S ITALIAN CHURCH
1039 North Broadway

This is to Certify

That Alice Skolfield
Child of Carl Skolfield
and Jane Geers
born in Los Angeles, California on the
5th day of November 1924 was BAPTIZED
on the 13th day of February 1944

ACCORDING TO THE RITE OF THE ROMAN CATHOLIC CHURCH

BY THE Rev. Michael Cecere, Cmf.
the Sponsors being Anthony LaBianca
and Corina Luizzi as appears from
The Baptismal Register of this Church.
Dated February 13, 1944

Rev. Michael Cecere Pastor
Book 4 No. 9 Page 26

February 14, 1944
Fort Ord, California

Dearest, darling Alice,

Honey, I am truly sorry that I was not there with you to talk to my parents. I guess it was a tough ordeal. I sent my letter to them immediately, but I guess it arrived too late. Honey, marry me as soon as possible, please. Don't think it is because I think we are going overseas and I wish to get the most out of life. My life is but a series of empty hours without you. I don't know exactly when I can get a three day pass, but I will make it as soon as possible. There is a rumor that we are going on maneuvers for a few weeks.

Yesterday we hiked five miles to a Camp Huffman, which has an "infiltration course." We crawled on our stomachs for one hundred yards with real machine gun bullets firing over our heads. Don't think I didn't keep my head buried in the ground, either! Every so often a dynamite charge would go off nearby, scattering dirt over our heads. After traveling the course, we set our pup tents up and dug fox holes. When it got dark, they sent us through the course again. We could look up and see the tracer bullets whizzing over our heads.

In your last letter you voiced a doubt as to whether I would continue to love you after a few years. Honey, I want to convince you that no matter how I tried not to love you, it would still be impossible until I die. These are not just words! Come up here and I will prove it to you; or do you dare?

I had better leave now. Hoping very much to see you Saturday.

All my love and devotion,
Leno

February 18, 1944
7:30 p.m.

Dearest Alice,

Before I get started, I want to warn you that this is going to be a very disgusted letter. I feel as if I would like to walk out the front gate of this camp and never look at anything GI again as long as I live. It is a series of disappointments I have endured since I came into this XXXXXX Army. These include being made an M.P., the

140

long wait and most likely failure to get into the A.S.T.P., not being able to get passes to Los Angeles and being so close, not knowing a damned thing about the Army and having the officers expect me to know everything and always jumping down my throat and a flock of other things like the possibility of going overseas so soon.

We are going on maneuvers Wednesday, but are moving into the Main Garrison by Monday night. Besides my platoon's being restricted for weekend passes, I just found out that I am on guard duty Sunday, which means I probably will not see you Sunday night. Besides all this I had to bungle up today when my name was called. My thoughts were far away in L.A. and on my honey, and I didn't answer. Well, our first sergeant is *rather* grouchy anyway, and he about blew his top. He practically said I would not get any weekend passes for a long time and would probably be put on some work detail.

Oh, honey, I just can't wait to have you sympathize with me and love me up. I would give anything in the world to have this war over and you and I living happily together.

I had better leave now, sending all my love.

See you tomorrow,
Leno

5

WE headed for the East Garrison at Fort Ord early Saturday morning—three hundred miles from Waverly Drive. I freely called Anthony and Corina Mom and Dad now and we were excitedly happy as we headed north together. Mom had cooked for two days in preparation for the trip. She had fried zucchini, asparagus and artichoke hearts and brought along a jar of her best home-made tomato sauce, grated cheese and spaghetti.

"Those soldiers will really enjoy a home-cooked meal," Dad announced cheerily.

"What if they won't let you bring the food into the mess hall?" I asked.

"I was a cook in the Army, remember? They'll be happy to have our food for a change."

We arrived about four-thirty p.m. The air was cold and damp and the small wooden buildings of East Garrison were shrouded in fog. We located Leno's hutment, where he had just returned from K.P. duty. He was happy to see us, but embarrassed when Dad asked if he had cleared everything with the mess sergeant for serving the food.

"I didn't ask him," Leno announced quietly.

"What do you mean?" Dad asked impatiently. "Why not?"

Leno lowered his gaze and said, "I don't want to remind everyone that I'm Italian. Can't we eat somewhere else?"

"You're ashamed of being Italian?" Dad's anger flared.

"No, Dad, but these guys would kid me unmercifully if you fed them spaghetti. Please try to understand."

"My son! You should be proud of your heritage. If you acted proud, they wouldn't tease you. It's your embarrassment that makes them do it! Can't you see that?" He continued his outcry, now in Italian.

"I didn't have the nerve to ask the mess sergeant," Leno apologized to Mom as we all climbed into Dad's 1941 black Buick sedan and headed for the nearest park in the fog.

February 21, 1944

Dearest Alice,

Well, you have been here and left again, honey. It really was wonderful to have you near me and be able to express my views and opinions to you verbally. I also like very much to express my love physically!

As things stand now, we will go on maneuvers Thursday. We should leave Hunter's Liggett after maneuvers on March 24th. I hope this is changed to an earlier date; but if it isn't, we can probably set the date for our wedding at Sunday, March 26th. Would that be all right, honey? (If you know what I mean.)

Some day this will all be over and we will be living on our little estate (1,000 acres) in the country with eight little boys running around the house dirtying up your living room; but still cute. Do you look forward to that day, honey?

Arrange everything for the wedding and let me know more about the physical exam. I will find out as soon as possible when I can get a pass.

Love me always,
Leno

March 12, 1944
Hunter's Liggett
7:10 a.m.

Dearest, darling Alice,

I hope you have not worried too much about not hearing from me for such a long time. I don't usually like to gripe (much!) but, honestly honey, this is tougher than anything I have ever done before in my life. Twice I have been sent way up in the mountains with several other fellows for periods of three days each. We live in pup tents and sleep on the ground. We eat "C" rations, which are not too bad but you get very tired of eating the same "stuff" every day. We are put on eight or ten hour "posts," guarding a washed-out bridge or keeping mules from slipping off a cliff (any odd job they can find), then get three or four hours sleep and go back on a "post" again. Walking to and from these posts is the most "fun." They are usually in the most isolated spots they can

143

Catholic Baptism
with my Godfather and Godmother

M.P.
in the fog
at Fort Ord

find, it seems. To my two posts in the mountains I have walked respectively ten and twelve miles, and the same distance back. This is with "full field pack" and several extra blankets.

When we are not on mountain posts, we are on posts around headquarters. This usually keeps us busy saluting, as there are always Generals or Colonels all over the place. Our job on these posts consists of stopping traffic and checking their "trip tickets." (Ticket giving them authority to use the vehicles.) I have really been wanting to write you for a long time, honey, because you are the only one who really understands me and to whom I may "blow my top."

Is everything coming along O.K. for the wedding? If I get there on the 25th, Saturday, the Health Certificate will be all right, won't it? I hope so. I am going to ask the C.O. for the pass tomorrow. Keep your fingers crossed, honey!

By the way, Masi sent his best regards since I told him we were to be married. Would you like to call everything off? I am just kidding, I hope.

I am sending my Health Certificate to you. Try to get the marriage license without me, as you said, and, hopefully, I'll be there on the 25th.

> Your loving, tired-of-waiting
> husband-to-be,
> Leno

> March 21, 1944
> Hunter's Liggett
> 10 a.m.

Dearest, lovable Alice,

Just think, honey, only five more days and we will be one. After all these years of your patient waiting (mine, too) and understanding, we are finally to be married. I can't believe it yet. Can you? Of course, it won't be a bed of roses for either of us until this war is over, but we will be together as much as possible for as long as possible.

I think it is swell of my dad to go to the trouble of getting a hall, etc. I really didn't expect anything so exclusive in times like these. I am happy to hear that everything is coming along so smoothly and that your mother will be able to be there.

I will probably arrive in L.A. about 10:30 a.m., Saturday, and will meet you at Emma's house. We will have to get our marriage license, buy me a uniform, cap (since mine is crushed and needs blocking), pair of shoes (have a stamp ready), starch my shirt collar and probably a million other things. If you can get any information about where I can buy an enlisted man's uniform, please do so in a hurry.

I can't think of more to say except that I love you devotedly and am living for the day when we can be together forever.

Your humble servant,
Leno

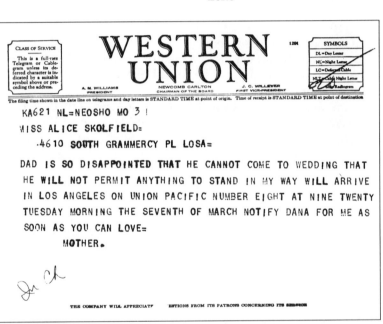

6

WE had each had our blood test, required by California law and only good for thirty days, not knowing when Leno would get his three day pass. He arrived on schedule Saturday morning on the last day our Health Certificate was valid.

The marriage license bureau was only open till noon and Mom and Dad had to go with us since Leno was only eighteen and needed their permission; a law not required for girls of eighteen.

As we sat at Emma's dining room table after the rush downtown and the afternoon shopping for last-minute necessities, I couldn't take my eyes off of Leno. We were to be married at last and my heart was so full of love and excitement. Would I ever get my fill of watching him and being with him?

Our wedding day was perfect, thanks to Dad. We were married at the 10 a.m. High Mass at St. Peter's Italian Church on Passion Sunday in the middle of Lent with special permission from the Bishop. The statues were covered and we were not allowed to have music, but we were too excited to notice.

Howard was Leno's best man, Ann was my Matron of Honor and Sammy Bruno, Jr. was our ring-bearer. My father gave me away—I think the only time he ever sat through a High Mass. My dad's brother, Uncle Herbert and his wife, Elaine, refused to come to the wedding because they thought my marrying an Italian was beneath a Skolfield. But Nana and Pop were there and adored Leno and his family. Mother came out from Neosho, Missouri on the Union Pacific number eight and joined Edith and Dana, but step-father Joe, Jane and Bobbie couldn't come.

ST. PETER'S CATHOLIC CHURCH
Our wedding day with
Ann, Howard and Sammy, Jr.

216 West Spring Street
Neosho, Missouri
March 10, 1944

Dearest Alice & Leno,

I guess this is the way I'll be addressing almost all of your letters from now on. I am very glad that it is Leno's name that I am adding to yours, Alice, as I have always liked you, Leno, and hoped that some day you would be my brother.

There is no one any sorrier than I am, that I can't be there to see you marching down the aisle, Alice. I know you will look beautiful in your gown and Leno will look very handsome in his tuxedo.

We all know, though, that the thing which will make it beautiful, will naturally be the meaning behind it. I am so very happy that Mother was able to get home for the wedding. I know just how she felt when she arrived there at the station, knowing she would be seeing you all any minute; and then, when she saw you coming, I can see you all running toward each other, crying, laughing and embracing all at the same time.

I will be thinking of you every minute of your wedding day and I want you both to know that I wish you every happiness in the world and hope you may be together always and forever.

Thank you, Alice, for all you have done for me, including the lovely Christmas gifts, which I have never thanked you for. Please forgive me when I do not write and thank you for things as I should. I know that it is through all your thoughtfulness that I received the beautiful robe and slippers for Christmas, and I really do love them. Thank you also for the sweet Valentine's card and Bobbie thanks you, too. I could go on and on thanking you for things which you have done for Bobbie and myself, but it would take much more paper and time than I have.

I am afraid that I have said and done things to you during my life which hurt you very much, when all the time you were very sweet and I was just plain spoiled. Please, please, forgive me, Alice, for all that I have ever done to hurt you, for I have suffered very much thinking of some of the mean things I have said to you, which I did not mean and you did not deserve.

I do love you, Alice. You have always been my favorite sister and sort of a second Mother to me. I truly hope that someday I may be as good as you, although I don't see how. I will never be

149

able to repay you no matter what I do. Thank you from the bottom of my heart.

Your loving sister,
Janie

I cherished this letter from my thirteen year old sister. I had forgotten whatever it was she had done to feel so remorseful, but in later years, when through an unknown illness, she wouldn't speak to me because of her hatred toward me, I remembered the letter and read it often.

Stella told me I never looked prettier and added that all brides were beautiful on their wedding day. I *felt* beautiful in the white flowing satin dress that Leno's mother had bought for me and the white veil that covered my face and swept down to the floor behind. Leno was handsome, nervous and smiling, though he couldn't find a new uniform to purchase and was wearing his ill-fitting one, albeit cleaned and pressed.

The immediate family, some seventy-five brothers, sisters, aunts, uncles, cousins, nephews, parents and grandparents, had lunch at the Mona Lisa restaurant on Wilshire Boulevard after our pictures were taken. Some two hundred more joined us for our reception at the Thursday Afternoon Club in Glendale.

I was too excited to remember much about our reception, except that there was lots of good food and plenty of friendly well-wishers. Most of our presents were money, handed to us in white envelopes as our guests passed through the reception line. I insisted on having no music or dancing—why, I don't know. I guess I wanted to be different.

I do remember that most of our friends from high school were not there. The husbands were stationed at various places in the United States and the wives were with them. All of Leno's friends were in the service and either overseas or far from home. Howard and Ann were there, of course, since he was lucky enough to be stationed about fifty miles away at the Santa Ana Army Air Base, but they had to leave early to get back to base in time.

We left impatiently about eight-thirty p.m., after I threw my bouquet right into Tish's eagerly awaiting hands. Since I had caught the bouquet at Emma's wedding, I was sure Tish would be the next to be married. I think she was.

We checked in at the Biltmore Hotel in downtown Los Angeles; adjacent to the Biltmore Theatre that we had frequented so often in the past four years. In those days, the Biltmore was the best hotel in town.

150

Leno wasn't sure how to register and was obviously nervous and embarrassed when the hotel clerk made reference to our being newlyweds. How he could tell, I don't know.

Leno had to be back at Fort Ord by five p.m. on Monday, and his dad was driving us back. He called to awaken us at six a.m., but we were not asleep. Our hotel bill was only five dollars and fifty cents since we had no room service.

We had taken Dad's car and arrived at Waverly Drive a little late. Dad was visibly annoyed and asked, "Was it worth it?"

We didn't answer—just looked at each other and smiled.

September 26, 1944
APO 5955

My very darling Alice,

It's kind of a wet, dreary day today; the kind of day I'd like to sit by the fireplace and pop corn, play cards and listen to the radio, with my slippers and bathrobe on, if I were home.

It's our seventh monthiversary today. I sure wish I were there to celebrate it with you. Remember all the trouble about the marriage license and church and hall? But it all worked out. Remember how late we were getting to the folks' house from the Biltmore Hotel the next morning, honey? Dad pretended to be angry with us, but I'm sure he understood.

We had an awful time on our trip to Fort Ord, getting two blowouts and having to wave down a ride. I was a couple of hours late getting back to camp and we were afraid that I would be restricted for some time. Although we couldn't stay together that first night in camp, we did spend three fun days and nights there before you had to leave.

Honey, the happiest days of my life have been spent with you, especially since getting married, which meant no more goodbyes at the end of a perfect evening. It meant that we had started a little family of our own; that we could live our lives the way we saw fit. It meant all the little things, so hard to describe, that go to make two people sublimely happy. Of course, my coming overseas has interrupted our little "paradise," but it won't be for long. I just know that.

Good night, honey. You're in my thoughts a little more than usual, tonight, if that is possible. I'll love you always as I do now.

> Your devoted husband,
> Leno

7

SALINAS, California: Salad bowl of the nation, home of the California rodeo, population 11,586, 95 percent white, measuring three and one-fifth square miles, altitude 49', annual average temperature 67 degrees, annual average rainfall 14.7", eight parks and three banks, nine churches and seven hotels, four theatres, two private and one county hospital, seven schools with 194 teachers, one fire department with seven men and fourteen volunteers, fifteen miles from Fort Ord—to be our first home.

I had read the statistics and wasn't disappointed as I got off the army bus that had brought me from Fort Ord where I had been allowed to stay only three days.

We hadn't found a place to live yet and I didn't know where to look in this strange town. We had left Dad and Mom three days before by the side of the road, changing a tire, and I thought they were back in Los Angeles by now.

Was I happy to see them as I stepped off the bus and they came toward me! In fact, I was so glad that I burst into tears.

"Now, none of that," Dad said sternly. "Come on, I've found you a room."

They had been touring the town all morning looking for a place for us. They talked Ethel, a widow who had been married to an Italian, into renting us a room behind her house off of the garage, with only cold water and no shower.

"You can use my kitchen and bathroom whenever you want," she said.

That was our "paradise" for three months. When Leno could come home on a pass, I cooked dinner in Ethel's kitchen. We used her bathroom for showers and I did our laundry in her laundry room.

On the nights Leno did get home, he had to be back at camp by six a.m., which meant our getting up at four-thirty and leaving for the bus depot by five, unless he got a ride in with one of his buddies. We were so

153

happy to be together that the inconveniences went unnoticed.

To fill my lonely hours when Leno was away, I got a job at Montgomery Ward as an accounts payable bookkeeper at one hundred dollars a month. Each day brought new war rumors and we knew our "paradise" was to be short-lived.

The 524th went back to Hunter's Liggett for maneuvers in May. They streamlined their outfit and got rid of men considered unfit for Combat Military Police duties. One of the oldest M.P. outfits in existence, they had earned a good reputation and the men were given a final polishing and tuning-up in preparation for work in an active war theatre.

May 10, 1944
Hunter's Liggett, California
10:15 p.m.

Darling Alice,

Gee, honey, I haven't been so disappointed in a long, long time. Here I was all set to come up to Salinas to see you and snuggle up to you tonight and "blooey" the bottom fell out from under another of my plans. I got off duty at five-thirty, all hepped up to leave as soon as I got into camp. When I arrived, Jack Geer informed me that I was one of thirty fellows that was leaving for Fort Ord at five a.m. to represent the Company in a physical fitness test; that includes running, push-ups, etc. Don't think that I didn't feel downhearted! Worst of all, the thirty "chosen" men had to see a training film on the execution of these exercises which just finished five minutes ago. I know you had a wonderful dinner waiting for me tonight, and being unable to even phone you to let you know I wasn't coming in, really burnt me up! There was a line by the phones the length you see waiting for See's candy in L.A.

I was on duty from seven a.m. until twelve-thirty p.m. yesterday at the airport. All I did was stand and wait for the "General" to arrive in his plane so I could blow a siren to let everyone in Camp know that "He" had arrived. He never showed up!

Believe it or not, I have not gambled once since coming up here! Aren't you proud of me? I got paid today; exactly sixteen dollars and thirty-five cents. What shall I do with it? Don't worry, honey, I won't gamble *all* of my money.

Good news! I'm definitely scheduled for a two week furlough

Weary soldier

Chow line

starting May twenty-fifth. Do you think you should quit your job or can you get a leave of absence? How about our little house? Will Ethel keep it vacant for two weeks? Would you rather stay in Salinas and go home with me or would you rather leave before? Start making plans for a glorious two weeks in good old L.A...

We had our furlough in L.A.; a taste of freedom for two fun-filled weeks. Montgomery Ward gave me a two week leave and we rushed excitedly to the Greyhound bus station in town.

We needn't have hurried. The whole town, it seemed, was going home on furlough. The lines were endless. Busses came and went, arriving on their way from San Francisco to Los Angeles; too crowded to pick up any passengers in Salinas.

We dared not leave the station for fear of losing our place in line. Snacking on crackers, cheese and root beer and taking turns going to the rest room, kept us from losing our coveted spot and eight hours later we squeezed onto an over-crowded bus with standing room only.

Heading south, we overlooked the frequent stops and long delays at each one—we were finally on our way! A phone call to Waverly Drive at four a.m. brought Dad to pick us up. He seemed happy to see us, not minding the early-hour arrival.

"We have to have our own car, Dad," Leno stated as soon as we were on our way to Oak Terrace.

"We thought we could get one with the thousand dollars you gave us for a wedding present," I added.

"All right," Dad answered, surprising us with no argument. "We'll go look for one."

Two days later, the three of us went to a used car lot in Glendale and found a black 1940 Chevrolet business coupe for nine hundred and ninety-five dollars, while Dad showed us how to buy a car properly.

"Always be sure to have them pro-rate the license fee and give you, at least, a ninety day warranty," he advised.

Then, "Of course, I'm not in favor of buying a used car. I wish you could wait to buy a new one."

"Who knows when that would be," Leno answered sadly.

I hadn't received my Confirmation into the Catholic Church which was also on the agenda for our furlough. On Sunday, I walked down the aisle at the Old Plaza Church with the twelve-year-olds and noticed how harsh the nuns were with them. "It's part of their discipline," I thought, "but did they have to be so rough and unfeeling?"

Our two weeks passed all too quickly and we were on our way back to Salinas in our 1940 Chevrolet; not knowing what would come next.

General Dwight D. Eisenhower had been appointed Allied Supreme Commander of the Atlantic war and on June sixth he launched the long-awaited second front with the invasion of the Normandy coast in France. The newspapers were full of exciting details:

As H-hour approached, the British Bomber Command began to bomb coastal batteries while the U.S. Ninth Air Force launched the largest airborne invasion yet with an air fleet of 900 planes and 100 gliders. Parachute and glider landings were difficult as they ran into heavy and persistent anti-aircraft fire, fog and generally poor visibility.

In spite of handicaps, they managed to seize important exits from Utah Beach, a code name given one of the planned locations for ground troop invasion, and secured bridges and access roads. The Eighth and Ninth Air Forces sent more than a thousand B-17s and B-24s in to soften the beaches before landings. Their pay load had to be delayed a few seconds to avoid hitting the landing forces.

At Omaha Beach, the second code name given for an invasion point, this delay caused failure to detonate German mines and destroy obstacles to the invading troops. Some 1,285 tons of bombs damaged enemy defenses and destroyed land mines inland from 300 yards to three miles, but was little comfort to the soldiers pinned down on the beach.

German fire, floundering craft and a high tide raised casualties on part of the beach to 66% on D-day, but by afternoon the Americans had established a foothold.

Eisenhower's plan, the air drop behind Utah, naval gunfire, seamanship on the beaches, demolition teams, men who left the sea wall at Omaha to continue the fight, and courageous GIs and junior officers everywhere are a few of the factors which contributed to success.

The Battle of the Beachhead continued until July twenty-fifth with the capture of Cherbourg, the most strategic port on the Normandy Coast. Paris fell to the Allies on August twenty-fifth, after an invasion of Southern France. Antwerp fell to the British on September fourth and the Germans retreated toward the Siegfried Line, along the German border, and hurriedly tried to reinforce the West Wall. Allied forces were struggling with problems of supply and Eisenhower wanted a general advance toward the Rhine River where German forces were preventing the use of Antwerp.

EXTRA

9 A.M. FINAL

Los Angeles Times

SOCIAL · SPORTS · LIBERTY UNDER THE LAW · TRUE INDUSTRIAL FREEDOM

9 A.M. FINAL

VOL. LXIII   ★   TUESDAY MORNING, JUNE 6, 1944   DAILY, FIVE CENTS

INVASION!

WHERE ALLIES STRUCK—Arrows show major points where invasion army hit France.

4000 Ships and 11,000 Planes Hit at French Coast

SUPREME HEADQUARTERS, ALLIED EXPEDITIONARY FORCE, June 6. (AP) Allied forces landed in Northern France early today in history's greatest overseas operation, designed to destroy the power of Hitler's Germany and wrest enslaved Europe from the Nazis.

The German radio said the landings were made from Le Havre to Cherbourg, along the north coast of Normandy and the south side of the bay of the Seine.

Prime Minister Churchill told the House of Commons today that more than 4000 ships with several thousand smaller craft had carried Allied forces across the Channel. He added that 11,000 first-line aircraft are sustaining the operations and said that massed airborne landings had been made successfully behind the German lines.

Allied headquarters did not specify the locations, but left no doubt whatever that the landings were on a gigantic scale.

Eisenhower Issues Statement

Ringing in their ears, the American, British and Canadian forces who made the landings had these words from their supreme commander, Gen. Dwight D. Eisenhower:

"You are about to embark on a great crusade. The eyes of the world are upon you and the hopes and prayers of all liberty-loving peoples go with you . . .

"We will accept nothing less than full victory."

The German radio filled the air with invasion flashes for three hours before the formal Allied announcement came at 7:32 a.m. Greenwich mean time (12:32 a.m., Pacific War Time.)

It acknowledged deep penetrations of the Cherbourg Peninsula by Allied parachute and glider troops in great strength.

The assault was supported by gigantic bombardments from Allied warships and planes which the Germans admitted set the coastal areas ablaze.

A senior officer at Supreme Headquarters said rough water caused "awful anxiety" for the sea-borne troops, but

Turn to Page 3, Column 1

LAST MINUTE INVASION BULLETINS

LONDON, June 6. (AP)—The German radio reported today that four British parachute divisions had landed between Le Havre and Cherbourg in France. This was four times the size of the Nazi parachute force dropped on Crete in the Mediterranean.

BY THE ASSOCIATED PRESS
The Berlin radio broadcast a D.N.B. dispatch today saying that one Allied cruiser and a large landing vessel carrying troops had been sunk in the area of

St. Vaast la Hougue, 15 miles southeast of Cherbourg.

SUPREME HEADQUARTERS, ALLIED EXPEDITIONARY FORCE, June 6. (AP)—United States battleships are supporting the Allied landings in France and U.S. Coast Guard units also are participating in the operations, it was announced today. American marines likewise are in the fighting, manning secondary guns aboard the big ships.

NEW YORK, June 6. (AP) The Berlin radio, in a broadcast recorded by N.B.C., said this morning that strong Allied air attacks have been launched in the Dieppe area.

LONDON, June 6 (Tuesday.) (UP)—The German Transocean agency broadcast a report, unconfirmed by Allied sources, of heavy fighting with "Invasion" forces in the area of Caen, about 8½ miles south of

Turn to Page 4, Col. 4

Special Invasion Edition

Times readers will note that this is an unusual edition of The Times—made necessary by the greatest news story of all time—the invasion of Europe! Not a single line of advertising appears in this issue. Every inch of available space has been devoted to invasion news, maps, pictures.

This is in keeping with The Times policy of serving, above all else, the interests of this newspaper's readers. The Times regrets that it must omit the messages of its many advertisers and hopes those advertisers will realize, as The Times does, that a newspaper's foremost obligation must be to its readers!

The second front had become a reality, but the end of the war seemed as far away as ever as the Germans held on tenaciously and the Japanese made the Allies pay dearly for every inch of territory they were slowly recapturing in the Pacific.

December 26, 1944
Holland

My darling Alice,

It's funny how quickly life can and does change patterns so often. Just nine months ago today everything seemed perfect and life was beginning to look rosy for a change. Since then so many things have happened it hardly seems possible. We were happy for a time, but for some cruel excuse, fate always seems to give, I had to leave you. Since then life has been almost unbearable. I'm sure no one can miss anyone the way I miss you. Maybe nine months from today we will be together and happy again. Life is funny that way. You never know just what to expect. But then I know we must have hope and faith that things will turn out for the best in the end. Without this faith, life would not be worth living.

Remember how happy we were and how much fun we had in Salinas, honey? There wasn't much to do, but just being together made anything we did, fun. We never did take that case of pineapple to those people in Santa Cruz for my dad because we wanted to be alone.

There's not much that's new to write about tonight so I'll close this letter now, sending you my deepest admiration and love.

Your devoted husband forever
Leno

8

THE latter part of June the 524th moved by train to what was undoubtedly the hottest, most miserable spot this side of Hades—Camp Howze, Texas. They went through a period of processing of personnel, packing their equipment for shipping and winding up their overseas training program. It was so hot, perspiration rolled from their bodies even when they were sitting motionless in the shade. Wives and sweethearts sweltered in nearby Gainesville.

And I was one of them.

I headed for Gainesville from Salinas in our new car with a wife of one of Leno's buddies. We drove to Waverly Drive to pick up Dana, who had reached eighteen in April and was going with us on his way to Neosho, Missouri to visit Mother before being drafted.

Anthony and Corina had tried to talk me out of going to Texas.

"It's such a long trip across the desert," Dad warned.

"Leno may only be there a short time. You might have to just turn around and come back," Mom added.

"I don't care," I assured them. "I want to be with Leno until he's shipped overseas, no matter how long a time that is."

They had learned by now that I had a mind of my own, and their worrying about me was not going to change that. Early the next morning, I was on my way with Dana and Henrietta across the California desert on Highway 66.

Dad was right. It was a long, weary drive on endless stretches of two-lane highways with nothing as far as the eye could see. The heat was unbearable. There were no air conditioners in 1940 Chevrolets.

On the third afternoon, we arrived in Amarillo, Texas, having stopped overnight in Flagstaff, Arizona and Gallup, New Mexico. How strange the Greyhound bus depot was where Dana was leaving us for Joplin, Missouri. "I guess we are in the south," I thought, observing the signs on rest rooms, designating separate facilities for blacks and whites.

When Dana boarded the bus with a big smile and a little-boy-lost look, how alone I felt. I had been so brave back at Waverly Drive and on the trip, so far, with Dana at my side. I didn't feel very brave now. I managed to hold back the tears to avoid embarrassment, but when we arrived in Gainesville that evening, I fell apart.

I dropped Henrietta off at her planned destination with no idea when I would find Leno and where I would spend the night in this dusty, run-down, miserable, sweltering town full of soldiers. I managed to make my way to the old, broken-down hotel where we had planned to meet. I sat in the lobby with a lump in my throat, until I saw Leno coming toward me with a broad smile.

"I've found us a room, honey," he announced after kissing me and holding me close. "It isn't much, but it will be our little place," and it was a "little place"—our room. We had no privacy and the people who lived there were so different from anyone I had ever met before. They were friendly enough, but not in a hurry to do anything.

The local Montgomery Ward didn't need my bookkeeping talents, so I took a job as a housekeeper, working in a home several blocks away every day from eight till noon.

Leno needed the car to get back and forth to camp, which meant I had to walk to work. The heat was debilitating and the thunder storms that arrived without a moment's notice terrified me. By the time I arrived home each day, I was exhausted and dripping wet. But Leno got a pass almost every night and that made it all worthwhile. Most of our recreation was attending the movies in town. That was the only place we could go to get cooled off.

The rumors were flying thick and fast almost from the day I arrived. When Leno was given a ten-day furlough, we knew overseas was imminent.

We headed for Neosho, an eight hour drive, to see Mother, Joe, Dana, Jane and Bobbie. They all lived together in one large room, infested with cockroaches, with four beds; sharing a bathroom with three other families. Leno and I joined them in their one room for a week, sharing the biggest bed with Jane and Bobbie. We didn't seem to mind the inconvenience. It was so great to be with the family.

Neosho was another army town, teeming with soldiers, small movie houses and a picturesque town square. Camp Crowder was just outside, where Joe was stationed as a radio instructor. We visited all the points of interest, including Joe's tour of Camp Crowder and the time passed all too quickly.

CAMP CROWDER
Outside Neosho, Missouri
with Dana and Joe
Our last furlough

Bobbie and Jane

SUMMER IN AN ARMY TOWN
by Dana F. Skolfield

Missouri summer.
Could the trees be greener anywhere?
Neosho summer...
An Indian name, an Army town, swelled by soldiers,
Their wives and children.
Neosho summer... People on the dusty side-walks,
Need some rain...
Humanity U.S.A. swelling Neosho because of war.
This Neosho summer you can see—
Ice-cream parlor jammed with barefoot kids,
A few self-conscious grownups.
Lazy, mingling mass of farmers from out-of-town
Bunching on the street corners and drawling "Howdy,"
  as you pass by, in a friendly way,
As farmers do.
Lilly's tavern crowded with soldiers on a pass
Quenching thirst and quelling the heat
With Lily's draft beer.
Good, plain folks
Lily, behind the counter, accommodating,
But "serving no liquor on these premises."
Good, warm-hearted Lily. How do you keep cool?
This Neosho summer you can hear—
Girls and boys splashing and screaming
In the pool under the sleepy green trees of the park.
Sound of many shoes on the sidewalk:
Khaki pants, frail skirts, mostly.
An arm with sergeant stripes around a girl's waist
A loud radio blares from an open window.
Ringing cash registers.
Distant thunder.
And mothers tell their children dwarfs are bowling
In the Ozark hills.
A sudden scurry for shelter
As rain descends from heaven.
That ageless sound of pattering rain
On the sidewalks and window panes.
The whir of automobile tires
On wet pavement...

We enjoyed and appreciated being together, never forgetting that it would end soon and we would all be going our separate ways.

We were right. When we returned to Gainesville, Leno received his orders to ship out to an unknown Port of Embarkation.

August 6, 1945
Straubing, Germany

My darling Alice,

Well, as you know, today was my birthday. It wasn't much different from most of the other days I have spent here. I worked in the office, as usual. Early this morning, I received your very sweet and thoughtful cablegram. Honestly, honey, I'll never be able to tell you how much I have appreciated the way you have gone out of your way for me. I don't mean only since I have come overseas, but always.

On my last birthday, when we were in Gainesville, you went to the trouble of arranging a little party for me. I may not say too much about things of that sort, but, believe me, I never forget them. We were very happy that day a year ago. I know I was. We weren't too well acquainted with the couples you invited, but, at least, we were together. Flies were buzzing around all over the place and it was uncomfortably hot, but that didn't matter too much. We had ice cold watermelon after finishing the ice cream and pie. Some day soon, honey, we will have days with just as much fun and happiness. Only this time they will last forever.

I saw the movie "From Pillow to Post" tonight, with Ida Lupino and Sidney Greenstreet. It was funny and entertaining. I wish they would send more comedies and musicals to us overseas. They help make us forget our troubles for a few hours, anyway.

Well, honey, I still don't know too much about this outfit's future plans. I just keep hoping for the best.

Good night for now, honey. Maybe we can spend my birthday together next year with me in civilian clothes again. Anyway, that's something to aim for.

Your ever-loving and deeply
devoted husband,
Leno

9

WHEN Leno left our room for the last time to return to camp, I thought I couldn't survive without him. I cried and cried and felt desperately alone. As soon as I could pull myself together, I left for Neosho and Mother with a terrified emptiness.

After driving a long eight hours, I fell into her arms, sobbing uncontrollably. How lucky I was to have my mother—to have her there to love and understand.

I knew I couldn't stay in Neosho long and was anxious to return to Oak Terrace and my job at State Wholesale. I needed to bury myself in my work, hoping it would ease the pain in my heart. No one wanted me to drive back alone, but who could go with me except, possibly, Jane. An army town wasn't the best environment for a girl of fourteen and when I approached her with the idea, she pleaded with me to take her.

I wrote to Leno's mother. "You'll be busy at work and I can't take the responsibility of a teen-age girl," she answered.

I wrote to Nana. "Yes, bring her with you, Alice," she answered. "We'll find room for her here, somehow."

Through tears and long talks, Mother decided to let Jane go, but the look of sadness, the tears streaming down her face as we drove off, have never left my memory.

After only six short weeks with Leno in Texas, I was on my way back across the desert to Oak Terrace to wait and pray for his return.

August 20, 1944
Camp Howze, Texas

My darling Alice,

I will remember today as being one of the unluckiest days of my life. It just doesn't seem possible that when I left you this morning we were saying good-bye for possibly a year; or even

165

two or three months. I can't quite get used to the idea that I won't be able to see you tonight. I just won't believe it!

I guess you have left Gainesville by this time. Please take care of yourself, honey. I think I would die if anything happened to you. Don't forget when you start back to Los Angeles to keep it under 45 m.p.h. and be sure to check the tires every seventy-five miles. The tires are not going to be as strong as they were coming out here, I'm afraid. Another thing, don't leave Neosho until you have at least a couple of riders. In case you get a flat, you won't be quite so helpless. Honestly, honey, be careful and I will do the same.

We're leaving in a couple of days so you probably won't be hearing from me for awhile. They won't let us write while we're on the train this time. When you answer my letters later on, be careful what you say as they can be censored also.

I just can't get it through my head that you and I might be miles apart in just a short time. I keep hoping that something will happen at the last minute to keep us together.

> Your faithful husband,
> Leno

August 28, 1944

Darling Alice,

I want you to know that everything is o.k. I am in good health and feeling fine. At present I am somewhere in the eastern part of the country. The weather here is rather pleasant and somewhat reminds me of California.

I'm sorry, honey, but I am not allowed to talk about the trip. I am sure you will understand.

I had a letter from my mother. She said that whenever you get ready to return to Los Angeles, they will be waiting for you. She told me not to worry about you, as they love you very much and are anxiously waiting for you.

I heard that Roxie was in town and was married last week. I am sure that he and Terry will be very happy and hope they can be together for a long time. I received a letter from Mike Radogna saying that he was all right, but that it was pretty rough over there.

You asked whether I was excited about leaving. I think you

know my feelings on that subject. The job has to be done and the sooner it is, the sooner I get home to you. That's the only thing that excites me!

Think of me always, honey, and I'll try to get back as soon as possible.

Your ever-loving husband,
Leno

PART IV

Endless Months in Europe

"How could two people go through what we have...
and still believe they could be exactly as they were..."
Dwight D. Eisenhower

1

LENO'S letters didn't arrive every day, the wartime mail system being what it was, but they were written every day during our long separation, except when his endless hours of work and poor living conditions made it impossible. Time and space have necessitated the reproduction of only a precious few.

September 19, 1944
A.P.O. #5955

My very darling wife Alice,

First of all I had better tell you that I am somewhere in France at present. Please do not worry about me, honey, for, truthfully, everything is all right and I'll take care of myself, I promise.

I'm sorry I haven't written recently, but I just haven't had the chance. I'll write you as often as possible, from now on, but if you don't hear from me at certain times, please don't worry as I am probably busy.

You asked what took so long for my letters to get to you. They must be censored by our unit censor and possibly again by the base censor. This probably takes a while to do. But I will try to write regularly so that you will receive a letter a day, if possible.

We are not allowed to say much about what we are doing. I am living in a pup-tent eating canned rations. I'd give anything to be in our little room in Salinas. I had my hair cut very short again today, honey. I wouldn't have, if you were here, but I figure there's no sense trying to look nice here and my hair is kept clean a lot easier short.

I wish I knew for sure whether you had arrived in Los Angeles safely yet. It's really not so good not knowing where your wife is or how she is...

Give the folks my love. Hoping to hear from you soon.

Your ever-loving and devoted husband,
Leno

Jane and I started our long trek across the desert. How happy I was that she was with me and I didn't have to do this alone. Our first mishap occurred as I was relaxing on a deserted, sleepy desert road. Suddenly I saw a car ahead and believed it was traveling at about the same speed as I. When I realized he was crawling with an apparent problem, I immediately applied the brakes, but at the speed of fifty miles an hour, I mis-judged the distance and ran into his rear end. Fortunately not much damage was done to either car and we were able to agree that we would each take care of our own expense.

I was unnerved and proceeded most cautiously from that point on. The car over-heated several times, but we managed to make it to the nearest town without stopping. Gallup, New Mexico, was a scary town to me, although I didn't let Jane know how nervous I was. We stopped to eat before dark and went quickly to our motel room and locked the door securely. I didn't sleep too well and was glad to "hit the road" at four a.m., just before sunrise.

The drive across the Arizona desert, over the mountain into Needles, California was the hottest part of the trip. When we finally arrived at our motel, I collapsed on the bed, my face as red as a beet—afraid I had had a sun stroke.

But by four a.m. the weather had cooled off and we were on the final leg of our journey. I wondered how the women had managed in the covered wagons so long ago, as we came down the Cajon Pass and into the fertile Inland Empire. As we ascended the steep driveway at Oak Terrace, Dad and Mom welcomed us exuberantly, much more relieved than I realized at the time.

September 25, 1944

My darling Alice,

Another day, another $1.67. My, my, think of all the money I can make in the Army.

Well, I guess today is the big day for Dana, or should I say the bad day. Today he'll probably experience one of the biggest changes in his whole life. I sure hope he gets a decent break in the Army, because if anyone deserves one, he certainly does!

Well, honey, believe it or not, I went to church this morning, a small one. I had to stand up outside and the sermon was in French, but the Mass was very nice. It took me back to our wedding day in St. Peter's Church. That was really the luckiest and happiest day of my life...

I haven't heard from you for so long, I hope everything is all right. By the way, hon, when you go anywhere in the city alone, please be careful. From what I hear, L.A. has become pretty rough lately. Is this true?

I guess I'll hit my "bunk" pretty soon and dream about my beautiful wife. You're the only thing in the world that means anything to me and I'll go through hell to get back to you if I have to. Let's hope I don't! ...

October 2, 1944

...I finally received two very welcome letters from you. You can't imagine how happy I was to get them! They were both written on Sunday the 17th and from the contents of them, I can assume that there are quite a few letters between the 9th and 17th that I haven't received yet. I am relieved to know that you are safe in Los Angeles, but I am sorry to hear that you had to get a new water pump for the car because this probably means that you had some trouble on the trip.

I am hoping with you that you get your "B" gas ration book. I am also glad that you had the Power of Attorney taken care of.

You asked about my laundry, probably referring to my last station. Well, we had to do our own laundry there and are still doing it. I guess it will be that way until we get back to the States.

So, you're for Dewey now, huh? Well, I haven't heard any of his speeches, but if he is for getting us home sooner, he's the man for me, too!

I had an interesting letter from Alice Ruth today. It amuses me because in almost every one she writes, your dad is asleep on the couch.

Today was payday for us. It was a little later than usual, but there is nothing to spend your money on except gambling.

You say you feel funny or bad because you're living in comfort and I'm "heaven knows where," as you put it. Well, that's just what we are fighting for; to make the ones we love happy and comfortable. I'll sleep better nights if I know you are comfortable and love me, too...

October 21, 1944

...I would like you to know that I have moved a short distance from my previous location and the mud doesn't bother us so much anymore because our living quarters are better. We are staying in a rather old building which doesn't have all the conveniences of home, but, at least, there's a roof over us and quite a bit of improvement.

It's really quite a treat to be able to go to sleep at night with dry feet for a change, hon. As yet we are sleeping on the floor, but we are hoping to get some cots.

In case you don't hear from me regularly, don't worry, as I will more than likely be doing regular M.P. duty.

According to Lloyds of London, the European war is supposed to end in nine days, but it looks as if they are going to be wrong. However, the Pacific war seems to be progressing at a much faster pace than before and the span of time between the ends of the two may not be as great as was first expected.

I was happy to hear of the Philippine invasion at first, but then I stopped to think that maybe Mike Radogna and a lot of our other friends might have been in it and then I wondered. But I suppose somebody had to do it and no matter who it was, they would have friends and relatives and somebody would worry.

In this letter you'll find two five-franc notes. The larger and older of the two notes was used before D-day and is still in use. The smaller note is called "invasion money" and was brought to France on D-day and is backed by the American Government. I also have a few English coins which I'll send you one of these days.

Well, it won't be long before our President is elected or re-elected. The choice of one or the other will probably make a great difference as to whether the peace is won or lost. The worst part of it is that the people probably won't know if they chose the right man for years to come...

October 29, 1944

...This will probably be the last chance I will have to write you for a short while, but please don't worry about me. I'll try to let you know what the score is as soon as possible, if I can.

That's very sweet of you to be assembling our old snapshots into another album. I am not sure just which ones they are, but I'll

174

bet there are really some "dillies" among them. No, I don't think we should include that picture of Angie and me and I certainly don't want any of your old boyfriends in it!

I received a letter from the folks today and I answered them concerning Christmas. Don't any of you dare keep from celebrating Christmas on my account, because spiritually I will be there with you.

In your letter of the 12th, you said Dad wasn't feeling well, again. Please don't hesitate to tell me things like that, honey. It worries me, but I would rather know the truth.

So, they stuck Dana in the infantry! Boy, the more I see of the whole thing, the less I like it. You'd think they could find a lot more useful places for a kid with his education and abilities. It just makes me cringe when I think about it.

I had such a large batch of laundry the last time that I sent it to be done by some old French woman who had been doing laundry for a lot of the other fellows. It's really comical trying to figure out what day your laundry will be ready and how much it will cost. The Army issued us a French-English guide book which helps somewhat. As a rule, though, American soldiers and French civilians do very little talking to each other. Both groups are not too pleased about our being here.

Yes, honey, baseball and football seem to help take my mind off of everything temporarily. We haven't had much time to play lately, but we do whenever we get the chance.

Give my love to the folks and tell my dad to get well soon...

November 5, 1944

...At present, I am somewhere in Holland, but please don't worry about me and I'll be home again before you realize it. We're sleeping in a building, which makes it much nicer than living in pup-tents, which we have been doing most of the time since we arrived overseas. I can't say that I enjoyed our trip up to Holland, because we traveled in the French "40" and "8" box-cars and besides being so darned crowded that at night half the time you had someone else's foot, leg, or arm in your face, the cars were naturally very bumpy. I know there are a lot of fellows in this Army a lot worse off than I am.

The people in Belgium and Holland seemed a lot happier to see us than the French did. However, that could be because they hadn't seen as many Americans as the French had when we arrived. Or then, it could be that these people were treated worse by the Germans than the French were. Some of the stories the Dutch tell Dutch-speaking soldiers are really gruesome and hard to believe. I used to laugh at propaganda pictures put out by Hollywood producers, and still do for that matter, but it's hard to laugh at things right before your eyes and at people who have encountered actual experiences.

I hope you didn't think I had forgotten today was your birthday. I knew you would be interested in knowing how and where I was first. You can't realize how much I wish I could be with you today, but then we'll spend so many birthdays together you'll get tired of seeing me around. The war can't last forever (I'm beginning to wonder) and we'll be together again for years and years. (We'll live to be a hundred.)

I wasn't going to mention anything about robot bombs, but I suppose you have read about their using them over here already. Don't worry about my safety, though, as they have not been landing in our vicinity. I have, however, seen quite a few of them as they travel on their way to their destination. At night all you can see is a small round ball of orange-ish light moving through the sky. They make a loud putt-putting sound that sounds like a giant outboard motor. They're really weird. If the noise stops, the light, which is caused by jet-propulsion, goes out and the buzz-bomb gets ready to drop. To tell you the truth, the first one I saw really scared me, and probably lots of others, but we're getting accustomed to them now and don't think about them much anymore.

We haven't received any mail for over a week now. I really miss your comforting letters. Here's hoping they are able to start using the port of Antwerp soon. They claim this will get our supplies (I guess that includes mail) through to us much quicker...

Thanksgiving,
November 23, 1944
Holland 9 p.m.

...Just about now you should be sitting down to a Thanksgiving dinner. Dad is late as usual, but has finally arrived and the dinner gets underway. How I wish I were able to be with you, honey. I just got off K.P. duty. It wasn't too hard a day, but it was rather tiring. For dinner we had turkey, dressing, cranberry sauce, sweet potatoes (dehydrated), peas, cake and coffee. It was really quite a treat and everybody was very well pleased, I'm sure. But, of course, all this "fancy" stuff meant extra work for the K.P.s and that's where I came in. Seriously, though, hon, I had a rather nice Thanksgiving Day, considering—I sincerely hope you did too.

Would you like to know just what's going on in the day room, where I am writing? Well, I'll tell you, anyway. In one corner of the room a fella is "shooting" basketballs at an improvised hoop. Several fellows are reading the "Stars and Stripes," sitting on what was designed for a billiard table, which has been used as a card table by us, as there are no balls or cues around. Almost everybody is writing, however. Some are sitting on benches, as I am, writing on a piece of cardboard or some other hard surface. Others are writing on the floor, on tables or chairs. There are two groups playing cards on another of the billiard tables. The radio is on, playing "I'll be Seeing You" at present having just finished playing "Star Dust." They are both beautiful songs and really make me homesick. You can come into the day room almost any time of the day and you'll find the men off duty doing just about the same things I mentioned. I think we should consider ourselves lucky to have such conveniences and I know most of us do.

Censorship regulations were eased up a little and we are now able to say that we're in the Ninth Army. You have probably read about it in the paper lately. However, we continue doing regular M.P. work, so please don't worry about me. I'll be home before you realize it. Even if they decide to send me to the Pacific after this mess is over here, I'll more than likely get a furlough back to the States first. Here's hoping they don't find me "indispensable" and leave me in the States for good. The news is looking pretty good now that the First and Ninth Armies have started the big push. Here's hoping they can batter their way straight on through to Berlin this time. You can hear planes droning overhead all day and night going to and from their objectives.

I'd better close for now, hon. I can hardly keep my eyes open. Think of me often any time of the day and you can be sure I'll be thinking of you at the same time...

December 17, 1944
Holland

...I haven't written you for several days, honey, but honestly it's been impossible. Besides working in the office days, there are some times that I have regular M.P. duties to do at night also.

Those are the only times I miss writing you.

I added another "great" accomplishment to my wonderful record. I was awarded the Good Conduct Medal. You can now prove to the people who were doubtful of my conduct that it's all right. (Ha! Ha! Ha!) Truthfully, I hope it's the last medal I get. I have no aspirations of being a hero.

You asked about my English coins. Well, I haven't many of them, but I told you we passed through England. People would flock to the windows of our train and ask for American coins in exchange for English coins. I exchanged several dimes for sixpences and several pennies for halfpences.

The mail situation here seems to be getting worse. It's not bad enough that it takes so long to get here from the States; now they've got things so messed up that if you don't happen to be around during mail call, you don't get your mail until the next day. This happens quite frequently, as we are on duty most of the time. I'll have to write to the President and have him clear up the situation immediately! Am I kidding?

I think your wanting to put so much of your money into War Bonds is a good idea... I'm glad now that we bought the car when we did, hon. When I come home again, all we'll need is a home, which shouldn't be too hard to find.

Well, I can now say I have been in "Hitler's Holy Land," Germany. It doesn't seem possible, even to me, but it's true. However, someday soon, I hope, I'll be able to write you saying I have been to Berlin.

I've been thinking of you all day and wondering how it's humanly possible for a person to miss anyone the way I miss you. I also thought of how a person would feel if he knew he would be unable ever to return to the one he loved. It's too terrible even to think about so I put it out of my mind. The day I return to you, honey, will be the happiest day of my life...

Christmas Day 1944
Holland

...I go on all-night duty tonight. I haven't received any mail for some time now. Emma and Pete probably have a son or daughter, but I haven't heard any "official reports" on it.

Things still seem to be pretty tense regarding the Nazi counter-offensive, but it should get increasingly better since the weather

Leno with Hallickson
Somewhere in Holland

Sunday without Leno
Polishing our
1940 Chevrolet

has cleared up and allowed our Air Force to get a crack at "Jerry." Just as I finished writing this last sentence, honey, they started playing "I'll Be Seeing You" on the radio. I take this as sort of an omen that we will be together again before long.

Say, hon, it's getting pretty close to the time when you should enroll at night school if you're going to. Honestly, I've been thinking it over and I'd rather you didn't. First of all, I'd be worried about you all the time. We can work it out some way or another (our program, I mean) when I get home again, I'm sure. Besides this, you'd really be doing too much work with your job. I hope you don't mind and take my advice. Of course, it's entirely up to you.

You've probably been reading the fairly bad news in the newspapers lately. Don't become too alarmed about it though, honey. I am very confident that General Eisenhower knows what he is doing and I'm sure as he says, "the enemy may give us the chance to turn his great gamble into his worst defeat." Anyway, I think everyone is working just a little harder now over here trying to make his words come true.

There's no more news tonight, hon, but remember I love and miss you more every day. My mind is always filled with vivid pictures of our wonderful past and silent prayers for our wonderful future...

                            Your devoted husband forever,
                            Leno

2

DANA left Neosho for Jefferson Barracks, Missouri, soon after Jane and I departed for California. From there he was sent to Camp Joseph T. Robinson in Little Rock, Arkansas and placed in the infantry to start his basic training with the 103rd Infantry Training Battalion. He developed a serious case of bronchitis, ending up in the hospital there for over six weeks.

Dana had had diphtheria when he was six years old, leaving him with a susceptibility to throat and lung infections. He had nearly died in the Los Angeles County Hospital isolation ward while we were quarantined at home on Leslie Avenue. Mother was concerned when she heard about Dana's being in the Army hospital and she and Dad took the bus from Neosho to Little Rock to see just how sick he was. He recovered quickly after their visit and started basic training over again with a new group of recruits—the 116th Infantry Training Battalion, applying for Officers Candidate School (OCS). He was tested by answering one hundred questions, passed the physical, and accepted into OCS by the time the 116th was suddenly flown to Belgium. The "Battle of the Bulge" was raging by now and most of the 116th didn't return. His attack of bronchitis probably saved his life.

On December fifteenth, the Allies were confident of an early victory in Europe. However, victory by Christmas, as Eisenhower had predicted the year before, was now only a remote possibility. Eisenhower's strategy was criticized by Britain's Field Marshall Montgomery, who also suggested that Eisenhower should hand over the executive command. Eisenhower ignored the suggestion, but lost a bet to Montgomery on the issue, writing on the sixteenth, "I still have nine days, and while it seems almost certain that you will have an extra five pounds for Christmas, you will not get it until that day."

On the morning of December sixteenth, Germany launched a counter offensive against the front of the U.S. First Army in the Ardennes, a hilly, wooded sector where the Germans had chosen to stage a "blitzkrieg" four years earlier, producing the capitulation of the West. The surprise assault of twenty German divisions burst the front wide open, being aided by blizzard-like conditions and heavy fog, which prevented the Allied Air Force from bombarding the advancing armored divisions.

Sixty thousand fresh troops were moved to the threatened area, and a hundred and eighty thousand diverted there in the next eight days. Many of the troops from the north were led by the military police of the 524th, including the 7th Armored Division on the eighteenth of December and the 84th Infantry on the twentieth. By that time, the town of Bastogne was completely surrounded by the Germans. This became known as "The Battle of the Bulge."

Part of the forces promised to the German command were sent to the raging Russian front, and the planned converging attack on Maastricht, where Leno's Company was billeted, was dropped. Thus are the fortunes of war.

The foggy weather persisted until the twenty-third, and with the aid of the Air Force, the U.S. Third Army, under the inspired command of General George S. Patton, spearheaded by the 4th Armored Division, drove into the besieged city of Bastogne, relieving its eighteen thousand defenders on the day after Christmas.

During their unprecedented drive from the south, the Third Army moved farther and faster and engaged more divisions than any other army in the history of the United States.

The Allies had come near disaster at the beginning of the Ardennes battle, but it became the last futile attempt at conquest by the German armies under Adolf Hitler.

I had gone back to my job at State Wholesale in September with a new intensity. The accounts payable bookkeeper soon left to join her husband in another state and I was moved into her position. Now I knew it all, I thought, and could see room for improvement—not much, but my eagerness for bringing meaning into my desperately lonely life without Leno, led me to suggest changes in the office procedures. This obviously annoyed the office manager, Lenore, who was perfectly satisfied with the way things were, right or wrong.

My conversations with Dad in the evening over dinner led to disagreements that I felt were unfounded. Why couldn't he see that my suggestions were changes for the better? I became disgruntled and my days were nothing but frustration as I argued with Lenore at the slightest provocation.

Emma was expecting her first child in December and became irritable and uncomfortable as the day drew near. She wasn't much fun to be with and I missed her jolly camaraderie. Stella had us over for dinner frequently, which I enjoyed. Her apple pie was the best I ever tasted. But Pete, the personality kid, thought he was funny when he kidded me about what Leno was doing.

"I'll bet he's having a great time in those haystacks with the French girls," he chided.

He didn't know how that made me feel, how I wanted to cry and run from the room. He didn't realize how full of anxiety I was over Leno's whereabouts and activities, to say nothing of his fidelity. I began to hate Pete for kidding me in this way, with Stella laughing in the background. "They just don't understand or even care," I thought. I refused to go to their house anymore and Mom and Dad couldn't understand why.

Jane became my constant companion on the weekends. I picked her up at Nana's and brought her to Waverly Drive. As I was trying to live on my government allotment of fifty dollars a month, I could only afford to take her to the Temple Theatre in Glendale where the seats were twenty-five cents each and the movies ancient.

Leno didn't want me to go to night school to help pass the long, lonely nights. Maybe he would consent to my helping the war effort.

December 31, 1944
Holland

My darling wife Alice,

Here it is New Year's Eve and I'm writing and thinking of you instead of actually being with you. The other fellows are either writing, reading, or working. Oh, yes, some of them are gambling, too; shooting dice or playing poker. I'll probably end up doing the same tonight since we got paid this afternoon and there is nothing else to do with the little money I received.

As you can see, I was made Private First Class (PFC). That's nothing to rave about, but then it's a raise in pay of four or five dollars a month and that helps.

In your letters you mentioned not going over to Emma and Stella's homes very often anymore because of some of the things their husbands say about me. Honestly, honey, you shouldn't take them so seriously because I am sure they are only kidding you and do not realize that you take it to heart. However, even if they are not kidding, you shouldn't let it bother you and have the utmost confidence in my faithfulness to you.

I see that you and Dad have quite a few discussions on

business problems. I am glad to hear that, but if you can't agree on certain points, wait until I come home again and I'll decide for you...

January 5, 1945
Holland

...I just received your letter of December 20th and, of course, was very glad to hear from you. However, when I read the part about your being a Nurse's Aid, truthfully, I wasn't very pleased. Honestly, honey, I appreciate your good intentions very much, but as far as I am concerned you are doing enough work as it is. Your work is directly connected with the war effort and most of your money goes for War Bonds. That's plenty. Besides, the very reason we are overseas is so that things at home will be right. As a Nurse's Aid, the nurses just dump the dirty work onto you that they don't care to do themselves. I want you to give up the idea, and from now on, ask me before doing anything like that. Please don't think me too harsh.

I finally hit a lucky streak for a change. I won close to one hundred dollars in last night's poker game. You will be receiving a seventy-five dollar money order shortly in one of my letters. Do whatever you want with it, hon; it's sort of a late Christmas present.

I am looking out of the window of our room. The rooftops, vehicles, trees and streets are all covered with snow. It is not snowing at this moment but looks as if it's going to start again.

There is a small package with English, French, Belgian and Dutch coins on the way to you. There are not many of them; just enough for souvenirs. You'll notice that some of them are made of lead. They were put out by the Germans when they occupied the different countries. Let me know when you receive them.

I will be glad when the weather clears again to give our planes a chance to rip up the German Army. It gives me a rather confident feeling to see and hear our bombers and fighters stream overhead. This may sound silly to you, but I don't know, they seem to say "there's lots more where this came from."

According to the Stars and Stripes, the Japs claim that Luzon has been invaded. The boys are really doing all right in the Pacific. If it is necessary for us soldiers in the E.T.O. (European Theatre of Operations) to go to the Pacific when this is over, maybe we won't have to stay there as long as previously expected. The paper also reported that Admiral Ingram expects V-bombs to hit the United States within the next thirty or sixty days. I certainly hope he is wrong. I'm glad you're in the west and most likely out of danger.

As yet I haven't heard any news about Emma's baby and it's very nerve-racking. By the time this letter reaches you, I suppose I will have received some news about it. I hope so.

We are fortunate to have a roof over our heads now. I hope our good luck holds out until summer. Most of us know what the infantryman is putting up with and feel indebted to him a great deal. I won't say that our work is a "bed of roses" by a long shot, but in comparison it seems trivial...

January 26, 1945
Holland

...Yes, we hear American programs on the radio now and then. We also have German propaganda stations that broadcast in English for the "benefit" of the Allied soldiers. They try to make us homesick and tired of the war by playing sentimental songs and telling us the war will last for a long, long time yet. Most of us just laugh at them.

You say Dana is growing a mustache now? He certainly must have gotten hairy all of sudden. Oh, well, this Army will do wonders for some men, so they say.

I am relieved to hear Emma had her baby. However, there must be quite a few letters I'm missing, as you said "it" was getting cuter all the time, without mentioning whether "it" was a boy or girl, how much "it" weighed or when "it" was born. I take it for granted you have written all of this information in one of your earlier letters and by the time this letter reaches you, I will know.

You say that things keep piling up at the office and it's making a nervous wreck of you. If things get too rough, take a few days off. I'm sure the office will be able to "stumble" along for a short time without you. And I know I can't! Besides, we can't have two nervous wrecks around our home when the war is over. I'll probably be one myself, having lived away from you for so darned long.

The news is looking a little brighter of late, isn't it? The Russians have started their winter offensive and seem to be doing all right. The "Belgian Bulge" has been straightened out and MacArthur is doing well in the Philippines.

I guess Ann and Howard's folks are really proud of his

graduating and becoming a pilot in the Army Air Corps. It even makes me proud... He's done a darned good job and fooled a lot of people by sticking to it. I only wish I could do something to make you proud of me, honey.

I agree that New Year's Eve is definitely one time we should be together. This year made the second one in a row we have spent apart. However, let's hope and pray we do not make a "turkey." Speaking of bowling, that's one of the things we will have to do when I get back; get into a bowling league.

I know just what you mean when you say that life is miserable and seems not worth living at times. I feel that way myself most of the time. Whenever I do, I think of a phrase your grandmother wrote in a letter to me: "All things shall pass." That's a comforting thought. Just think, no matter how trying a situation may be, it has to end sooner or later.

You asked if Paul Salata played football. I don't know if he played in high school or not, but I am pretty sure he is the one that's playing for USC now. Howard mentioned it in a letter to me quite some time ago. He was such a punk when we last saw him it hardly seems possible, does it?

At present I'm doing regular traffic duty again instead of driving. You say you worry about wine, women and smoking. You know darned well I don't drink or smoke. As for women, we have gone over that subject a hundred and one times. Please have faith in me, honey. I'll never fail you.

I am having a small pair of wooden shoes made for you as a souvenir. They won't be large enough for you to wear, but they're pretty cute...

February 8, 1945
V-Mail

...I received quite a few letters from you today written between December 26th and January 3rd. Most of them cheered me up very much, but I must admit there were several things that didn't please me. I have every reason to believe your intentions are of the best and you wish to join the Red Cross Motor Corps because you think it might help me in some way. However, I have already written to you, telling you how I feel about the Nurse's Aid job, and I feel the same way about the Motor Corps or anything else like it. I wish you would write me before you decide on something like that instead of letting me know after you have already begun.

It's a helpless feeling having to wait so long to let you know how I feel about anything. If you care to please me, as I hope you do, just keep loving me forever. I'll love you as long as I live and if there is a hereafter, I'll love you there, too.

Devotedly yours,
Leno

3

WHEN Howard completed his training in the Army Air Corps he was sent to Nebraska to await his orders to go overseas. Ann had to stay home as she was expecting their first child any day. Bumpy wasn't with her when Howard Jr. was born, their one and only child. Ann had had a difficult pregnancy, and the doctors had marveled that she was able to conceive at all.

By the time the baby was five weeks old, Howard had moved to Oklahoma. Some of his group shipped out to the E.T.O. from Nebraska, but Howard, along with several others, was sent to Oklahoma to train on a new fighter plane which was to be used in the Pacific. Ann was ready to meet him there and I drove her and Howard Jr., formula, diapers and all, to the infamous Union Station to take the train. How brave she was and how lucky they were. I would have given anything to be on my way to meet Leno.

Mike Radogna was in "the thick of it" in the Philippines, sweating it out in the heat of the jungle and Sammy Bruno was in the Navy on Guam. The war news began to be a little more encouraging, but word began to reach us that many of our school chums wouldn't make it back. Don Gustafson, who had lived next door to us when I was in the fourth grade, was killed in action. He had made a name for himself on Franklin's basketball team and was Archie Wilson's best friend. Paul "Chubby" Roussel, whom I had known since kindergarten and had a crush on all through grammar school, was killed on Guam. There were others, but their names have escaped my memory. The times were sad and fearful.

Mother was far away in Missouri and missed me as much as I missed her. Bobbie was the only one left with her in that miserable army town now that Jane and Dana were gone, but of course, she still had Joe. Thank goodness he hadn't been sent overseas!

When Leno finally made PFC, his family laughed, finding it amusing that it had taken him so long. I was disgusted with their attitude and thought them inconsiderate and without compassion. I was desolate with Leno so far away and in such danger and became impossible to live with. I was in a state of feeling sorry for myself constantly and resented anyone who was leading a somewhat normal life. Mom and Dad took the brunt of my misery, placing obligations on me that I thought unreasonable. Leno was the only member of his family who had to serve his country and I felt they didn't understand what either of us was going through.

Pete Smaldino's deferment as a welder had been cancelled when the need for more men increased. He was drafted into the Army and then rejected when his physical exam showed a problem with his lungs—probably brought about by his welding. He and Pete DeSantis, my two illustrious brothers-in-law, were safely at home with their families for the duration. Emma finally had her baby, over two weeks late, with great difficulty on January fifth. Being their first boy, they named him John, after Pete's father, as was the Italian custom. Stella was expecting her third child, Louis now being over two years old, and their lives were progressing quite normally while mine was at a dead standstill.

We were all concerned about Dad's frequent bouts with the flu. The doctor finally told him that he had diabetes and would have to start taking insulin. He had apparently had it for several years without its being detected. He improved significantly after going on the insulin and we all breathed a "sigh of relief."

But "life on the home front" was for me a time of desperation and my attempts at keeping a positive attitude toward those who weren't waiting for someone were futile.

February 12, 1945

My darling Alice,

I received three more wonderful letters from you today which I enjoyed very much. Your letters are so sweet and sound so natural, I can almost hear your voice. If I weren't sure you were so far away, at times I could swear you were whispering in my ear. I hope you don't think I am going crazy.

I am sending you the soldier's newspaper in the E.T.O.—the Stars and Stripes. I thought you might like to know how we get our news. Besides that, if you will turn to page six, The Question Box, you will notice my name. My squad sergeant and I had a little argument as to who had won the most games between

Southern California and Notre Dame. Being from Michigan, he naturally took up for Notre Dame. As you can see, I lost the argument. But it was fun waiting to see if they would print the answer.

I see you're really "socking away" the cash, hon. I hate to think of your working so hard for it and hope you don't overdo. All the money in the world isn't worth one of your eyelashes to me. I wish there were some way I could help you save, but I guess there's not much I can do unless I get awfully lucky in poker.

It hardly seems possible today that I will miss you more tomorrow than I do now, but I will. It's been that way from the day we parted. Remember me in your dreams...

February 16, 1945
Holland

...I hope you don't think I have been neglecting you the last couple of days, because you have been in my thoughts constantly. However, I haven't been able to write since we have been awfully busy and have made another short move. There is very little change in our living conditions and our work continues to be the same—maybe just a little more of it. The only difference is that I am again sleeping on the hard floor, which is difficult getting used to after those swell mattresses.

It doesn't make any difference what my family thinks about my making PFC. I certainly do not plan on making the Army my career. If they have cracks to make, let them have their laugh. Maybe someday I'll get the chance to prove myself in a field where my brain is the basis of success and not my mouth. However, I'll always know that I have your confidence and faith no matter what I do. Please keep the faith in me, honey, because I promise someday to make you very proud of me.

I hate to think of your being so lonesome and despondent, honey, because I know what a terrible feeling it is. Sometimes it's hard to figure out why life should be such that two people so much in love as you and I should have to be separated. But I guess we are just a minute part in the enormous plan of the world. Maybe somebody with greater intelligence and fewer human instincts can understand. I can't!

As you probably know by now, the Ninth Army along with the First shoved off again, this time across the river Roer. The artillery barrage preceding the attack was really terrific and could be heard from some distance. I hope, more than anything, that this is the final push, honey. I want so much to return to you soon and hold you in my arms again...

March 1, 1945
Germany

...I guess you thought I had forgotten you, but as you can see, we have moved again. This time a little farther than usual and well into Germany. From now on I guess it will be just a series of jumps straight on through Germany until she capitulates.

I can't say that everything is "gravy" here because our living conditions are naturally not what they were in Holland. However, being here gives me a feeling that we are accomplishing something at last. We are living in a deserted Ghost town, one of many which comprises "modern" Germany. The buildings are mostly flattened to the ground, but occasionally you will find one room of a house left standing by some miracle. I am living in a room such as this but some of the other fellows are living in barns and basements. The roof isn't very stable and if it rains, I'm afraid it will leak. I'm not complaining, though, because it could be much worse. There are no showers or running water, but I suppose they will form details where we can get cleaned up at Shower Units.

We will probably be working longer hours than before, if possible, but just so I get six or seven hours sleep, I'll be satisfied. I am very thankful we will still have hot meals because they really make a difference.

I'm not sure how the mail situation will be, but just before I left Holland, I received several wonderful letters from you and a package from Mom. She sent me a sweater she had knitted for me, some cookies and the Rose Bowl Game Roster. I also received a nice letter from Stella in which she enclosed some snapshots. I was rather disappointed because there were none of you. I wish you would send more snapshots, hon.

There is very little to do around here. There are no movies or other forms of recreation. If we work days, we can't even read or write at night since there are no lights. If we work nights, we sleep most of the day. I guess I will have plenty to keep me busy with my laundry, etc.

So far I have seen only one or two German civilians, but plenty of German soldier prisoners of war. Thousands continue streaming towards the rear and it really does my heart good to see them. The only thing that burns me up is to think that the Americans have to feed them. Personally, I think we should let them starve to death as they have made others do. Please don't think me bloodthirsty, hon, but I am sure you would feel that way, too, if you knew of some of the things they have done...

> March 6, 1945
> Germany

...Well, we made another move yesterday. We are living under practically the same conditions as before. We don't have running water or electricity, but we have a fairly nice room with a stove and mattresses to sleep on.

There has been mail here for me the last three days or so, but since I have been on duty during "mail call," the mail clerk refuses to give it to me. If you think that doesn't burn me up good, you're sure wrong! I "sweat out" the mail for days and when it finally gets here, they won't let me have it because I'm on duty. There I go griping again. It's just that I miss you so darned much and letters are my only way of talking with you, honey. Your wonderful letters give me hope and patience which I need very badly when my morale drops.

As for your mentioning my "breaks," I have no one to blame but myself for anything. I guess I haven't been interested enough in the Army, or lack the abilities to get anywhere. All I seem to care or think about is getting home to you again where there is some incentive to live and work. However, most people can't understand that and I can just hear Dad and the "brothers-in-law" now. Oh well, I can take it if you can. You are right there and get the "brunt" of the attack. Sometimes I wonder which they are more interested in—my safety or my progress.

I'll leave you for now, much as I hate to. When I start closing a letter to you, it makes me feel as if I am saying goodbye and going home like I used to so often in Highland Park. However, your memory never leaves me, night or day.

> All my love and devotion,
> Leno

4

THE days and weeks dragged on interminably as I worked and put all my money into War Bonds. We listened to the news, holding on tenaciously to each encouraging word with hope that the war would end soon. My letters to Leno became more despondent, as Dad and Mom encouraged me to be more cheerful. My discouragement must have been evident. How they knew I didn't write cheerful letters I never knew.

Dad frequently suggested that we drive to Hollywood to see the latest war movie. Somehow, seeing the war action on the screen made me feel closer to Leno, as if I were sharing in his danger and discomfort.

Suddenly, in the middle of our accelerating move toward the capture of Berlin and complete capitulation by the Germans and Italians, President Roosevelt died. We all panicked. As a nation, we had become totally dependent on this man to see us through to victory. Harry Truman had been pretty much in the background as Vice-President and we didn't know how he could step into Roosevelt's shoes at such a critical time in our history without committing serious blunders.

Dana had made it home to Neosho for Christmas and left for OCS at Fort Benning, Georgia, on the day that Roosevelt died. The armies in Europe continued their advance toward Berlin and Leno was showing them how to get there. On May 8, 1945, less than a month after Roosevelt's death, Harry Truman announced complete and total surrender of Germany and Italy and we were finally celebrating victory in Europe (VE) day.

Before that eventful day arrived, however, Stella had her second boy and according to Italian custom, named him Anthony, after her father. This threw me into a state of complete despondency. I wanted our son to be the first "Anthony" and resented Stella giving our name to her son. To further my animosity, she gave him the middle name of "Leno," which hurt me beyond all reason. No one understood why I retreated into myself after that event. I couldn't stand to be around any of the family and began to rebel against their most simple requests. "I have made a mistake," I thought, "to come into this family with its unyielding traditions, traditions which give no consideration to individual thinking or feeling."

When the end of the European war was announced prematurely in the States, nearly a week before the last gun was fired, my heart was heavy and my joy incomplete. But by the time VE day was officially confirmed, I had forgotten Stella's inconsiderate gesture and joined in the festivities with two very dry martinis.

> March 26, 1945
> Germany

My darling Alice,

How are you on this very memorable evening? I hope you are not as lonesome and homesick for me as I am for you. I wouldn't wish that on you. We were so very happy just one year ago tonight that it hardly seems possible conditions can change so drastically in such a short time. Well, all I can say is if they changed so much so rapidly once, they can change again in reverse.

You apologized for not sending me anything for our Anniversary. The best present would naturally be you, wrapped in cellophane, delivered C.O.D.!

I've received a couple of letters from Mike Radogna from the Philippines. He says he has seen action and has sent a Jap flag home to his mother. He sends his best regards to you. He's a darned nice kid and I sure hope nothing happens to him.

You mentioned that "they" tell you to write cheerful letters. Well, don't believe what "they" say. Just write what is in your heart at the time. If you feel tired or blue or sad, tell me about it. I want to know your true feelings and do not need "pep talks" to cheer me up. Just talking with you, through our letters, as we normally would if we were together, makes me as happy as can be expected, so far from you.

It makes me sore when other people get my news before you and I know how it must make you feel, honey. But no matter how the mail system works, you can be sure that I always write you first about anything of any importance...

April 10, 1945
Germany

...Please forgive me for not writing to you for several days, but we have been moving continuously and it has been impossible. You asked if I was trying to be the first one to Berlin. Well, we probably won't be the first ones there, but we'll be right in there close. We have run into a lot more German civilians lately and the roads are lined with Dutch, Belgian, Polish, Italian, Russian, French, etc., slave laborers and former Prisoners of War in Germany, who were freed by the Americans and are now heading westward trying to get back to their homes, or, at least, out of Germany. You see old men and women carrying enormous loads of clothing, furniture and other belongings on their backs or in carts and you wonder how in the world they can do it. You can't help feeling sorry for them. I guess they have suffered plenty under the Germans, too.

So, you're not going to take a vacation this year? You're pretty ambitious, aren't you? Maybe it would do you good to just lie around and do nothing for a week or so. You have been working pretty hard, I know.

In one of your letters you said, "It always takes you to bring out the best in me." I thought about that for awhile and realized how true that was in my case, too. It made me think of how much we are a part of each other. Without you, I am not me. It's as if half of me were gone...

April 13, 1945
Germany

...Well, I guess yesterday was a day that will long be remembered. Roosevelt's death at the time when Allied Armies were drawing awfully close to Berlin, came as a great shock to me. It's really too bad he wasn't able to see Germany defeated. Oh, well, such is life! Just when a person gets to thinking things are running smoothly for him—bang—something happens to knock the props from under him again. I am very confident Americans will meet this crisis as they have met countless other crises in the past, and pass through it safely.

I'm feeling terribly blue and homesick for you tonight, honey. There's an awful hollow feeling somewhere around my heart, which is where you are meant to be.

The Stars and Stripes had in it a map (which I am enclosing) showing the Ninth Army's advancement since March 24th, a record which I think everyone in this Army should be proud of. I know I am. Mainly, I am happy because it places this Army in position to deal Germany the final and fatal blow which we have all been waiting for, for so long. I hope and pray it comes soon, placing the day of our reunion that much closer...

April 28, 1945
Germany

...The linking up of Russian and American troops is really swell news, isn't it? People the world over have been waiting for this news for so long now that it sounds almost too good to be true. I guess I had better start learning to speak Russian, as it shouldn't be long before we will be using it quite regularly.

The spotlight is also on the West Coast now with the World Conference being held in San Francisco. The results of that meeting are likely to shape future events for years to come. Here's hoping everyone cooperates with one another to make worthwhile all this fighting and loss of life the world is witnessing today.

We are running into a lot more German civilians as we advance. On further investigation, many of them turn out to be German soldiers and are carted away to a Prisoner of War camp. Much of our trouble is caused by the displaced persons—Russians, Poles, etc., who were used as slave labor by the Germans. They get drunk and shoot German civilians. Somehow you can't blame them since they have been treated as slaves by the Germans for four or five years. However, the American Army can't tolerate lawlessness, of course, and it must be stopped...

May 2, 1945

...You seem much closer to me tonight than you have in a long time. I guess it is because of the swell news I have been hearing all day; the German Armies surrendering unconditionally in Italy, the death of Hitler, the capture of Von Rundsted, and the continued progress on all fronts. Of course, I know this doesn't mean that the war is over as yet, but anyway, it's a big step toward the end.

At our newest location we haven't been doing much of anything except catch up on some much needed rest. We have a radio to listen to and I'm telling you honey, it certainly is welcome. Actual fighting on our front is over except for mopping up operations. We listen to news bulletins all day, hoping to hear that Germany has surrendered totally. The surrender of German forces in Denmark, Holland, and Northwest Germany was really good news. There isn't much territory left to the "Jerries" to fight for and it should all be over before long.

I finally received the package you mailed so long ago with the Catalogues. I've really been having a time with them figuring out courses I'd like to take and the requirements for a degree. I've decided that Merchandising with Marketing as a Major would suit our purpose best. What do you think of it, hon? By the way, have you sent my grades yet? Going to school together again will really be perfect, honey, and I can hardly wait to start.

I know what you mean by not wanting to be with a lot of people now. I feel the same way myself. But I wish you wouldn't spend so much time alone. It worries me. If anything ever happened to you, I think I would die...

> May 8, 1945
> V-E DAY
> Germany

...Well, it is finally over! Impossible as it seems to me, the war in Europe is really over. We have waited an awfully long time for this day, honey, but God at long last rewarded our patience by bringing it to us. It will be that way with all our hopes and dreams. At times we will wonder if they are ever to be realized, but in the end they will all come true and these trying days will be forgotten.

Right now, all that anybody is talking about over here has to do with discharges, furloughs home and China-Burma-India. I have no hopes of getting a discharge right now since I haven't been in the Army long enough. But I do have hopes of returning to the States on furlough before too darned long. I must see you before long, honey. Life just isn't worth the trouble without you. Please pray with me that we shall be together again shortly. I'm sure that God will answer our prayers.

We should have a little more confidence for our future happiness now that this war is over. Give my love to Mom and

Dad, and the rest of the family.

Now and forever your loving
and devoted husband,
Leno

5

THE war in Europe was over. But how much longer would it take to
end the war with Japan? We were making progress, but each day seemed
an eternity without Leno. My patience was at an end and I blamed the
condition of the world onto those closest to me. I became belligerent and
Dad and Mom responded defensively. They minimized my complaints
and fears which meant to me that they didn't understand and I stopped
communicating my feelings altogether.

The Sunday afternoon dinners at Oak Terrace with Mom and Dad
and quite often Stella and Emma and their families became an endless
round of complaints of their restricted lives due to the war.

"We can't go away anywhere, because we don't have enough gas
coupons."

"The rationing of meat and other food makes it impossible to serve a
variety of meals."

"I need another pair of shoes, but I don't have any more stamps."

"These children are driving me crazy!"

On and on it went until I thought I couldn't face another day. "They
don't know what real sacrifice is," I thought. "How can they be so
unfeeling? How can these petty things matter? They're together, they
have each other."

There was an endless obligation to attend weddings and showers,
mostly of Italians I had never met. The women communicated in Italian
which, of course, I couldn't understand. Going alone to weddings where
there was much gaiety and dancing made my heart break almost beyond
repair. The only person who might understand my feelings was far away
and I continually burdened him with my unhappiness. His placating
responses only served to depress me further as I felt he didn't
understand either. Our separation was alienating my love for him and
especially, for his family.

I needed religious inspiration which I couldn't find in the Catholic
church. The Latin Mass held no meaning for me and the sermons

continued to be in Italian at St. Peter's. Attending services there brought more tears, reminding me of our beautiful wedding day.

I started going to Christ Church, Unity, off of Wilshire Boulevard in Los Angeles, after attending Mass. Dr. Ernest C. Wilson's inspirational messages gave me a new patience and hope for our future. I didn't tell Leno's parents, who seemed to receive all the inspiration *they* needed from St. Peter's. The more I went to Unity, the more I realized that Catholicism was not the answer for me, yet I felt an unexplained guilt.

When Leno said there wasn't much hope for his returning soon, I wasn't able to stop crying long enough to go to work. Six more months of this seemed more than I could bear.

"Why don't you take the day off?" Dad suggested, after demanding that I pull myself together.

Emma spent the day with me while Mom took care of Johnny. We went shopping in Glendale and had lunch together. Emma was fun to be with again, as she escaped the demands of motherhood for one afternoon.

"Leno will be back before you know it, Alice," she suggested kindly. "We all miss him. At least the shooting is over and he'll be safe now."

"She does care," I thought. "I have been stupid to think otherwise."

When the news came that Leno was taking a furlough to Wales to look up Pete DeSantis' brother, Johnny, envy reared its ugly head again and I felt I had been a fool to cater to every whim of Leno and his family, doing nothing but working and saving my money. I called my high school chum, Helen, to suggest we do something together.

Helen Coupe, who had been asked to join the Lamb Dabs in the eleventh grade, had married her beau from Franklin, Elmer Black, who was now in the Coast Guard somewhere in the Pacific.

Helen, nicknamed "Toady," was a great "outdoors" girl and suggested that we go camping in the mountains.

"I have a tent and all the equipment," she said enthusiastically.

"I've never been camping, Helen," I answered apprehensively. "Aren't you afraid of snakes? Do you have cots to sleep on?"

She laughed derisively. "Don't be silly, Alice. There aren't any snakes where we're going. We'll go to the Blue Jay campgrounds, up near Lake Arrowhead. I do have cots though."

When I announced my plans to Mom and Dad, they were delighted that I was going to take a vacation.

"I'll see if I can get you some steaks and bacon," Dad suggested. He managed enough stamps for choice meat for our entire week.

We headed out on the sixty-mile trek to the San Bernardino

mountains in Helen's Model A Ford four-door sedan. When we arrived at Camp Blue Jay, Helen picked out a beautiful campsite close to the stream. She wrapped our precious meat carefully and placed it in the stream to keep it from spoiling. I was afraid that someone would steal it or the water would wash it away, but she assured me it would be safe.

We hiked over the hill, about a mile, to a small lake and spent our days tanning and swimming. I received the worst sunburn I had ever had and complained incessantly about the long hikes each day. I talked about Leno and Toady talked about "Hank," Henry being Elmer's middle name. He had decided that "Elmer" wasn't quite "hep."

I had a wonderful time, in spite of myself. Helen prepared the meat deliciously at dinner time and the bacon to perfection in the morning. The air was clear, the water cool and the nights relaxing, though the trek to the "out-house" I found annoying. By the time I returned to Oak Terrace, I felt renewed and glad I had made the trip—a trip I made only because I was upset that Leno had a furlough somewhere other than home to me.

May 13, 1945
Germany

My darling Alice,

You'll have to excuse my not writing last night because we moved again. The set-up here is about the same as the last place except that now we are doing a little work, mainly riding around in a jeep to let these Germans know we are around so they won't get any funny ideas.

Censorship Regulations have been let up a little so I will be able to tell you some things I wasn't able to before. I can't tell you where I am right now, but I can tell you most of the places we have been.

To start from the very beginning, we left the U.S. from the Port of Boston, Massachusetts on September 7th, 1944. We had spent about ten days at Camp Miles Standish in Boston getting final training and processing before leaving for overseas. After a very boring and tiresome boat trip, on which our outfit pulled guard all the way over, we arrived at Liverpool, England on September 14th. We stayed on the ship until the 16th—why, I don't know—on which date we boarded a train and headed for the south English port of Southampton. We spent that night sleeping in an old warehouse right on the docks. That's one night I won't forget for a long time because it was so darned cold and miserable trying to sleep on cement with our clothes on. Aside from that, my mind was filled with all sorts of thoughts because things were happening so darned fast I didn't know what to expect next. I'll admit I was plenty nervous and scared as this was something altogether new to me and my thoughts kept returning to you and all the wonderful times we had had in the past.

Anyway, the next morning we boarded an old English boat on which we crossed the English channel. We spent about three days on the "tug," anchored in the harbor most of the time. We landed at Utah Beach, one of the original Normandy beachheads on the 19th. Things were much quieter than I had expected (I don't know why I had expected any action there as the front had moved up long ago) but signs of the bloody battle that had been fought still remained. Unexploded mines were all over the place so we had to take it easy after wading ashore from our landing craft.

We then stayed in between the towns of Valognes and Montebourge, on the northern side of Normandy, for almost two months. They had been pretty well battered up and made us appreciate the fact that our American cities have not been bombed. Then part of us were sent to a small town on the southern side of the Peninsula, Barneville. We spent about ten days there and then were told we were going to Holland. We traveled to Holland in boxcars and were so crowded that all of us could not lie down and sleep at the same time. We traveled about five days and passed through Argentan, Paris, Mons and Liege in Belgium, then stopped in Maastricht, Holland. We stayed in Maastricht for about a month, then moved to Valkenburg about seven miles northeast of Maastricht, where we spent the worst part of the winter. We were there about two months. From there we moved to Heerlen, still in Holland, where we stayed for a couple of weeks. The area in which we stayed while in Holland is sometimes referred to as the Dutch Panhandle. It is in the Province of Limbourg and is in the most southerly part of the Netherlands. From Heerlen we moved into Germany when the Roer was crossed and the big push to the Elbe began.

Our platoon was commended by General Simpson for the way we handled the enormous amount of traffic flowing across the Roer River. This was in the Linnich area. From there it was just a series of hops through a lot of small and large towns, including Erklenx, Rheindalen, Munchen-Gladbach and Heinsberg on the Rhine River. When the Rhine was crossed we were moving all the

"We had to hike over a mountain to get to the lake. If we had camped any closer, we would have had to pay 75¢ a day! Helen is more of a miser than I am."

Final days in Germany

time, passing through Wesel, Munster, Bielefield, Hereford, Hannover, Goslar and others to our present location.

The main topic around here now is the Army Demobilization Program, which was just officially announced over the radio a few minutes ago. I haven't near enough points to qualify for a discharge, but there are quite a few fellows with four years service and several children who do qualify in our outfit. For each child under eighteen, a soldier gets twelve points. This gives a married man with children a very decided advantage and makes it practically impossible for single men or married men without children to get out, regardless of length of service. I honestly believe that the childless men were handed a raw deal.

What makes the War Department think that one child should be equal in points to six months of overseas duty, sweating out buzz bombs, bombing, shelling, strafing and the rest of it? Or that one child should be equal in points to one full year duty in the States; training, hiking and doing the rest of the work that makes a man sick of living? It's really pathetic to look at some of these fellas with four or more years in the Army who were deprived of wives and families because of the Army, now that they realize they're stuck in here for only God knows how long. A person just doesn't know how badly 99 percent of the fellows (myself definitely included) want out, so they can return to their normal lives again.

Well, now that I've got that out of my system I can continue with the letter. There is still no word as to what we will be doing in the near future. I haven't had any mail from you for several days but I am hoping to hear from you tomorrow...

May 19, 1945
Germany

...You came pretty close when you figured I had twenty-five points. I have thirty-six. I received five extra points for the Battle of Germany star and the other point was because I was actually inducted into the Army on November eleventh, instead of December second when I left you. I am not sure about getting five more for the Ardennes. We led convoys to the Bulge, including the 7th Armored Division, 84th Division and others, but we were not living in the immediate area at the time, but were in Valkenburg, Holland. It still leaves me a long way from the critical score of eighty-five.

204

This has been a day of surprises. I was told this morning that I was to get a seven day furlough to England. I don't expect to enjoy myself, but at least I will get away from this army routine for awhile. We leave sometime tomorrow so you see we weren't given much notice. I'll write you every chance I get while traveling, and every night while in England. We can go to any part of the country we want, so if Johnny De Santis is still in Wales I'll look him up...

> May 31, 1945
> Wales, England
> 2:00 p.m.

...We arrived here in Cardiff, Wales, late last night and found rooms waiting for us at the Red Cross here in town. It's a pretty good deal, honey, sheets and all. They are the first we have seen since leaving the States. I didn't write you while traveling because we were on the go all the time. It was really a long and tiresome trip taking about five days. We drove about three hundred miles by truck over bumpy roads. The cities in the Ruhr area are flattened down to rubble. We waited twenty-four hours for our boat in Le Havre and arrived in Southampton, taking a train to Cardiff. The hospital that Johnny was attached to had been disbanded about two weeks ago so I just missed seeing him. I will just sit around and take it easy here, eating as much as possible and taking in shows. I can't enjoy myself without you. I feel something missing no matter where I go or what I do that tells me that my love for you is soul deep and never-ending...

> June 22, 1945
> Straubing, Germany

...You probably think I have forgotten you, but believe me, that is not the case. The last time I wrote you was from Verviers, Belgium. At that time we were awaiting transportation back to Germany. We got it sooner than expected and learned that our Company Headquarters was in Regensburg, Germany and my Platoon was thirty miles further east, in Straubing. Both of these towns are fairly close to the Czechoslovakia border and a long way from our last station. We traveled all the way in an open truck (a distance close to four hundred miles) and I mean to say it was a rough, dusty trip. We ate "C" and "K" rations most of the way (poor excuse for food). We finally caught up with the

Company here in southeastern Germany several days ago. That same night, we all got sick to our stomachs, one by one. The doctor blamed it on the water we drank on our trip, which was polluted. They took us to the hospital here in town and we have had nothing but juices since. We should be able to eat solid food soon. We're all feeling pretty good now, so please don't worry about me.

Our Battalion was awarded the "Unit Meritorious Service Plaque," which I consider quite an honor. We are now attached to the Third Army, temporarily, for administrative duties. The Ninth Army is getting ready to return to the States.

You sound utterly despondent, tired, and about ready to give up all hope. Needless to say, this worries me to death. If anything were to happen to you, I know I would die. I've known the same deep pains of loneliness you feel, honey; the familiar feeling of discouragement and disgust; the feeling of growing old way before our time. Those are terrible feelings and all of them come from being away from the one you love. Possibly you feel them more than I, but I honestly can't imagine anyone doing so and still living. Anyway, I find that thinking of the wonderful times we have had in the past together, thinking especially of our future—our home, where and what it will be—our children, their names and how cute they will be (they will all have gray eyes) working out our problems we will run into later—all these things help to give me hope and courage, and I find myself thanking God that things aren't worse than they are. Honey, you've been wonderful to me while overseas. There's nothing I've asked that you haven't done, and I sincerely appreciate it. You have had to put up with a lot during our separation and I'll never forget it. It's probably much harder for you, being a girl and physically weaker (you'll probably hate to admit that). I know it must be especially hard when no one around you understands how you are suffering. Over here, at least, almost everybody feels the same way and there is some satisfaction in that alone.

You asked me what I thought of your going to Christ Church, Unity. As far as I'm concerned, honey, if you get spiritual help there that you don't at the Catholic church, that's the place to go. No, my folks probably wouldn't understand that, but then they probably don't understand how lonesome you are, either...

June 25, 1945
Straubing, Germany

...I am writing to you while sitting on the edge of my cot and using a magazine to write on. I'm feeling well now, but they are still keeping me in the hospital for a few days to make sure. I finally got off that liquid diet and started eating again. It's a good thing because I was starting to get weak from hunger.

The rest of our platoon is guarding a jail full of Nazi War Criminals here in town. From what I hear, I will be going back into the office again when I get back. They are running into a lot more paper work now that the war is over.

I received two letters from you today. One knocked me right back on my heels. It surprises and hurts me that you can look at things the way you do. You must think that whatever Dad says is final. Just who did you marry, me or my dad? Who cares whether he likes your going to college with me or not? When I get home, first thing we are going to do is take our honeymoon. When we get back, we are both going to college. After school we can both work if you care to. And if Dad doesn't want us to work for him, we can work elsewhere! I don't mean to sound rude or ungrateful to my folks because they have done an awful lot for me, but it's our life and we'll run it our way!

In your other letter you asked if I were kept here for occupation would there be any chance of your coming to be with me. I don't know if you are still interested or not, but there was another article on that subject in today's "Stars and Stripes," which I am enclosing. Honey, if things come to pass that I am stuck over here and you decide to come over, I hope you realize that conditions in Germany are nothing like those in the States. Transportation, food, living, entertainment; in fact everything is a big headache. It would take a lot of patience to put up with everything. I'm not trying to discourage you; I just want you to know what you would be getting into. I would hate to have you put up with all those discomforts, but just being with you would make me the happiest person in all this world. However, I am doubtful that we will be staying in Germany.

There's a fellow in this ward who has an infected eardrum. I was surprised to find out that he is receiving penicillin shots for it. I've heard a lot about the healing qualities of the drug, but I didn't realize its extent. I guess they use it for just about everything...

July 8, 1945
Straubing, Germany

...My letter from you today was written on June 27th and you hadn't heard from me for a week. I'm really sorry, honey, because I've been writing to you every day. You sounded so happy because the Ninth Army was returning to the States. I guess you haven't received my letter saying that we're now attached to the Third Army. Ninth Army Headquarters is probably all that is returning. The Headquarters Unit always precedes the operational units, except into combat.

You asked about some of my buddies. We had several casualties leave the Company, but I don't think you knew any of them. No one you know is entitled to a discharge yet; most of them don't have children. Generally, we have been between two and fifteen miles behind the first line of defense, so we were pretty lucky.

I was happy to hear that you had a nice rest up at Lake Arrowhead with Helen. But I wish you wouldn't go on such long trips with a girlfriend, especially into the mountains. I'm glad that I received the letter you wrote when you arrived at Arrowhead and the one you wrote when you got back home, at the same time. I just think it would be safer if you went with your dad or my folks. I guess you think I'm an old drip, always nagging at you, but I worry about you, hon.

No, I wasn't too disappointed because I couldn't see Johnny in Wales. In a way, I don't blame you for feeling envious because I want to see anyone I know. I remember how I felt when you flew into your cousin Tommy's arms on Joy Street. I got a letter a few days ago from Johnny saying he was in Verdun, France and expecting to come to Germany soon. And here I thought he was on his way to the Pacific!

I also received a letter from your mother hoping we can have a reunion when Dana finishes his training, if and when I get home, and if and when the Army drops the age limit to thirty-eight and Joe gets a discharge. People would really get a laugh out of the "man home from the wars" being a PFC in the presence of a Lieutenant and a Corporal who haven't even left the States. I guess they really think I am some dodo.

You want me to promise that I'll take you to all the cities and towns I have been through, someday. Well, honey, I can't say that I'll ever want to leave the States again once I am home for good,

208

but if you honestly care to come, maybe someday, a long time from now, we can make the trip. We would really have a lot of traveling to do, I'm telling you!

In one of your letters you said your heart was full of anger and bitterness towards people you once loved. I am truly sorry that things have to be that way, but I also know that you must have good reason for your feelings. I had so hoped that you would be happy living with my folks, although I should have known how difficult and non-understanding they can be. I know that they love you very much, honey. If they have hurt you in any way, I am almost sure they have done so without knowing or thinking. I love you more than anyone else in the world, and our happiness together means more to me than anything. However, I naturally think a lot of my parents, too, and hope that someday you will be able to forgive and forget. Is your misunderstanding too great to ever forget, honey? I suppose it is more a lot of little things than just one issue, or is it? If you are unable to explain on paper, maybe it would be best to just disregard this letter for now and explain everything when we are together again. I am a helpless human and cannot give you hope and strength, so all I can tell you is to remember that I will love you forever and always, regardless of what anyone says, thinks, or does.

The latest news is that we are scheduled to eventually go to the Pacific, but that we will get thirty day furloughs in the States on our way over. Doesn't that sound wonderful, honey? Once we are in the States, our orders could change or the war could end. I'm quite an optimist, huh?

I was happy for Howard and Ann's sake to hear that they were coming to L.A. for twenty days. He has been lucky so far; I hope this doesn't mean overseas for him. Ann and little Howard really need him now...

August 11, 1945
Straubing, Germany

...I'm both happy and very tense tonight. I suppose millions of others feel the same way. I'm happy because the Allies accepted the Jap offer, provided we rule Japan through the Emperor. I'm tense because it's a "toss-up" whether Japan will accept our latest proposal or not. This is very hard on the nerves, isn't it? To think that the whole world could be at peace again within a very few hours is just too good to believe, I still say. I'm afraid I wouldn't believe it for a long time, even if the announcement came over the radio. Gee, honey, I wonder how you're taking all of this excitement. These last few days have certainly been full of spectacular developments—first, the Atomic Bomb, then Russia's declaration of war on Japan, and now this latest peace offer. God has been very kind to the world, honey, giving us so many pleasant and unexpected surprises. I am really very thankful. I guess I am very selfish, though, because I am thankful mainly for the wonderful possibility of seeing you again in the near future. Also, I'm thankful because of Mike Radogna and our other friends already in the Pacific. I was very worried about them because of the great possibility of their participating in the invasion of Japan. But now it seems very unlikely that there will be an invasion, even if Japan rejects the new offer. I'll be a very impatient "Joe" once the war is over. They claim there will be a speed-up of the return of soldiers to the States, but they can't make it fast enough for me.

I suppose everybody in the States is talking about the new Atomic Bomb. I know all the GIs over here are. The average opinion is that it's a great invention and will speed up the end of the war, but everyone seems to be afraid that it will fall into the wrong hands someday. That would really be a terrible thing, don't you think? Of course, the way we are using it isn't exactly according to Hoyle, either, but the Japs are not exactly sportsmanlike and the bomb will certainly save thousands of American lives.

I saw "And Now Tomorrow" at the movies last night. It was one of those pictures Hollywood should make more of. In a way, the title seems to fit the cases of all the soldiers, wives, and sweethearts in this war who have hoped, dreamed, and planned, and have finally realized their dreams. It's a meaning of constant, unending hope and faith finally rewarded extravagantly. (Don't get me wrong, honey. I'm not trying to write an essay!) It's just that I was very much impressed.

Remember the letter I wrote to you in which I griped about the Bronze Stars that were issued to all the wrong people, I thought? Well, the other day, ten men from our Company were awarded the "Certificate of Merit" and very much to my surprise, I was one of them! Imagine me getting an award of merit? I don't think I am entitled to one because I can't honestly see where I have done anything more than the average guy in the outfit. But then the Army never rewards the person who rightfully deserves anything,

Last get-together with Jacobs,
Hallickson, Geer and unknown buddy

EUROPEAN THEATER OF OPERATIONS
UNITED STATES ARMY

This

CERTIFICATE OF MERIT

is awarded to

PRIVATE FIRST CLASS LENO A. LA BIANCA, 39716562

COMPANY C, 524TH MILITARY POLICE BATTALION

IN RECOGNITION OF CONSPICUOUSLY MERITORIOUS AND OUTSTANDING PERFORMANCE OF MILITARY DUTY

Citation

PFC LENO A. LA BIANCA, 39716562, SERVING AS A MILITARY POLICEMAN
DURING THE CAMPAIGN, RHINELAND AND CENTRAL EUROPE, FROM 16 DECEMBER
1944 TO 9 MAY 1945, UNDER EXTREMELY ARDUOUS OPERATIONS PERFORMED HIS
DUTY IN AN OUTSTANDING MANNER. HIS EFFORTS WERE IN ACCORDANCE WITH
THE HIGH TRADITIONS OF THE MILITARY SERVICE. ENTERED THE MILITARY
SERVICE FROM CALIFORNIA.

JOE P. PRICE
Lt. Col., CMP.,
Commanding.

anyway. The Army seems to specialize in blunders, delays and confusion. This award is not a medal; it is just what the name implies, a "Certificate." As soon as I get it I will send it to you. It will be a nice addition to your scrapbook.

Who was it that said eleven months wasn't a long time? It was probably someone who had never left home or been away from his wife for more than a weekend. No one can possibly realize how very long even a week can be until he has spent it away from one whom he loves more than life itself. I know how long eleven months is, honey. Believe me! These last eleven months or so have been the most miserable days of my life, and they have dragged by. Oh, how they've dragged by! Don't ever think your letters are boring, honey. I think they are beautiful because they sound so very much like you. As for your being too much of a dreamer—don't be silly. What would our life be now if we didn't have our dreams?

We got in over two hundred prisoners yesterday. I really get a kick out of watching a Jewish kid in our outfit handle the Germans. Among the prisoners was a German General who commanded the German 15th Army at one time. This kid made the General shine his shoes, stand at attention for an hour, and scrub the floor on his hands and knees with a small brush.

I heard a tune on the radio several days ago for the first time and haven't been able to get it out of my mind since. It's called "There, I've Said It Again" and I like Vaughn Monroe's arrangement of it the best. I think of you and I dancing at the Civic or Palladium, or even in the front room of our house...

August 14, 1945
Straubing, Germany

...I guess I should date this letter the fifteenth, because it's now past one in the morning. News just came over the radio that the Japs have officially accepted unconditional surrender. We have been waiting up for the news all night, but now that I've heard it, I can hardly believe it's true. This means that the war is over, honey. We've waited so long for this day and now it's finally here. I had to write to you, even if it is awfully late. This is one time we should be together, but since that is impossible, the next best thing I can do is write. I feel very close to you when writing.

Right now I guess it's about three in the afternoon back in Los Angeles. You're probably still at the office and the place is probably in an uproar. However, I may be wrong and you may be taking the news very calmly. I can't see how, though.

Most of the radio commentators seem to think that everyone will be sent home quicker, but I'm skeptical about that. The "rank" in the Army won't be in too much of a hurry to discharge GIs. The more men in the Army, the higher their prestige, rank and pay. I guess I sound pretty hard on them, but I've lost all respect for the abilities of most of the men running this Army.

By the way, honey, I'll probably send you a cable tomorrow asking for fifty dollars. The cable should reach you before this letter does. Honestly, honey, I really hate to have to ask you for money, but that's what I get for gambling. I don't like to get into these poker games, but there is hardly anything else to do in our spare time. Yes, I know I said I was going to send you forty or fifty dollars this month, but then I lost part of it, and the only way I could get it back was to invest the rest. Well, I lost that, too, and figured the only thing to do was to borrow. I should have better sense, I know. I'll use better judgment next time. I hate to be in debt. Please forgive me, will you, honey? If you won't, I guess I can't blame you. When I am home again, I promise never to gamble unless we are together.

I heard from Howard today. He's now stationed at Monroe, Louisiana. He didn't make it plain whether Ann was there with him or not, but I suppose she is.

When we were separated nearly a year ago, I couldn't get it through this thick skull of mine that we were not going to see each other for long months or years. I guess I'll never forget those first few days after we had landed in France, when it finally struck home that I was to be here a long, long time. That was a terrible realization, honey, especially when I thought of the possibility of never returning again. It wasn't so much the thought of dying, but the fear of not being able to live and enjoy all the wonderful days we had planned to share, so long ago. I hope all this doesn't sound too dramatic to you, hon—I guess you know how much I dislike insincerity and over-dramatization, myself.

I'll love you till my dying day and then, if there is another world, I'll find you there if I have to search the whole universe. Until tomorrow, I'll see you in my dreams.

All my love and undying devotion, forever,
Leno

MacArthur–Settles Score With Japs

VICTORIOUS LEADER—General Douglas MacArthur, supreme Allied commander in the Pacific theater, whose determination to carry the fight to the enemy spurred his troops into island-by-island conquest.

Unconditional Surrender by Japanese Announced

WASHINGTON, Aug. 14.—(AP)—Japan has surrendered unconditionally, President Truman announced at 7 P. M., EWT (4 P. M. PWT) tonight.

General of the Army Douglas A. MacArthur has been designated Supreme Allied Commander to receive the surrender.

Offensive operations have been ordered suspended everywhere.

V-J Day will be proclaimed only after the surrender has been formally accepted by MacArthur.

6

"WE'RE building the apartment behind the garage so that you and Leno will have a place to live when he comes home," Dad was saying.

"We'd like a place of our own," I answered coldly.

"How will you be able to afford that?" he challenged just as coldly.

We sat in the living room at Waverly Drive engaging in our usual after-dinner confrontation. At the same time Dad was building the apartment behind the garage for Leno and me, he was making plans to build both Stella and Emma three-thousand-square-foot homes five blocks away. That was not upsetting to me, but why did Leno and I have to live behind the garage? I decided not to pursue the issue further.

I was excited about the affairs of *my* family at the moment. Dana had completed his training at OCS and was now a lieutenant in the Army. I felt great pride in his achievement. He spent his two-week furlough in Neosho with Mother after a sixteen-hour train ride to get there and was now in Camp Hood, Texas, in charge of a platoon, awaiting further assignment.

"I ran into Pat Billinghurst here," Dana wrote. Pat was a friend of ours from "Little Theatre" days in Kathryn Offill's drama class at Franklin. "Pat was captured in the fighting at the 'Bulge.' He's quite thin, but otherwise o.k. It was wonderful to see a friend, so far from home. We'll be leaving here soon, I think."

Dana soon travelled by train to L.A., receiving a short furlough and announcing his engagement to Dorothy, a girl he had been corresponding with from UCLA. Dorothy was a pleasant girl and pretty, but a little domineering for Dana, I thought. His furlough was over quickly and he was on his way to Camp Adair, Oregon.

"This is a replacement depot," he wrote. "We have no idea whom we are going to replace. The rumors have it that we're on our way to the Pacific somewhere and Dorothy's father has called his congressman to protest our being shipped out. I don't think it will do any good, though."

A month later Dana was sent to Fort Lewis, Washington and then to

215

Seattle, on his way to Okinawa for at least a year, which saddened and frightened me. "We waded ashore here after two weeks at sea," he wrote. "Planes that crashed in the ocean are still in the water and skeletons are lying around, especially in the caves. I am attached to the 24th Infantry Regiment, which is all black. All of the officers are white, however."

But before Dana arrived on Okinawa, the telegram came from Mother. "We'll meet you at Aunt Pearl's in Palm Springs on October fifteenth." Dorothy and I headed for the desert with anxious anticipation. She hadn't met the family and was in for a big surprise!

Mother and I had a tearful reunion and Aunt Pearl was her usual stoic self, being "terribly busy with property matters" and "too busy to entertain us." Aunt Marjorie, Mother's sister who lived in Palm Springs, ushered us to her "place on the side of the mountain" and she and her husband, with drapes closed to keep out the sun, proceeded to serve alcoholic beverages to all who would partake. Being only noon, I thought it rather scandalous and abstained. I don't know what Dorothy thought, but her conservative personality was a bit out of place with this crowd. By five o'clock they were all "feeling no pain" and I announced that I had to be at work in the morning and Dorothy and I departed.

Looking back, that was a wonderful afternoon and one that I would like to have a chance to do all over again. But in 1945, it all seemed a little depraved to me and I was happy to return to the stability of Oak Terrace.

August 30, 1945
Burglengenfeld, Germany

My darling Alice,

There have been quite a few changes in the past couple of days, as you can see. They are not the changes I've been hoping for yet, but at least they are changes. Yesterday, the Second Platoon moved back with Company Headquarters and we hadn't any more got settled than I was told to get packed and ready to leave for Battalion Headquarters in Burglengenfeld, about fifteen miles northwest of Regensburg. I was the only guy coming up here from "C" company and was brought up by jeep several hours ago. It seems the reason I was sent here was in order to be assistant to Corporal Evans, Company C's company clerk. He has enough points to be discharged, so they want me to learn his job. He takes care of allotments, service records, bonds, pay, etc. for about two hundred men.

I haven't seen much of the town yet, but it seems to be a small farm town, not too dirty. We are billeted in an old schoolhouse, but the rooms are not bad. We have lights, running water, showers, a radio—that's about all that's necessary.

Now that I'm here with Battalion Headquarters, I will be able to hear any news about our leaving as soon as the outfit receives it. I hated leaving some of my friends in "C" company, but this is a much better job.

I'm learning to do the payroll. Evans had typed out the payroll in the middle of August in quadruplicate, listing all the deductions; such as insurance, Class F allotments (wife), Class B allotments (bonds), and sent it to the Battalion Finance Officer who figures out the exact amount each person has coming. We received it back and put his figures on our copy. It's pretty complicated with all the promotions, demotions, furloughs, transfers, etc.

I started the course in business law through correspondence. It's divided into twenty-seven assignments and I can do them as fast as I want, but at least one a month. I've already done the first assignment, but the book is over a thousand pages and pretty hard. Maybe I can learn something which will help both of us later on in college.

I'm sending you the V-Day edition of our weekly publication, "Yank" magazine. The picture represents the exhausted gratefulness of the average "Joe" after hearing the wonderful news about the end of the war....

September 6, 1945
Burglengenfeld, Germany

...I'm feeling more depressed than usual tonight, because I'm getting so fed up with this uncertainty, or should I say "slow death." If the War Department would only let us know where we stand! They announced tonight that all men with seventy points would be out of Europe by Christmas and also a "limited" number of men with less than seventy. They went on to say that the point score for the Army of Occupation had not been decided yet, but that it would probably be men with under forty-five points. According to the revised date on the scoring system, I have at least forty-four points and a possible forty-nine. They've been squabbling over that third battle star of ours for the last four months and they're still undecided. If they're going to give it to us, I wish they would make up their feeble minds! While the war was

217

CONTINENTAL EDITION—STRASBOURG

YANK

THE ARMY WEEKLY

3 FR.

AUGUST 19, 1945
VOL. 2, NO. 4

By and for the enlisted men

on, I realized that there was a job to be done, even though I wasn't very happy about being here. But now that the war is over, I want to be with you and this waiting, waiting, waiting is really getting on my nerves. Every day seems like an eternity. The minutes and hours just seem to drag on and on until it seems as if I can't stand it much longer.

It seems to me that the Army is doing a darned poor job of this demobilization. If we had just one child (like Jack Geer who came into the service the same day I did), there wouldn't be a thing to worry about or "sweat out." It doesn't seem right to me that we should be punished because we thought that it wouldn't be right to the baby if he were born at this time, when everything was unsettled and unsure. But then, who am I to say?

Enough of this rambling for tonight. Things might turn out a lot better than I expect. It's just the idea of waiting! I worry a lot about you, honey. I read of all the accidents that occur every day, and I think about you speeding down Figueroa or Riverside. Please take it easy.

Another thing, hon. I wish you could get along with my folks a little better—just for a little longer now, anyway. When I get home again, I'm sure that things will work out. By asking you this, I don't mean to say that it's your fault. I know how sensitive you are at this time and I know how cold my folks can appear to be. I grant you that they are hard to understand, but, believe me, I know they love you as their own.

Besides, when you married me you knew there would be many difficulties and that you would have to put up with a little of the unpleasant for a time. But of course, if you've lost some of that love for me, I can understand why it's so repulsive to live with my folks. Please don't be offended by what I've said, hon. It's more than likely mainly my folks' fault, but I can't very well write to them about it because as you know, they probably wouldn't understand and it would just make matters worse.

Have you heard any more from your mother about Joe's discharge? I think I'll feel a little more at ease about you when you will be able to see them once in awhile. I feel that your mother understands your problems very well and I think her being close will make your life more bearable.

I heard the "Hit Parade" a little while ago and "Dream" was number two. I know you like it, and it made me think of you more than ever. I guess you've already sent the money order I asked for, but if you haven't, I won enough to repay my debts already. I'll return your money when I receive it...

September 10, 1945
Burglengenfeld, Germany

...It's been another busy day for me today, and I'm glad. The "70" pointers left this morning about ten. I would have given anything to have been able to go with them. The way things look now, I don't think I could even make a good guess at how long I'll be here. If I'm home by Christmas, I'll be darned lucky. If Congress would apply pressure on the Army, they might be forced to work out a better rotation plan and give some of those "USO Commandos," who have never left the States, a chance at it over here. About one-third of the Battalion left, and I feel like crying when I realize so many of them have gone when we all came over here together. Oh, honey, I pray that my score is high enough to get me home soon. I miss you and love you so much, it's killing me. Why should life be this miserable?

I wrote to Roxie congratulating him on his newly born son. We are getting way behind everyone having children, honey. We are going to really have to go some to catch up, aren't we? I am looking forward to it very anxiously, myself! I cancelled my enormous ten dollar bond deduction as of August thirty-first. I'm getting tired of contributing to something that is keeping me in the Army that much longer.

Your adoring husband (maybe a little worn out, disgusted, lonesome, sick of the Army, tired of this life, but still), your adoring husband...

September 17, 1945
Burglengenfeld, Germany

...The days continue passing by and as yet there seems to be no easing of this aching pain in my heart. It's been here since the morning I left you at Camp Howze and I'm afraid it's going to stay until you are in my arms once more. Believe me, honey, when I say I've missed you. Only God knows how very much.

Well, as you can see, they finally decided to break down and make me a corporal. A lot of good that does, though. It certainly doesn't get me any closer to home. It helps a little financially. A corporal draws sixty-six dollars base pay. Then I get 20 percent overseas pay; that makes a total of seventy-nine dollars and twenty cents. Subtract twenty-two dollars for your allotment, ten dollars for your Class "E" allotment, and six dollars and forty cents for Life Insurance, and that means I draw forty dollars and eight cents over the pay table each month. If anyone has any smart remarks about the promotion, don't get mad, hon. I certainly don't care what anyone else thinks.

Yes, I like this job much better than guarding the prisoners, hon. It's really not much of a town; all the places in Europe are so darned filthy. In this town, and many others over here, the toilets drain right out into the side of the street. The drains are open and a person has to keep his eyes open when walking around!...

September 24, 1945
Germany

...I received two letters from you this afternoon and to say that I was happy to receive them would be putting it mild. In the letters you cleared up many things which have troubled me for some time. I think I have a better understanding of the way you feel about my folks and the family in general. You seem to be mostly worried about how I feel about family affairs, visiting, birthday parties, doing everything the folks want, etc. And I want you to know that your fears are all unfounded. Believe me when I say that, honey. You are the most important thing in my life and you will always come first in everything. I think you should know me well enough by now to know that I won't allow the family to run my life. I hope you haven't grown too independent in my absence. Of course, though, I would much rather take orders from you than the First Sergeant.

You mentioned in one of your letters that my cousin, Mary, was getting married the first part of the year to Louis and that you hated to think of going alone. That makes me happy to know that you dislike going anywhere without me, because I feel exactly the same way myself. However, it's my honest opinion that you should go. Not because it's the conventional thing to do, but because I really believe that Mary and her folks would like to have you there and would feel terribly hurt if you didn't show up. Of course, if it would be too unbearable for you, I'd a lot rather you didn't go.

You asked me how my German was coming along. I'm afraid that it's not very good. I talk to these Krauts only when I have to, especially when I stop to think that if it weren't for them, I would be home with you.

No, hon, I haven't taken up smoking and I certainly don't plan to. You should know by this time that even if I were practically dying for a cigarette, I would do without, just because so many people think that I am bound to start smoking one of these days. Not that smoking is such a terrible thing—I guess it's just a little streak of stubbornness in me...

9:30 p.m.
Sunday, September 16, 1945
3301 Waverly Drive

My dearest Leno,

I have spent a very lonely Sunday without you, honey. I want so much to be with you. Surely, it must come soon. Help me to keep that faith. Without it, I would be lost. If you only knew the terrible things that have gone through my mind about you, and the horrible dreams I have had. I have honestly waked up hating you for being such a "cad"; and thanking God when I remembered it was just a dream. It's just part of this horrible nightmare of being separated. If you feel a pang of jealousy or uncertainty about what I'm doing, just imagine how I feel about you, especially when you went on your furlough. I also have to contend with the sneering remarks that people are always making about what you're doing. And if you don't think that hurts, honey, you'll never know how much. It has only been your constant reassurance and faithful letter writing that have helped me at all.

There are other wives that go to dances; they're perfectly harmless, I guess; but they couldn't get me to go. They have often laughed, and said, "Don't you think Leno ever goes to any?" This hurts a lot when they say that, honey, perhaps because I'm not completely sure you haven't been; but, of course, I always say that you don't.

Your dad said today that he thinks he misses you more than I do. And don't say he was just kidding, because it was a very serious conversation, honey. Of course, I told him that was impossible, but he didn't seem convinced. It rather upset me, but I soon got over it.

One thing this separation has taught me—I can take quite a bit from people. I've had to for so long now...

October 14, 1945
Burglengenfeld, Germany

My darling Alice,

I've just come back from a long ride to Nuremberg to see a football game. It was a rather cold, tiresome ride, but I would say it was worth it. We saw a swell football game, the first I had seen since last year in Maastricht, Holland. The First Infantry Division beat the Ninth Infantry Division forty to nothing, but the game itself was a lot closer than the score indicates. The game was played in the Nuremberg Stadium which Hitler had built for Nazi activities. It's a pretty nice looking place, but the funny part of it is that we had to sit on the ground. I can't imagine why such an elaborate place would have terraced rows of dirt seats. Maybe they ran out of materials.

There was no mail waiting for me when I got back from the game, which was very disappointing. There's always tomorrow, though. It seems that of late our whole life is being spent living in "tomorrow." I hope and pray that "tomorrow" comes soon, very soon.

Believe it or not, somebody in the outfit scouted around and found two Ping Pong tables plus paddles and balls. I guess it is sent overseas, but the Army seems to thrive on making things hard to find. So now we have something to do in the evenings. Remember when we used to play on our off hours, across the street from LACC? Gee, honey, we've had so many wonderful times together. I'll never forget them. Wouldn't it be swell if we could spend our second wedding anniversary in our own little home? Even a cozy little three room place sounds like heaven to me. All I care about is being with you. Nothing else matters. I hope you feel the same way.

I've been doing a lot of thinking and dreaming lately, even more than usual. It has been about you and me, our family and our home. Honestly, honey, I'm actually looking forward to having grown children of our own. I want them to be handsome, intelligent, and successful, but most of all I want them to be happy. Maybe I'm getting to be an old sentimentalist, but that can't be helped. You know I've come to the conclusion that the reason life is so cruel and harsh to people at times is only to make them truly appreciate the everyday things. It's a terrible price to pay for happiness, I know, but I guess there is someone higher than us who has the final say so.

On the lighter side, the food here at Battalion Headquarters has been surprisingly good. That goes to prove that it isn't so much the food but the way that it's prepared which counts. At present, we have a cook who used to have a job as chef for Melody Lane in Hollywood. He really takes pride in his cooking and usually goes out of his way to bake a pie or cake for us every day. The greatest percentage of cooks in the Army just don't give a darn and fix a meal so that it will mean the least possible work for them. I guess you can't really blame them too much, though, because they are thoroughly disgusted with the Army too, and are only thinking of getting home to their old jobs (which in most cases wasn't anything like a cook). Out of the twelve million men in the Service, I doubt if there were fifty thousand who really wanted to get into the war. But somebody had to do it.

I'd better be getting some sleep or I'll be putting you to sleep. Goodnight, honey. I love you and miss you more than I can ever tell you in writing. Don't ever stop loving me...

October 28, 1945
Germany

...I received three wonderful letters from you today and I'll try to answer some of the questions which you asked. First of all, I was very happy to hear that Dana was able to get a pass to Los Angeles before leaving for Okinawa. It's too bad that he has to ship out now that the war is over. It was nice of him to say that he would like to replace me, but even if that were possible, the unhappiness would still be "all in the family."

I went to the movie again tonight and saw "The Unseen," with Herbert Marshall and Joel McCrea. It was an interesting show, I thought... more of a murder mystery. Naturally, I had it all figured out before the picture was half over.

Don't believe the stories you hear about unfaithful men in the service. I'll grant you that at least seventy-five percent of the married men never step out on their wives. At least that holds true in this outfit. And a couple of the boys have received terrible shocks from home, in the form of a baby born to their wives after being overseas for a year.

Yes, March is a long way off, but at least it's a goal to shoot for; a date at which we can expect, or reasonably expect, all our troubles to vanish. That is a lot more than we had a few months ago. I know how long six months can be. Besides, March isn't six months off—it's only four and a half! I had a hard time going to sleep last night. All I could think about was how I will react when I first see you again. Usually, our reunion is at the Union Depot, with you running into my arms, tears in your eyes and as pretty as a picture. We probably won't meet there at all. I don't know if I will smile, laugh, scream or cry. It will be such a happy moment for me, and it's been so very long since I've enjoyed true happiness that I just don't know what will happen.

I received your packages along with the mail today. Two of them were for Christmas from Emma and Zi Zi. They contained everything from tooth powder to handkerchiefs. In your package there was a can of apricots, a bag of almonds, candy, a bottle of Lucky Tiger hair tonic and a Liberty magazine and newspapers. In the Highland Park Review there was an article about Dana. It was a good article and Dana looked very "rugged" in his battle attire. Honestly, hon, you must spend all of your time buying, wrapping and preparing packages to send to me. I'll never forget your thoughtfulness.

I'm really happy to hear that your mother, Joe and Bobbie arrived safely in Los Angeles at long last. I guess you had a beautiful reunion at Aunt Pearl's in Palm Springs. I sure wish I could have been there. I hope they can find a nice place now that they're back. The Stars and Stripes says the housing situation in Southern California is really a problem. Is that true?

So, Howard received his discharge! I'm very happy for him, Ann and their little Howard, but, as you said, somehow it just doesn't seem fair. It seems to me, too, that the fellas who have been overseas any length of time at all should be the first ones out. A great many of the men here feel as if they have been left "holding the bag" and that the "powers that be" are truly ungrateful. That goes for the longshoremen and other workers striking in jobs affecting the speedy return of servicemen.

I received a letter from my old Squad Sergeant, Spangler, who left the 524th about a month and a half ago with seventy-six points, having spent four and a half years in the Army. He, along with a bunch of other men who left the 524th about the same time, is still sitting around a staging area in France waiting to ship home. Isn't that a dirty deal? They were ready to leave a couple of weeks ago, but due to the shipping shortage their trip was postponed. He had no idea how much longer they would be waiting...

225

November 15, 1945
Germany

...I hope you will forgive me for not writing the past two days. But the situation has changed around here and a lot of extra work has been thrown on my shoulders. About three hundred and sixty-five men from the 524th are to be transferred into another M.P. battalion stationed in Munich and the remaining sixty or so men in the battalion will be transferred to Vienna. I'm scheduled to go with the group to Vienna; mostly clerks, cooks, mechanics, supply men, medics and a few M.P.s who are commanding officers and first sergeants. We are to be the Cadre of a new M.P. battalion to be formed in Vienna for occupation. We will break in new men as M.P.s and then, hopefully, head for home. We personnel clerks have been working our heads off the past couple of days and nights. There are only fifteen of us from "C" Company going to Vienna. Out of the fifteen or twenty who came into the Army on the eleventh of November two years ago, Clayton Hallickson and I will be the only two left. Jacobs and Jack Geer are going to Munich. I spent some time in Straubing saying goodbye to most of my buddies and taking pictures.

Gosh, honey, I wish that I could get away from all this and return to you! Usually, if a person wants something in life very badly, he can most likely fulfill his wishes through patience, initiative, suffering, endurance, and common sense. But what can I do about wanting to see you? I have never felt so completely helpless. Don't think for one minute I haven't thought over the different angles I could use to get home. I've thought of having you send me a cable from the Red Cross saying you were ill and that you needed me at once. I've thought about applying for OCS back in the States and once that I got there to fail all my examinations and get a discharge. I've thought about feigning sickness, but Army doctors are pretty well up on all the tricks of goldbricking. Please don't think me terrible for feeling this way, honey. It's just that I get so darned mad seeing men with four or five months overseas duty going home only because they have a couple of children. I read in the paper today where the Army wasn't sending men overseas anymore who had twenty-one months service. Well, that's all fine and dandy, but who's going to relieve the guys overseas, or don't they matter anymore now that the war is over? And, honey, when we are finally together for good, I promise to make you the happiest woman in the world. I'll be the best husband any woman could ever hope to have. Oh, yes, you lost two dollars in a pool, didn't you? Well, I guess I'll forgive you this time, but don't let it happen again. (Look who's talking!)

You mentioned recently driving Jane to the Civic Auditorium for a dance. Isn't she quite young to be going there already? She's only thirteen, isn't she? Come to think about it, I guess I wasn't much older than that myself when I started going. We have had some wonderful times at the Civic, but I'm not at all sorry that those days have gone by.

I received a post card from your mother and Joe sent from the Rosslyn Hotel. It really makes me mad to think that they can't find a house to rent. There should be a ruling of some kind which would give persons who had lived in California all their lives and left to fight the war priority for housing over the newcomers, who are mostly draft dodgers of one kind or another. I guess that wouldn't be the most democratic thing to do; although something's wrong somewhere!

Goodnight for now, honey. I would gladly sleep out under the stars tonight if I could be with you. (And it's snowing now!) I wouldn't let you freeze either, honey, believe me! ...

30 November 1945
Vienna, Austria

...We arrived in Vienna last night, but I was unable to write you until now because there was so darned much to do in getting set up. There were no accidents on the trip for which we are all thankful, but we did have some trouble in Linz, Austria the first night. We stayed over night there because it was just about the halfway mark to Vienna and we couldn't make it to Vienna in one day. While we were sleeping, our trucks and jeeps were looted, most likely by civilians. Not everybody lost something, but naturally I did. All the candy, cookies, canned goods, etc. which were sent to me in packages from you and others were stolen. Also I lost combat shoes, a couple of shirts, a couple of pairs of pants, my camera (with a roll of undeveloped film which I took in Straubing and was going to send you), and probably a lot of stuff which I haven't missed yet. It really burns me up to think that anyone could be so darned low as to pull a trick like that and I'd give anything to have caught them in the act. There was supposed to have been a GI guarding the convoy, but he must have been "goofing off."

The latest news out is that our "55" pointers are leaving for home about December sixth or seventh. One of the men leaving will be our First Sergeant, McDonald. I really hate to see him go, too, because he's such a swell guy. I'm hoping we won't be getting another First Sergeant like Beckenbaugh. That would be too much. But then, I don't think I will be in "C" company much longer, anyway. I think I will be officially transferred into Headquarter's Detachment when the "55 pointers" leave.

As you no doubt know, Vienna is a very large city. I would guess that the population is just a little larger than that of Los Angeles. It is not too badly torn up in comparison to other cities we have seen. Rubble piles are still heaped up in the center of the streets or on the sidewalks, waiting to be moved away. The city is split up into four areas: American, Russian, British and French. When American M.P.s patrol the city in jeeps they are accompanied by M.P.s from each of the different Allied armies.

You asked what I thought about your moving into a place until I get home. Well, truthfully, hon, I would rather you didn't. I've heard so many things about L.A. criminals lately that I would be worried stiff about you all the time. Jane would be swell company, but I'm afraid she wouldn't be much protection! Those pictures you sent of you and Bobbie are really cute, honey. He's a cute little devil and the ocean sure does look good, too.

This nightmare has got to end soon. I pray to God that it will...

15 December 1945
Vienna, Austria

...It looks as if I'm not going to be able to write you as often as I have in the past, honey. I sometimes wonder if we will ever get caught up with our work around this place. But maybe I won't have to worry about anything pertaining to the Army in a very short time. Believe it or not, honey, our Ardennes Star and five beautiful points came in this morning. I could hardly believe it when Captain O'Neil came rushing into our personnel office to tell us about the star. That gives me forty-nine points now and should get me home at least a month or two sooner. The rumor down at VAC Headquarters is that men with from forty-five to forty-nine points will be on their way home by January fifteenth. Doesn't that sound wonderful, honey? I've taken over Sergeant Dickinson's job as Personnel Sergeant Major and as you can see, I was promoted to "Technician Fourth Grade" or "T/4" as the GIs say. I make the same pay as a sergeant, a raise of about fifteen dollars a month. The only difference is that there is a "T" under my three stripes. In this new job I have quite a few reports to submit to higher headquarters, but the company clerks make out reports which I consolidate into one total. It's interesting, but the Army isn't exactly the company I want to work for. If I have to stay around here much longer, I'm afraid I'll go nuts! Everything is so darned disorganized, and if there's anything I hate to see, it's an office without a system. That's the way the Army does everything.

At first they told me I would not be promoted unless I volunteered to remain over here for at least ninety days. Well, naturally, I told them I would not volunteer for even one day if they were to promote me to General. They decided to promote me anyway. It made me think that they do not expect me to be here ninety days which really gave me a lift.

I can't imagine that I might be on my way home next month. I don't want you to feel that the only reason I miss you so terribly is because of my intense sexual desire for you. I won't deny that it is one of the many reasons why I do miss you and why shouldn't it be, when you're so wonderfully luscious and desirable? Oh, honey, why do I torture myself, thinking of such things? I shouldn't be talking to you this way, I know. Please forgive me. I miss the wonderful talks we used to have, the long walks we used to take at Sycamore Grove so long ago. I miss the long drives we took along the beach on Sundays and on days we ditched school. Those happy moments will be ours once again very soon, I feel sure, and I can hardly wait.

Goodbye for now, honey. Love me forever,

Your adoring husband,
Leno

7

MY sister, Edith, was getting married in January. She had been corresponding with Mel Murry while he was in the service and when he received his discharge, it didn't take him long to pop the question. I was to be Edith's Matron of Honor and being involved in her happiness helped to pass the time, which was dragging unmercifully.

The closer the time came for Leno's return, the slower the time went for me and the more difficult it became to accept the fact that we would have to continue to live with his parents.

As was my nature, I tried desperately to solve the problem long before it even existed. Perhaps I could rent an apartment now and live with Jane. Then when Leno came home we would already be set up. Leno didn't like that idea, and besides, there were no apartments anywhere for rent.

Howard had received his discharge in October and he and Ann were living with his parents. Why don't we buy a place with them? That was it! We could buy something together and solve both our problems!

We found a cute duplex in Glendale for twelve thousand dollars which we all liked and thought would work out. The hitch was that Howard had to get the money for a down payment from Paul, Ann's father, who had finally forgiven them for getting married without his consent. And *I* had to broach the subject with Leno's father.

This confrontation was approached, on my part, with a vengeance. Dad listened to my idea attentively and then told me in no uncertain terms that it was out of the question.

"*This* is your home. It is nonsense to purchase anything else. Property is expensive now because of the shortage. When building starts increase, you will lose a lot of money."

I listened and decided not to argue about it, but I was heartbroken and knew Leno and I would never be able to live our own lives. Howard didn't have any luck either and I knew the only way for us to gain our independence was to have our own money. I had saved enough for half of the down payment on the duplex, but Leno and I couldn't swing it alone. I felt trapped, but knew my frustration would have to wait until Leno was back. My own ideas were being thwarted and I hoped Leno would take a stand when he came home. I wondered if he could.

January 6, 1946
Vienna, Austria

My darling Alice,

I haven't written you in several days and you must be thinking that I've completely forgotten you. I know I should continue writing often even if our reunion is not too far off. I sit down and try to write, but no matter how hard I try, nothing I write sounds sensible to me. So, I crumple up the paper and lie down on my cot and think and think and think some more. I sometimes wonder if I will remain in my right mind if our separation lasts much longer.

I was promoted to Staff Sergeant last week. But what good are promotions when I am eight thousand miles away from you, the only person in the whole world who means anything to me?

You must have heard about the War Department's latest statement about slowing down redeployment and the discontent among the GIs. I literally shudder when I stop to think of where I would stand in this picture if our Ardennes Star and five points had not come in! What makes me so darned mad is the fact that there are only about a hundred and fifty thousand men left in Europe with more points than I have. Unless they start sending over more replacements from the States, I'm afraid I won't be home until some time in March. Where are all the men who were drafted after I came in? There must be two million of them, at least. With all these demonstrations being put on by GIs, you would think that something would come of it!

I received two letters from you this afternoon; one was written on November twenty-sixth and the other on the twenty-seventh! They must have come by way of China. You suggested with the housing shortage what it is, that perhaps we should buy a duplex, living in one and renting the other. That sounds like a very sensible suggestion to me and a lot more logical than paying out rent for nothing. So, honey, if you're still interested, I wish you would look around and let me know if you find something you like. Since Dad knows a lot about real estate, if he thinks it's a good deal, I'd like you to get the place. What will you use for a

Edith May
and Mel Murry
January 12, 1946
(Mrs. Randall Pycha)

Dana
on Okinawa

down payment? With my soldier's deposits, I can probably scrape up three hundred dollars. Use any of the money you have that's in my name.

I received an invitation to Edith's wedding. Mel sounds like a real nice fellow. Since he owns some apartments, I hope your mother and Joe can rent one from him. I guess I won't be home in time for the wedding.

I was happy to hear that Mike Radogna is probably on his way back to the States. I guess you'll be very happy when he arrives. You two always did get along so well together.

This hasn't been much of a letter, I know, but I just can't seem to think of anything but returning to you. I hope you'll always love me, honey, and that I haven't changed too much in your eyes...

February 4, 1946
Vienna, Austria

...Well, honey, as you can see, they finally made me a Technical Sergeant. Besides boosting my ego a little bit, the promotion raises my pay to a hundred and fourteen dollars. In one of your letters you said that Mike Radogna is a Tech Sergeant. That's one of the main reasons I am happy about being promoted. I certainly can't let my "competition" beat me! I'm just kidding, honey. Anyway, the new CO, a Major, said he would make me a Master Sergeant if I cared to stay over here for a couple more months. What do you think I should do? Well, that's what I think, too, so don't worry. You said not to make myself too essential. I already have a man, Corporal Frausch, learning my job and he will take over as soon as I get shipping orders.

This letter should reach you some time around the end of the month and I'm almost certain I'll have left this outfit by then. But I don't want to tell you to quit writing until I am certain. If redeployment hadn't been slowed down this last month, I'd almost definitely be in the States right now.

I'm enclosing a few snapshots which were taken last month sometime. Sergeant Carlson, who I mentioned in one of my previous letters, is the First Sergeant of Headquarter's Detachment. He's really a swell guy and easy to get along with. I never thought I'd ever buddy around with a first sergeant, but then he's a lot different than Beckenbaugh. We went to the movies last night and saw Robert Benchley and Vera Vague in "Snafu."

We had quite a laugh over the show, being an orientation on how to handle the returning serviceman. Oh, well, maybe we are a terrific problem and burden to some folks in the States and just don't realize it...

February 4, 1946
3301 Waverly Drive

My dearest Leno,

I had a very nice and welcome letter from you today. You write so seldom now that I was quite surprised and happy about getting it. March or April seems so far away, but I'll be saving my money and getting ready for you. I have been getting ready for so long—it isn't fun anymore.

I'm sure glad you want to buy a house, honey, but I'm waiting for your opinion about buying a place with Howard and Ann. I really would like to wait until you're here before making a selection. For that matter our tastes are pretty much the same, so I'm pretty sure that we would both choose the same place. You mention using any money in your name for the down payment. If you say so, I know I can legally, but your dad has the money and I hope you haven't forgotten how he is about that, especially since you're not here. If I have to use that money to get a place, I would rather wait until you're home. Dad and I don't seem to agree on anything from labor strikes to young marriages, and about the only way I can avoid an argument is not to talk to him. So, you see where that leaves me in an issue of this kind.

Mom and Dad won a mattress in a raffle yesterday and said it was yours. I guess that means it is mine too, but they didn't mention me. It's things like that, that hurt, honey.

I'll say goodnight now, hoping you're well and thinking of me. Your oh-so impatient and eager wife.

With all my love,
Alice

February 5, 1946
3301 Waverly Drive

My dear Leno,

Another day has passed, another day closer to you. It seems every time I think you're within reach, you slip away for another couple of months.

Work was as boring as ever today, and dragged endlessly. When I look ahead on two months or longer, it seems like an awfully long stretch. But it has been that way ever since you left, so I should be used to it. I'm sure hoping you'll make it for our anniversary, but I'm certainly not counting on it. I think you'll be very lucky if you get home even soon after. But such is life; one disappointment after another. Emma said, "Oh well, it doesn't really matter if he's here or not for your anniversary. A few days one way or another won't make any difference." It's very easy for her to say that when her husband has been home for all of their anniversaries. But that's the way people are, and that's that.

It sounded so good, honey, when you said for me to get the luggage because we didn't want to spend too much time in L.A. That's exactly as I feel, but I was so afraid you wouldn't. I thought I'd like to go to Florida, but you said you didn't want to do much traveling, so perhaps, that's too far. Of course, if we're going to be gone for awhile, we could really take our time and travel at leisure. And it wouldn't be anything like the way you have been traveling for the past year and a half. I hope, too, it will be a little more enjoyable for you.

Somehow, in your last letter, you sound so much older. It's the first time I've noticed it. I expect you to look older and, perhaps, act a little older, but I sure hope you're still the same in other ways. You're so wonderful, honey, and I hate to think of your changing.

I'll say goodnight once more, hoping to see you very soon.

Your devoted wife,
Always,
Alice

235

February 9, 1946
Vienna, Austria

My darling Alice,

Honey, I can hardly express the complete happiness which fills my heart tonight. It's a feeling which I have not enjoyed for a great many months. At long last, I can tell you the exact date that I will leave Vienna and the 524th M.P. Battalion; this time in the right direction, home. We will leave on the 7:35 p.m. train, Tuesday the twelfth, for Linz, Austria. I am going to send you a cablegram Monday or Tuesday night, telling you I am leaving Vienna and to hold up all mail. I am expecting to spend two or three weeks in Linz, processing. Then I will head for the port, and you. I won't be able to sleep tonight, that's for sure! I probably won't be able to sleep again until you are in my arms—and then I'm afraid I won't feel anything like sleeping. So, I'll just have to be contented with spending the rest of my life awake.

I'd better say goodnight now, honey. I just lie on my cot and think and dream of the wonderful days which lie ahead.

Your adoring husband, always,
Leno

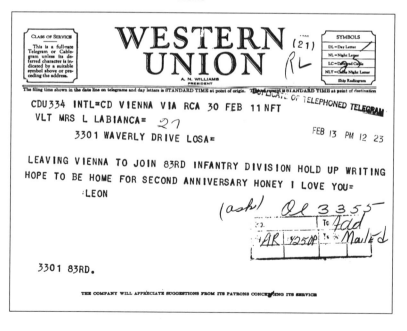

February 13, 1946
3301 Waverly Drive

My dearest Leno,

I do want to let you know about our housing situation as it now stands. The deal with Howard and Ann didn't go through, due to the fact that they couldn't get the money from Paul. Perhaps it's for the best, anyway. I decided to have a talk with your dad to see what his views on the subject were. I got exactly the answers I expected, but I was a little surprised at the way he had it all planned out in his mind.

In the first place, he reviewed the fact that 3301 Waverly Drive is our house—reason number one why we shouldn't buy a place. He figures that as long as we're so unsettled in our minds as to what we want to do (so he puts it), that the best thing for us to do is stay in the apartment behind the garage where Emma and Pete are now until such time as we feel we can use the front house. I'm not going to express my opinion at this point until I know what you have to say about it, because he made the remark that whatever I want to do will be all right with you. But he's wrong, and I don't think he knows you very well. So, honey, those are his plans.

As long as he feels that way and also feels that I am the one who wants to buy a house and not you, I think it best to wait until you're home and can get it settled once and for all with him. I'm not going to have anything to do with it, because I don't want them saying that I tried to get you away. I hope you understand all this, honey. I've done my best to explain it. He also has it figured out that if you get home before Emma and Pete move out, that they can move into the front house and we can have the apartment. There are no facilities for cooking, but he says that they can all be put in.

So, it's just like I told you, honey, we won't ever have to worry about anything. Our whole lives are planned and we'll be very well taken care of. Your folks will give us everything, and all we have to do in return is say thank you, and live with them the rest of our lives.

Forgive me, honey, if I sound a little bitter, but I don't feel too happy about the whole affair. I'll try not to worry about it until you get here.

Your perplexed and anxious wife,

Alice

Linz, Austria
February 13, 1946

My dearest, darling Alice,

As you can see, I've finally taken that first, important step in the right direction. You should have received the cablegram which I sent on the eleventh, telling about my leaving Vienna. By the time this letter reaches you, there is no telling where I will be.

There weren't many of us from the 524th who came down here together: Sergeant Carlson, Corporal Fletcher, a sergeant from the supply section, and the first sergeant of Company "B". We rode down here from Vienna in some beat-up old coaches and we had to sleep sitting up all night, but it honestly seemed like heaven to us because we're finally heading for home. We leave Linz for our port of embarkation on the morning of February twenty-sixth. Our sailing date is set for the eighth or tenth of March. Oh, honey, I write this all so casually, but if you only knew how I feel! These last few weeks are going to simply drag by, I know, but at last it is definite, honey. No more dreaming and hoping—just a little patience and courage...

February 24, 1946
Linz, Austria

...Well, honey, this will probably be the last letter I will write to you from Europe. I should be practically home by the time this letter reaches you. I've honestly enjoyed writing to you these past, long and lonely months, hon, but you'll never know the complete happiness which fills my heart every time I think that I will actually be with you in the very near future.

If I had been unable to write to you during these days of emptiness and bewilderment, I would have been completely lost. If I had not received your wonderful letters, full of love, warmth and encouragement, I would have died. But now I'm glad this correspondence via the Postal Service is all over. From now on our "communicating" will be done in person! I'll probably send one more cable from Le Havre, telling you our date of departure. We should reach Le Havre on the second or third of March. That's allowing us lots of time for usual army "snafu," too. I'm hoping and praying that for just this once everything will run smoothly.

I'm enclosing another snapshot of a couple of fellows who worked in the 524th personnel section and myself. As you can tell, I am trying to break you in gradually as to what I look like, all over again. I don't think I have changed that much myself but I'm not sure whether that's good or bad. Anyway, honey, I'm hoping you still love me, even though I'm not a "Gable" or "Taylor." Imagine me a civilian again, honey! It's almost too good to be true. I know it has only been a little over twenty-seven months since I was drafted into the Army, but it almost seems as if I've been in forever. I've lived for this day since the day we set sail from the port of Boston eighteen months ago. And now that it's drawing so close, it's hard for me to believe that these past long, lonely days, weeks, and months are almost over.

I'll miss your letters terribly for the next few weeks, honey, but, at least, I know I'm on my way home and won't have to worry about letters anymore.

I've been working in the personnel section since arriving here, helping to get the service records in order so that we won't have any trouble getting discharged later. There's quite a bit of administrative work to be done between now and the day we board ship.

We are going to Camp Phillip Morris at Le Havre for a few days of final processing immediately prior to embarkation. Our train (which is to take us to Le Havre) is already sitting on a sidetrack at the railroad station just outside of town. We are riding down in "40 and 8s" naturally, and have spent the last couple of days cleaning out the cars and installing stoves. The snow outside now is almost a foot deep, so I suppose it is going to be a pretty cold trip. At least it will be a lot more comfortable than the one we took a year ago last November from Valognes, France to Maastricht, Holland. This time there are to be only eighteen men to a car and that time there were close to forty. The trip is scheduled to take about four or five days and then we reach the port, at long last.

Remember, honey, I'll be thinking of you and loving you and missing you till the very moment we meet again.

Your adoring husband,
Leno

Leno and his 524th buddies joined the 308th Engineer Combat Battalion at Linz, Austria.

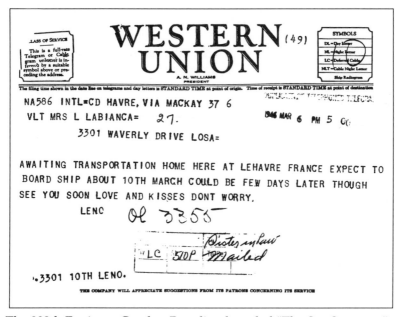

The 308th Engineer Combat Battalion boarded "The Sea Sturgeon" on March eleventh headed for home.

Charlie second from right

Waiting in the fog at LeHavre

8

March 20, 1946
Aboard the Sea Sturgeon

SOUVENIR EDITION

Homeward-bound GIs aboard "The Sea Sturgeon" have learned these past eight days that one of their choice phrases—"Things are tough all over"—is essentially correct. Although Captain T.R. Sorensen, veteran skipper of "The Waterman Lines," and other ship officials had the Sea Sturgeon under complete control at all times, there still were many uneasy moments and the Le Havre-New York voyage may grow into some tall stories in years to come.

The Sturgeon glided out of the harbor on Tuesday, March 12th, through the minefields and into the channel. Wednesday was "R" (Rail) day for a sizeable number of passengers. "Mal de Mer" was the vogue, although by no means popular. It was just as rough in the galley where mess sergeants were hard-pressed to maintain a favorable balance of manpower.

"Red letter" days continued on Thursday when a connecting pipe cracked. It was necessary to reduce speed and only 271 miles was covered for the day.

Anxiety ran the gamut on St. Patrick's Day when the Sturgeon was caught in an ice flow. Although a warning had been served, the size and quantity of the ice was not anticipated and the Sturgeon shattered some king-size cubes before breaking clear. But the ice came off the winner. A small hole about ten feet aft of the forecastle on the starboard side was the result. More than 350 GIs in lower number one were forced to move their quarters and

242

settled down to whatever space there was for the remainder of the voyage. Rumors ran rampant that the Sturgeon would have to put in at either St. John's or Halifax for repairs, but Skipper Sorensen continued to chart a course for New York.

Our trip is nearly over. Soon after you read this you will see "The Lady with the Torch," and then you will soon have your feet on U.S. soil again. One thing we all agree on—it has been a rough month.

...The 308th Engineer Combat Battalion sweated out nearly a month in or near Linz, Austria—then came the train ride. They started on February 26th in box cars. One delay after another, some for twelve hours and longer, and then a blizzard left the cold, exasperated, impatient shipment thoroughly disgusted. It took them 118 hours to get to Le Havre.

We have been glad to have had this part in getting you home again, and appreciate the way you have pitched in on the work that ship-keeping entails.

The loss and inconvenience that many of you have suffered as a result of the flooding of your quarters we deeply regret, but we have admired the soldierly spirit with which you have taken it. However, our Arctic adventure will be something to remember and talk about—an adventure we would not have had further south. Ahead of you now is another few days—maybe a fortnight—of Army routine, and at the end, the long-coveted little white piece of paper. On the pier the Red Cross will be waiting with the first fresh milk most of you have seen in years. There may even be a brass band.

Via ferry and train, the shipment will move to Camp Kilmer, New Jersey, where many stayed on their way in the other direction. The principal lure of Kilmer will be, for men on board ship nine days, a chance to shave in fresh water, maybe even hot water, and the chance to eat a good meal without the food sliding left and right. The process is said to never take more than thirty-six hours, but you will not be able to get away to New York —legally, that is.

Then you'll be sorted out according to discharge centers and after one more GI train ride—for some lucky few, a flight—there comes the last sweat. Once you get on a discharge roster, it should be only forty-eight hours more, but there's no telling how long it will take to get on a roster. You turn in the equipment you were issued by the Category IV Outfit and have carried across the ocean in the Army. You get a chance to convert your National Service

Life Insurance into a civilian asset and there is a real physical exam. By no means merely a shortarm, this time—the exam must protect the Army against possible later claims.

So, to all of you, our guests, we say, "Go with God."

9

THE telephone call came from New Jersey two days before our second wedding anniversary.

"Honey, I'm here in the States."

"I can't believe you're finally back," I cried.

"I'm here, all right, but it's going to take several days to muster us out. I'm not going to make our anniversary."

"It doesn't matter... a few days," I returned sadly.

"They're sending me to Marysville, California. It's about four hundred miles from L.A. Can you and the folks meet me there?"

"Of course, but I want to come alone."

"No, you'd better come with Mom and Dad. It's too long a trip for you to make by yourself. I'd worry about you all the way."

"Leno," I began to cry. "I don't want to share you with anyone."

"Don't cry, honey. If you'd rather come alone, it's o.k. Mom and Dad will just have to understand. I have to go now. There are a hundred guys standing in line waiting to call home. Remember, honey, I love you."

Then he was gone.

"Of course, we will all go together," Dad said immediately and emphatically, with Mom nodding her head in agreement.

I was too weary from the long months of waiting to feel happy, and their attitude was more than I could stand. I lashed out at them, unmercifully.

"I am going alone," I shouted amid my tears.

"That is nonsense," Dad returned, shouting even louder. "This is too long a trip for you to take alone. Leno is just as anxious to see us as he is to see you!"

"Of course," Mom interjected furiously. "He is our son, and we have missed him, too." I had never seen Mom so angry.

I became furious, determined to have my own way. "You haven't missed him!" I shouted. "You've had your precious business and your daughters and your grandchildren! Why, when Leno came to say

245

goodbye to you on his last furlough here, headed for overseas, you didn't even stop your card game long enough to say goodbye!"

Dad's face sobered. "If I had gotten up from the card game, I would have cried," he confessed. "I couldn't let him see me do that."

"I've been alone for nineteen months," I went on, not listening. "No one understood what I was going through. Now it's *my* turn and you're not going to spoil it for me!"

I didn't know where all of this bitterness was coming from, but it kept coming, in spite of the hurt in Mom's eyes and the rage on Dad's face. I felt nothing but their interference. They were intruding on my long-awaited reunion with Leno and it seemed unforgivable.

I ran crying to my room and continued to pack the new clothes I had been saving for what seemed like an eternity.

We had dinner together, but there was no conversation. Mom was dejectedly quiet, and Dad, speaking only in Italian to her, drank a little more red wine than usual.

I went to my room right after eating, not stopping to help Mom clear off the table. I planned to leave at five in the morning and wanted to get to bed early. As I began to close the Venetian blinds covering the windows, I looked out and saw Dad walking toward the garage door. He lifted it slowly and walked around my car, looking carefully at the tires.

He came out thoughtfully, closing the door behind him. He stopped by the huge mulberry tree, overlooking his extensive fruit orchard that terraced down to the fountain, and watched the city lights as they slowly began to appear.

PART V

From Southern Italy to Southern California

"They came... from far places... all wanderers
of one sort or another seeking peace or fortune
or the last frontier, or a thousand dreams of escape."
"A Place in the Sun" by Frank Fenton

1

THE sun was hot and it was not yet noon. Antonio LaBianca, at seven, was browned by the sun and strong. Strong enough to lift the heavy rocks from their place in the dry, hard ground and carry them on his back across the small piece of farmland that belonged to his family.

He wandered among the low hills, gathering the huge rocks. The yellowish-gray mud, dried hard, and the barren, cracked and wrinkled ground were harsh on his bare feet. Suddenly, the ground shook, not enough to open cracks as it had last year, but enough to startle and frighten Antonio.

"Line them up along that place on the ground," his father, Pasqualino, directed. "We'll build a wall to stop the rain waters when they come."

It was hard to imagine rain on this hot, August morning, but it would surely come and with a vengeance in a few months.

Pasqualino was not a tall man; bent from the years of tilling the meager soil that was his allotted farmland, but a handsome man, proud and stubborn, devoted to the Pope in Rome and to the well-being of his family.

He stopped for a moment to watch his son; his first to live after losing four before him to illness and disease by the time each had reached the age of three months. He looked at Antonio with pride as he dug the rocks from the earth and moved them to their place where the wall would be.

Pasqualino felt the sun getting hotter and knew it would soon be too hot to endure.

"It's noon, son, time to go home to eat," he called to Antonio as he dropped the sixth boulder in its place.

As they trudged toward town, about a mile from their farm, along the narrow, rough and dusty dirt road, they talked.

"Did I do good today, Papa?" Antonio asked eagerly.

"You did fine, son," Pasqualino replied. "You're a good, strong boy and a credit to your papa. Of course, you can't go to school anymore now

249

that you're old enough to help out on the farm. I'm sorry you couldn't go to school longer..." his voice trailed and his shoulders slumped a little at the thought.

As they approached the small impoverished town of Adelfia-Canneto, Antonio realized how hungry he was. He looked forward with eagerness to the noon meal, as he and his father had been working since sun-up and had only had a piece of bread for breakfast.

His mother, Stella, waved to him as they approached their stone house connected to many others on the narrow street. They had no plumbing or electricity, but were comfortable. Antonio didn't miss what he had never known.

Stella was beautiful but care worn and old for her thirty years—a strong, quiet woman with complete devotion and obedience to her husband. Antonio's brother, Saverio, and sisters Marietta and Carmela were already in place at the table anxiously awaiting their pasta. Antonio was hoping for a bit of chicken. He didn't remember ever being so hungry.

Adelfia-Canneto was just a few miles from the seaport of Bari on the southeast coast of Italy. It might as well have been a hundred. Antonio had never been there, only heard about it from the few people who had ventured that far. They had no means of travel to the land by the sea, and no time to go by foot. Their lives were spent in their community and the family was the focal point of their everyday existence. Their father was the undisputed person in charge, and Antonio, his mother, brother and sisters accepted his authority without question.

The following year, Antonio's brother, Saverio, joined him working on the farm and together they carried the rocks, tilled the soil and harvested the meager crops that kept the family fed. Their father became more impatient and often spoke harshly to the boys, who got the pitch fork on the backsides if they laughed or had too much fun, wasting precious time.

As Antonio grew in stature, he dreamed of a better life. He heard stories of those who had gone north where jobs were more plentiful and the ultimate dream, to America.

When he reached the age of twelve, his mother's cousin, Saverio Bruno, left for America with his new wife, Rosa, and her mother and father. How Antonio wanted to go with them! "We can't take you now, Antonio," Saverio explained. "We don't know how it will go for us there, and you're still needed here at home."

"I know, Zi," Antonio admitted sadly. "But if I save some money, my brother can take over for me here."

Tears came to Rosa's eyes. "You can join us in a few years, my dear Antonio. I promise you."

When Saverio and Rosa left for Bari on their long journey to America, Antonio was determined to follow them no matter what he had to do to make it happen.

The over-population and lack of natural resources in southern Italy in 1906 made it next to impossible to get a job, let alone save money for Antonio's ambitious scheme. The family needed him to help on the land for their existence. When he returned from the farm chores at noon each day, instead of taking a rest as all the other workers did, Antonio looked for work around town. His mother promised he could keep any money he earned in the afternoon for himself.

Their village, as all the villages of southern Italy, was dominated by a patron, a notable who controlled all important resources and was looked to for the necessities of life. He was the most respected person in the community, the one person who could help Antonio find work. Antonio's eagerness, willingness and persistence earned him the few jobs that were available in town and he observed the methods to inspire confidence used by the patron.

It is said that hardship builds character and Antonio's character was well established by the time he reached sixteen. His bank account had grown under the watchful eye of the patron and he was prepared to leave his home and family. His cousins, Saverio and Rosa, sent for him in 1910.

Pasqualino reluctantly said goodbye to his eldest son and Stella wished Antonio well with dry eyes. If it was possible for him to have a better life than what theirs had been, they could feel no sadness. Saverio was left to support his father on the farm, and the two girls to help out at home.

Antonio promised to send them money as soon as he could, and to return home when he had made his fortune in America. He kept the first promise but couldn't keep the second, as he fell in love with the beautiful land of freedom across the sea. He had to brave the long trip through Italy to Naples and the frightening ocean voyage that brought him to the "Lady With The Torch" before he came to that realization. As the boy of sixteen stepped apprehensively ashore on U.S. soil for the first time, no words could describe his exhilaration or excitement. This would be his home now, forever.

Antonio LaBianca
Circa 1910

2

TWO hundred thousand Italians arrived in America in 1910, and Antonio LaBianca was among them. The history books say the great majority of Italian immigrants settled in the east in slums, flooding the unskilled labor market, suffering the degradation of merciless discrimination.

But not Antonio. He had worked and planned too long to become a depressing statistic. He knew what he had come to America to accomplish, and he set about to do just that.

He left New York on a train headed for Chicago, where he boarded the Santa Fe railroad to California. Passing through the vast expanse of open land across the prairies and desert, over the Rocky Mountains, across the Colorado River to the last mountain range and the final descent through the Cajon pass to the floor of the coastal plain at San Bernardino, he came upon the orange groves of the inland empire, extending through the foothills to Pasadena. To describe his excitement at seeing this endless, productive land is impossible. Only a farm boy from Southern Italy with all of its arid land and resulting poverty could appreciate what he felt as he rode through the fertile countryside.

Los Angeles was a veritable Garden of Eden in 1910. The beauty sprawled from the mountains to the ocean. The sky was blue and the air was clear and the smell of orange blossoms was everywhere. On occasion, the fog rolled in from the sea and the beauty was shrouded for a time, which gave the basin the name of the "Valley of Smokes," by the Indians. The heat and dust of the deserts were far away behind the San Bernardino and San Jacinto mountains on the east and the Tehachapi range on the north, allowing the moisture from the ocean winds to form clouds.

"The weather is somewhat like home," Antonio thought, "without the sultry summer air or the mosquitos or the mistral winds."

The Union Railroad Station in downtown Los Angeles was adjacent to the old Town Plaza where the city had its beginning. The Plaza

Butcher shop on wheels
Circa 1917

Catholic Church beckoned Antonio and he stopped to give thanks to St. Anthony for his good fortune to have arrived safely in so beautiful a city.

Saverio and Rosa welcomed him into their home like the son they didn't have. They had settled in a small Italian community, along the streetcar tracks on North Broadway close to the downtown area, which made it possible for Antonio to go almost anywhere with ease.

He immediately set out to get work in the flourishing orange groves, alongside the Mexicans and the Japanese. He picked oranges until he thought his arms would fall off and his back would break. But there was no sweltering sun to impede his activity at noon, as a breeze blew in from the distant ocean to cool the air and there was plenty of water to drink and food to eat to keep his stomach from aching with emptiness.

"They call me 'Dago'," he reported laughingly to Zi and Zi Zi, Uncle Sam and Aunt Rose, his fast-becoming Americanized cousins. "Because I say that any day for work goes. It seems to anger some of the other workers, but Zi, I can't feel any anger. We are here with so much beauty and so much work. I am too happy to be angry."

He soon became Tony to all of his friends, a name which he accepted along with all of the Americanisms. But he never called himself anything but Antonio, later changing it to Anthony.

When Antonio had learned all there was to learn in the orange groves, and mastered some of the English language, Zi suggested he could earn more money and learn a new trade in the meat-packing houses. Zi was making a good living as a butcher after serving time there and introduced Antonio to his old boss.

Antonio's experience in the packing houses would live with him forever. The cruel manner in which the livestock was slaughtered and hung up for the blood to drain made him sick to his stomach for a long time. But he became hardened, even to that, and eventually was able to watch those who came to drink the blood. The impoverished who were anemic were allowed this privilege, thinking that drinking the blood would cure their illness.

Antonio worked every waking hour, finding no time to take part in the unrest among those of his Italian friends who turned to crime to avenge the persecution and the unfair treatment by their Anglo-Saxon bosses.

His was a dream that would be fulfilled for himself and his family to come by endless hours of work. Learning quickly, his packing house experience was short-lived and he was a full-fledged butcher by the time he was eighteen. No sooner had he learned this trade than he decided that being his own boss with a butcher shop on wheels, would be the next step in his climb upward.

His meat truck traveled up and down the streets of Cypress Park and Lincoln Heights, suburbs of Los Angeles, with fresh meat for grateful housewives, mostly Italian.

Antonio was working hard, but he was also having a lot of fun. His sense of humor attracted good friends and his developing keen knowledge of business matters gathered an entourage that would remain steadfast.

He remembered well his days and years as a poor farmer's son, gathering the strength and knowledge that was now standing him in good stead; preparing him to be a counsel to his loyal friends.

By 1917 he was not only operating a successful business with his meat truck, but he was the proud owner of a Model T Ford. On an infrequent Sunday excursion to the beach with family and friends, some twenty miles away, his car just wouldn't start. He became a little over exuberant when winding the crank, his hand slipped, the crank reversed itself vehemently, and broke Antonio's arm.

"That's what I get for taking a day off," he lamented.

3

ANTONIO had completed only the first three years of school as a boy in Southern Italy, but as soon as he arrived in America he wanted to learn to read English as well as speak the language fluently. This he tried to accomplish at the end of his long day's work, choosing to start with United States history.

He had learned about Christopher Columbus in Italy. The Italians were proud of this ancestral heritage and took full credit for the discovery of America. He had also learned that his country had been in constant turmoil with no advantages going to farmers or other workers. But in America there were jobs for all those who wanted to work.

He started at the beginning. He read about the Mayflower and the sacrifices of the Pilgrims. He studied the life of Benjamin Franklin and his many accomplishments, and Patrick Henry and Thomas Jefferson.

"We hold these truths to be self evident, that all men are created equal, that they are endowed by their Creator with certain inalienable Rights, that among these are Life, Liberty and the pursuit of Happiness," he painstakingly translated, reading these words over and over again.

"That's what separated America from the rest of the world," he decided. "The inalienable right to do and be whatever one's vision could imagine. That's it, Zi, we have the right to be whatever we want to be in this country. It's all up to us. And given the natural resources we have available, there is no end to what we can accomplish."

Antonio's learning and reading took on new meaning. He studied the Constitution and the lives of the great men who had written it. His examination of the lives of George Washington and Abraham Lincoln became an inspiration during the long, difficult days in the orange groves and packing houses. If Abraham Lincoln could learn the law of the land from books, he could learn all he needed to know about business by reading.

When America went to war in 1917, Antonio enlisted in the United States Army and earned his United States citizenship. His mishap with the Model T Ford crank and the broken arm delayed his induction into the Army, which may have saved his life. By the time Antonio's arm was out of a sling and he was ready to serve his country, most of the men who were in the service had already shipped out to Europe. Many of them didn't come back.

Antonio was placed in the Quartermaster Corps and sent to Fort Lewis in the state of Washington after his basic training. The Army made him a cook and he learned how to prepare food on a large scale. As was typical with Army assignments, he had never done any cooking, but welcomed the experience and camaraderie with his fellow servicemen. He had a great time and in the years that followed, he enjoyed talking about what a good cook he became while in the Army. But he gave up cooking as soon as he was discharged, except for family barbecues.

Antonio learned more of American ways while in the service of his country, perfecting his ability to speak and read the English language. When he received his honorable discharge in 1919, he was twenty-five years old and ready to conquer the world. He had sold his meat truck at a profit when he entered the service and after his extensive experience in the kitchen at Fort Lewis decided to try his hand at running a bakery. That lasted less than six months. There were two other attempts at business ventures with friends, which were more disastrous than the bakery had been. The experience taught Antonio two things: never attempt a business that you don't know anything about and never have an equal partner. Always be in control.

Antonio went back to work for someone else, this time as a butcher in a neighborhood grocery store. He watched, he listened, he learned and he continued to study and read.

Antonio had done rather well with the ladies, in spite of his natural shyness, although taking none of it too seriously. But when Corina Luizzi, the niece of cousins Sam and Rose, arrived from Italy to live with them, he began to get other ideas.

He was never able to get her alone, away from the family, which made it difficult for them to get better acquainted. They didn't know that Zi Zi had sent for Corina with the purpose of introducing her to Antonio, hoping to get them together. Antonio spent more time at home now and the four of them became inseparable.

Corina's father had died when she was only twelve years old, and she left her mother, step-father, brother and step-brother in Italy. Sam and Rose became her mother and father in America and encouraged the growing attraction between Antonio and Corina.

When Antonio asked for Corina's hand in marriage, it came as no surprise to anyone. After a respectable time elapsed for their engagement, they were married at St. Peter's Italian Church on North Broadway in a solemn, Catholic Mass. The reception was festive, the food and wine were plentiful and Antonio and Corina finally got to be alone.

4

CORINA was a quiet woman—quiet and obedient. She was strong with a fine figure, though she only stood five feet, three inches tall. She hadn't worked in the fields in Italy, as her husband had done, but her brothers had. The women in her family never worked outside of the home. Their duties were domestic and were dutifully performed for the sole purpose of serving the men in the family.

Her eyes were brown and beautiful, full of love and compassion. She had gone to school in Italy only through the third grade, but from the time she arrived in America, she began to teach herself to read English with Aunt Rose's help.

She knew instantly that Antonio was well read. He seemed to have the answer to everything, and his ready wit made her laugh. She tried to catch up with him, but soon realized he was way ahead of her and always would be. She liked it that way.

It was love at first sight for Corina and there would be no one else for her for the rest of her life. She knew of Antonio in Italy, but there were no boy-girl relationships there at age sixteen. On her long trip to America, she looked forward to seeing him again, and their first meeting was not a disappointment to her. He was more handsome than she remembered, four years older than she and twenty-six when they were married.

They continued to live with Uncle Sam and Aunt Rose, who, having had no children, made the decision to adopt an orphaned boy, calling him Sammy. They needed more rooms and purchased a duplex with Antonio and Corina in the predominantly Italian community of Cypress Park, lying west of North Figueroa and north of San Fernando Road.

Gathering together in the evenings after long days of working for others, they talked about having their own business.

"Zi is certainly the best butcher in town," Antonio laughed. "And I have learned all about the grocery business in the past couple of years," he continued. "I think it's time to try it on our own again."

Their store was planned on paper when Antonio and Corina's first child was born—Stella, named after Antonio's mother, as was the Italian custom.

At the corner of Cypress Avenue and Elm Street, Antonio found a suitable lot and built his first store, paying all cash. This time he had no partners, except his wife, whom he knew he could control, and he felt thoroughly knowledgeable on the subject of food.

Corina waited on the customers, Zi took over as the butcher and a born American, Tom, helped Antonio with the produce and grocery delivery. Tom didn't speak any Italian, enabling Corina to practice her English, which flourished under his tutorship.

By the time the store was well on its way to being a profitable venture, Corina announced they were going to have another baby in the spring. Antonio knew now that they had to have a bigger place to live, closer to their business, and made plans to add living quarters to the back of the store.

The baby was due in four months and construction was under way for the addition when the news came from Italy. Antonio's father had had a stroke and wasn't expected to live. Antonio couldn't realize how much time had passed since his arrival in America. He knew he had to go back home now, a decision he made reluctantly.

Corina accepted the fact that it would be too risky for her to join him, and expensive, but this was their first separation and how she hated to see him go, especially now. There were restrained farewells and promises to be careful and come back safely. Uncle Sam and Aunt Rose were close by to comfort, and, of course, little Stella and Sammy were a handful for everyone.

Antonio left with a heavy heart for the long trek back, alone. To return after thirteen years was more traumatic than he had anticipated. He found himself restless on the sea voyage to Naples and the long train ride to Bari was tiresome once he had finished reading the books he had brought along. His arrival in Adelfia-Canneto was both triumphant and devastating.

"How did I survive in such poverty?" he asked himself. There had been no change nor improvement to his town since he had left. In America, he was accustomed to seeing growth and progress and change. His attention was drawn to areas that could be restored and renewed as he traveled through the town.

His father was unable to speak to him, being completely paralyzed, and there seemed to be very little recognition between father and son. "He has aged so much in the last thirteen years," Antonio thought. "I wonder if he knows I'm here."

He sat with him for a long while, telling him about his adventures in the new land, but had to leave the room several times to hide his tears.

"The doctor says it won't be long," Stella confided to her son. "He wasn't feeling too good that morning he left for the farm, but times have been especially hard this year, even with your help. He felt he couldn't take the time to be sick. He collapsed and had to be carried back to town. He's been like that ever since." Her eyes were dry and her voice was quiet. "I'm so glad you are here, my son."

"Mama, I will be back for you and the girls if Papa dies," Antonio promised.

"No, my dear, I will never go to America," she said sadly. "Marietta will be married soon, and this is my home."

"Saverio will be coming over next year," Antonio continued. "And if Carmela wants to come then, we will make a place for her. Mama, you can't believe the beauty and freedom in America, especially where we live in California. You're happy to get up in the morning and you can work all day and into the night if you want to—there's that much work. There are beautiful trees and every kind of fruit and plant you can imagine. It's never too hot or too cold and the air smells sweet with blossoms and ocean breezes. I want you to see it, Mama, and enjoy the harvest."

Antonio's eyes were moist, and he felt an overwhelming homesickness for America as he spoke. "The wages are enough so you can save and get ahead. Now that we have our own business, there is no limit to what we can accomplish. And little Stella. Mama, you would love her. She is beautiful, just like you."

Stella listened to the enthusiasm of her son and was proud of what he had done in America. She knew her second son, Saverio, would follow and possibly Carmela, but Marietta would stay and that satisfied her. She saw the sadness in Antonio's eyes when she told him she couldn't go. But to live is to be sad, she thought, and she accepted her life just as it was.

Antonio was disheartened when it was time to leave. "All I can do is help by sending money," he thought. "Wherever I am, I will always be without part of my family. I have been successful in America, but we are now separated forever."

By the time he saw the Statue of Liberty again, his father was gone.

5

ANTONIO returned to his family with a thankful heart. The Cypress Market had flourished in his absence under the watchful eye of Corina. Of course Zi was a better butcher than Antonio, so that department was under control. And Zi Zi helped with little Stella and managed the domestic chores. It was a family affair.

Zi Zi was a meticulous housekeeper. She didn't allow Stella and Sammy to be messy, undisciplined children and from an early age, Stella learned to be a perfectionist.

Corina was as painstaking about the house as Aunt Rose and enjoyed her new living quarters behind the store. They moved in and were ready just in time for the birth of their second girl, Domenica Rose, named after Corina's mother, which was the Italian custom.

Domenica was called Emma from the beginning. She was a happy baby which eased Antonio's disappointment at her not being a boy.

Those were busy months for Corina as she continued to help out at the store after Emma's birth. Their prosperity increased with careful planning by Antonio, but their living conditions soon became crowded. Being right on the premises made it easier for Corina to be there when necessary, but Antonio needed more space. Stella was constantly underfoot and the teething process with Emma left little time or place for him to do his reading and attend to office matters. He became irritable and difficult to live with.

Corina was hurt. She thought she was doing something to cause Antonio's unhappiness. They found themselves arguing at the slightest provocation. "We shouldn't have had the children so soon," she thought.

"Having Stella and Emma so close together has put too much pressure on Antonio," she confided to Zi Zi.

"Nonsense!" Zi Zi retorted. "He's just going through what every man goes through when the children get noisy. Try not to confront him if he isn't as loving as you would like him to be. He will work it out in his own way."

Patience was the order of the day for Corina. She had the demands of the girls to meet. She had to make herself available to help when needed in the store as well as a grumpy, demanding husband to placate.

Just about the time she thought she couldn't stand it any longer, much to her delight, Antonio announced that he had bought a lot up the street from the store where they would build a house. Their rooms became a happier place to be. Antonio was engrossed in the plans with Corina at his side. After living behind the store for nearly two years, they could now look forward to having their first real home.

The house was completed and paid for by the end of 1924, ready for Antonio, Corina, Stella, and Emma. Standing on the side of the hill about half way up Elm Street, the house had a small yard in front leading up several steps to a small porch. There were three bedrooms, one bath, a living room with a fireplace, a dining room, kitchen and breakfast room. And, of course, the service porch in the rear to accommodate laundry and cleaning tools. The rear yard was a good size—they would plant fruit trees, maybe an olive tree. This was to be their home until 1940 and they were all pleased and happy.

Another surprise was in store for Corina. When she announced that August would bring another addition to the family, Antonio had an announcement to make, too. He no longer wanted her to work in the store.

"You are to stay home with the children now. Your brother, Vittorio, will be arriving from Italy soon and can help out until he gets a job," Antonio announced. "I think I'll put Rinaldo Natale in charge of produce. He's done a good job so far and I think he can handle the responsibility."

Antonio expanded the store where their living quarters had been and added a delicatessen. The front opening was only thirty feet wide where the fruits and vegetables were displayed in two rows of stands across the front, extending out to the sidewalk. There were at least two employees to sack produce at the customer's request. Each bag was weighed by the "produce man" and the price was marked, usually in black crayon, on the outside of the bag. The produce was rung up and paid for in that department.

As the customer continued into the grocery section through turnstiles, she selected canned goods from the shelves and was checked out again. Then on to the butcher shop and delicatessen, where she selected special cuts of meat, prepared individually by the butcher. A delivery service was provided for those who made large purchases. They had charge accounts in the beginning, but there was too much of a problem collecting. They offered competitive prices and friendly service, but everyone paid cash.

From Southern Italy to Southern California

This operation required several people to handle efficiently and courteously. And the Cypress Market was noted for its good service and outstanding values.

Women did most of the shopping, and came into the store on a daily basis. With only ice boxes to keep their food fresh, they couldn't buy too much in advance. Besides, they loved to come in and talk to Antonio.

Vittorio Luizzi arrived in the spring and came to work in the store. He was Corina's younger brother; handsome with dark, wavy hair, dark brown eyes and a winning smile. He wasn't as serious as Antonio and enjoyed having a good time during working hours.

"There is a time to work and a time to play," Antonio admonished him.

"I'm just trying to make the customers happy, so they'll spend more money," Vittorio laughed; then, "No, you're right, Tony. I shouldn't fool around so much. I will try to work harder, if you will remember to call me Vito."

Antonio's friends approached him to join the newly-formed Sons of Italy. He didn't do anything halfheartedly, and although his day was more than full, he took on the added chore of not only joining the organization, but becoming its most active member. He became responsible for gathering recruits from among his loyal following which took a lot of his time. But this allowed him to make more friends and he quickly became recognized as their leader.

August brought added responsibilities. Corina was more uncomfortable than usual when Antonio left for the store at five a.m. on the morning of August sixth. Her baby wasn't due for another week, but her back had been bothering her for three days.

"Maybe I should call the doctor," Antonio suggested just before leaving the house.

"No, I don't think so," Corina replied. "I'll let you know later," and kissed him goodbye.

"I'll go get Zi Zi," he suggested. "She should be with you today."

By seven a.m. Corina said quietly, "I think I should go to the hospital." She was glad Zi Zi was there as Antonio was nowhere to be found. The pains were coming every three minutes now and there was no time to lose.

The phone rang. "Did you call?" Antonio asked anxiously.

"I think I need to go to the hospital," Corina answered in obvious pain. "Can you come now?"

Corina had never been to a hospital. The two girls had been delivered at home by mid-wives with very little trouble. This time she felt different. The wrenching in her back became excruciating. She'd be glad to get the relief she had been promised.

She became apprehensive as she was led to the labor room—so stark and white and all the unfamiliar faces. Antonio held her hand until he was asked to leave the room.

The pain was soon over and Antonio was told he had a ten-pound baby boy. His life was complete, he thought, as he tried with great difficulty to hide his feelings.

"How is my wife?" he asked the doctor.

"She had a pretty rough time, but she will be fine. You can see her now."

"I finally gave you a son," Corina smiled weakly. "I knew there was something different about this one."

"We have our son now and two beautiful girls. You won't have to go through this again," Antonio announced quietly with tears in his eyes.

They named their son Pasqualino, after Antonio's father, as was the Italian custom.

6

THE next five years were what Antonio was to describe later as the best years of their lives. He had it all; an excitingly prosperous business, a loyal wife, two beautiful girls and a son to share his business later and carry on the tradition of his heritage, albeit Americanized.

"What was wrong with that?" he thought. "Hadn't America given his life fulfillment and meaning? There was no reason that the best of Italian traditions could not endure the American dream.

Antonio went on dreaming. He purchased his groceries from the wholesalers who were available at the prices they demanded. This created a situation where, in order to give his customers competitive prices, he had to cut corners in every other area to make his business profitable.

In talking to others in the business, he found they all had the same problem. "Why couldn't they band together somehow and buy in larger quantities directly from the manufacturer?" he reasoned. This would take more people and a lot of cooperation.

"If we form a corporation in which we all participate, we could make this happen," he told Zi. "I'd like to open more stores, too."

"You can count me in," Uncle Sam responded enthusiastically.

An attorney drew up the necessary legal papers and Antonio contacted first his family, then his friends. Their first meeting was held in August, 1929 and the attorney was there to explain the legal ramifications. Antonio presented his ideas regarding increasing the number of stores so they could buy in larger quantities and therefore, increase the profits.

"We'll call the stores 'Gateway' and get started on store number two immediately. I will put my store on Elm Street into the corporation as 'Gateway Store number one', although I will keep the building and property where it stands. The corporation will pay me rent for the use of the building," Antonio explained. He and Corina never parted with their original store property.

CYPRESS PARK DUPLEX
Zi Zi, Corina, Sammy, Stella, Emma, Zi

ELM STREET
As nearly as I can tell –
Vito, Corina, Mrs. Radogna, Antonio, ZiZi, Zi
Children in front–Stella, Emma, Lino
probably one of the cousins
Circa 1928

There was keen interest that first night. Some changes were made to the numbers the attorney had presented and a date for the next meeting was set.

Enthusiasm was running high during the next two months, but when the stock market crashed in October, Antonio lost many of his eager participants. He lost a little money in the crash, too—not much, but that was his last encounter with investing outside of his own business.

By July of 1930, the "survivors" were ready to get together again and the Articles of Incorporation were signed on July 21, 1930 by Antonio LaBianca, Saverio Bruno, Vito Luizzi, Saverio LaBianca and Rinaldo Natale; naming the corporation "Gateway Markets."

The sign went up changing the Cypress Market to Gateway Market and the plans were under way for the building of store number two on Cypress Avenue, six blocks from store number one. The original corporation allowed each stockholder one share, one vote and equal participation in the endeavor. Each shareholder purchased his one share of stock for one hundred dollars.

Antonio's contribution of additional money and store number one, as well as additional contributions made by other stockholders, were recorded as notes payable at the attorney's suggestion. As the business progressed, the noteholders would be paid interest on the loans and be paid off as cash permitted. No dividends would be paid until the noteholders were paid in full. In the meantime, all of the stockholders participated in the operation of the business.

By 1933 Antonio was ready for store number three and the first step toward warehousing and wholesaling. On January 30, 1934, the corporation was re-structured and the name changed to "Gateway Stores, Ltd, dba State Wholesale Grocery Company, Inc." The new stockholders signed their names and participation as follows: Antonio, now Anthony LaBianca, President, 191 shares; Saverio, now Sam LaBianca, Vice-President, 59 shares; Saverio, now Sam Bruno, Treasurer, 21 shares; Rinaldo, now Ray Natale, Secretary, 26 shares; Joe Renna, Assistant Secretary, 16 shares.

Vito Luizzi had had a little too much fun sometime between 1930 and 1934. He sold out and moved his family to the state of Washington, not to return until after World War II.

Store number three was built on Avenue Twenty-six, one block from North Figueroa, on the fringes of Cypress Park, one mile from Lincoln Heights. Gateway Ranch Market, positioned over a picket fence, was displayed on the store front in neon lights. Number three was twice as big as number two and three times bigger than store number one.

Anthony bought additional land behind store number one and added

269

a five thousand square foot warehouse to house his surplus purchases, enabling him to buy directly from the manufacturer.

By 1936, he was ready to restructure the corporation again. This time he divided his Company into two separate entities, increased the capital stock to five hundred thousand dollars for each corporation and set a par value of twenty-five dollars per share.

Now he was really getting sophisticated. He introduced "A" and "B" shares; "A" being non-voting. He issued sixteen thousand dollars in "A" and four thousand dollars in "B". At this point Anthony and Corina owned 60 percent of the voting and non-voting stock and Anthony's brother, Sam and his wife, Pauline, owned 19 percent. Ray Natale was the next highest owner with a share of 8.2 percent and Uncle Sam Bruno a share of 6.2 percent. And this was all happening during the great depression! No wonder Anthony had such a high regard for capitalism. Now he was ready to get into the wholesale business in earnest and rented an office and warehouse on the other side of the Arroyo, a low lying river bed that separated northeast from east Los Angeles. He moved Joe Renna to the order desk and hired other office personnel and warehousemen.

He contacted all his friends that had grocery stores in the greater Los Angeles area and solicited their business. They could join his membership by posting a deposit of one week's merchandise purchases in advance and the payment of two dollars and fifty cents per month dues. Credit was extended to one week's purchases and a patronage discount would be paid each quarter depending on profits. The net profit to State Wholesale would be less than 2 percent. The success of the business depended on volume, which Anthony built up quickly. In addition, it afforded Gateway Markets the opportunity to sell at prices competitive to other, much larger chains.

As the wholesale business grew, Anthony remained president of both companies, but left the day-to-day operation of the markets up to his brother, Sam.

Corina was busy taking care of their home and children. She attended the stockholders' meetings held each year, but was otherwise not involved in the business as it grew. She had no necessity to learn to write a check, but was never in need of money for good food, nice clothes for the children and interior decorating and stylish furniture for her home. She had indeed prospered in the New World.

Her children knew a strict father, who demanded obedience, and a kind, understanding mother whom they could turn to for comfort.

Now it was time to return to their homeland in style and introduce the children to their heritage from across the sea.

Antonio and his Model "T"
Circa 1917

GATEWAY RANCH MARKET
Store number three
Twenty-sixth and Figueroa
November 25, 1939

7

PASQUALINO, having long since shortened his name to Lino, was twelve years old and one of the most popular boys at Nightingale Junior High School on North Figueroa in Cypress Park.

He had been so bored when he was in the fourth grade at Aragon Elementary, that the principal decided to skip him ahead a year to see if he would pay more attention. That's how he came to be a year younger than the other boys in his eighth grade class.

His attention hadn't improved much, but he managed to get above average grades even though he seldom did his homework. He was more interested in girls and sports than he was in school work. Besides he had been working at Gateway Markets since last summer as a box boy and was responsible for mowing the front yard on Elm Street. That didn't leave much time for homework.

"I can't go to the malt shop with you after school today," he complained to Howard Bumpass, his closest friend since Aragon.

"Yvonne Watson's going to be there," Bumpy chided.

"Really? Gosh, darn it! My dad keeps me busy so I won't have time for girls, or football either. Now he's going to drag us all off to Italy before the semester is over," he continued.

"At least you'll get out of school early," Bumpy laughed.

Later that evening, reaching for a snack in the kitchen, he asked his mother, "Mom, do I have to go with you to Italy?"

"Of course you do. What do you think? Don't you dare tell your father you don't want to go. This trip means a lot to him and to me, too," she admonished.

The dinner table was quiet that evening. Dinner was late, as usual. Anthony hadn't returned from work until well after seven o'clock.

"I stopped in at store number two on the way home," Anthony finally began. "Ray Natale told me you came to work a half hour late this afternoon." He spoke quietly, but Lino knew he was angry.

"I had to stay after school," Lino lied. He had gone to the malt shop,

GROWING UP

Sammy, Stella, Emma, Lino

ELM STREET
Emma and Lino

Cousins Mary and Stella,
Emma, another cousin Stella,
Lino and cousin Lino

after all. The chance to see Yvonne again was more pressure than he could resist.

"Hm," Anthony observed disbelieving. He muttered something in Italian, under his breath. Then he changed the subject. "We will leave early next Saturday morning for New York," he announced. "I don't think it will hurt any of you to miss a few weeks of school. Besides you will learn more on this trip than your teachers have to offer."

Lino glanced at his mother, then spoke up. "How long do you think we'll be gone?"

"Well, the drive to New York should take about two weeks. We'll start at five o'clock each morning, but stop early in the evening to make sure we get a good rest. We want to see a few things along the way, too. Our ship leaves New York Harbor on the fifth of next month and will take about ten days. We'll do some sight seeing in Italy before we go on to Canneto and we'll want to spend plenty of time with the family there. I should say about three months," Anthony concluded thoughtfully.

"Oh," Lino moaned to himself. "How can I get along without my friends for three long months?" he wondered. Then aloud, "How will they do without me at store number two?" and laughed.

Anthony laughed too, and everyone relaxed.

On Friday they said their goodbyes to the family they were leaving behind, packed their new 1938 Buick with luggage and a picnic basket with fried artichokes and asparagus and plenty of fruit and drove down Elm Street Saturday morning before the sun came up.

Their trip could be an elegant travelogue, but suffice it to say, they saw the Grand Canyon and all points of interest on their way east, including Philadelphia and Washington D.C. They visited cousins in New York, and Lino didn't let anyone know how terrified he was at several thunder storms that raged before they embarked on the "Rex," their home afloat for ten days.

Lino had a great time aboard ship. There were girls his age and a lot of activities. For a time he forgot about all he thought he was missing back at Nightingale. Stella and Emma watched him like a hawk, so he managed to keep out of trouble. Anthony and Corina were elated to be going home in such style and proud of their three children, although Lino could be trying at times.

The Buick came along on the "Rex," which gave them their own transportation when they arrived in Naples. They had their gondola ride in Venice, but Lino never forgot how dirty the water was; they watched smoke rising from Vesuvius and visited the Vatican in Rome.

Their triumphant drive through the narrow streets of Adelfia-Canneto was a thrill Lino hadn't expected. To see the poverty, for the

TRANSATLANTICO "REX"

Hank, Harry and Lino

"Buona Vita"

Anthony, Corina, Emma, Lino

first time, that his mother and father had grown up in and managed to escape, brought him to the realization that if it hadn't been for their courage and daring, he would be living here, in this town.

He met his cousins, but could understand very little of their conversation. He was sorry he hadn't paid more attention when his folks had sent him for Italian lessons when he was only eight. He showed no interest in learning the language, so they had given up.

His Aunt Marietta was warm and loving and demonstrative—feelings he didn't quite understand. Her daughter, Jean, was pretty cute, but since she was his cousin, he didn't see any hope in that relationship.

His grandmother, Stella, sat quietly in her chair, rocking endlessly. She kept asking who the cute little boy was. Anthony explained several times that he was his son, but Stella wasn't sure who Anthony was either. Her health had failed some months before, leaving her memory vague and often non-existent.

Anthony often wandered into the center of town to see some of his old friends. The men in the Plaza were happy to see Anthony again, after he told them who he was. One afternoon the conversation turned to politics. Anthony bragged about conditions in America and espoused the democratic way.

"I don't see how you can tolerate Mussolini," he admonished. "He will only lead you into more war and disaster."

In less than ten minutes, a military car drove up and two uniformed men jumped out and asked Anthony to come with them.

"What did I do?" the astonished Anthony asked.

"Come with us. You will find out soon enough," one of them answered harshly.

Anthony was led into an interrogation room at the local jail. "Who are you?" he was asked. "Let me see your passport and identification."

"I am an American citizen," Anthony answered in his most polite demeanor. "I didn't mean anything by what I said. We were just having a friendly discussion."

"We don't appreciate talk like that about IL Duce. He is our respected leader and has done much good for our country. You Americans don't understand what conditions we had here before he took over."

The officer studied Anthony's papers for a long time. "How long has it been since you have been in this country?" he asked.

"About fifteen years," Anthony answered quietly.

"I suggest you leave as soon as possible. We will be watching you until you are gone. And don't congregate in the Plaza during the remainder of your visit, or next time you won't get off so easy."

After a month of living in a totally strange atmosphere, the LaBiancas were more than ready to leave. Anthony's experience had unnerved him and he wanted to return to his much appreciated freedom. Seeing his family and his mother, unable to recognize him, saddened him to the point of desolation. He and Corina even had difficulty with the living conditions—they were more Americanized than they knew—and never let on to Lino and the girls how happy they were to be heading back to America.

By the time they saw the Statue of Liberty again, Anthony's mother was gone.

8

ANTHONY gazed down the terraced slopes of his property—a city acre sitting atop the Los Feliz hills. His heart was heavy. America had been good to him, that much was certain, but he had worked hard for every dollar he had made. His body had grown tired and heavy under the pressure of long hours of stress and the debilitating diabetes that had been diagnosed a little over a year ago.

He had such high expectations for his son. Much to his disappointment he had married at eighteen, before completing his education. Of course, the war could be blamed for that, even though he started seeing Alice while he was still in high school.

Anthony remembered well the first time he had met Alice, hiding on the front porch, standing there with terror in her eyes. "She was a pretty girl—a little on the thin side," he thought. "She had a lot of spunk, though, even then," he laughed.

"She called me to say they were both planning to go to college. That took a lot of nerve. I guess I wasn't very nice to her, but Leno wasn't running his life the way I wanted him to and I took it out on her. I just can't get used to the American custom of boys and girls going out unchaperoned at such an early age," his thoughts continued. "They are bound to get into trouble."

Anthony sighed, trying not to think about how frustrating it was not to be in charge of his son's life. "He is the one I did all of this for, from the day he was born. Coming to America has taken away the authority that is rightfully mine. Of course, what did I do to my father? I left him—but we were so poor!

"Now I have all this and I don't have the respect of my son's wife. She is telling him what to do and he is going along with her. She won't even let us go with her to meet him. I just don't understand this generation. We've done too much for them. We've given them everything and they don't appreciate it." His anger was building again.

"But what is it, really?" he questioned himself. "A young couple that wants to be alone. I can understand that. After all, it has been a long time for them. When they get back from Marysville, we can work all these things out. After all, Leno is coming home and that's what is important."

Anthony found himself laughing again. "What a pushover I am. I talked myself right out of being angry at two people that I love more than my own life, who have treated me rather shabbily. I guess that's what parents are for; to understand and to forgive.

"I hope she doesn't have any problems with the car. She doesn't realize the danger of a young woman traveling alone all that distance."

Anthony had to laugh again. "I wonder how my father and mother felt when I left for America at only sixteen. And I didn't see them again until they had forgotten who I was. That must have been their protection against their sorrow at my leaving."

His eyes were moist. "It was only yesterday. Where have the years gone? Who knows how many are left? I must have time to prepare Leno to take over for me. Alice must give me that chance. I must not have done all this for nothing."

Anthony was tired; tired of being angry and tired of always being there for others. When was his rest to come?

"As long as others need me," he decided, "I'll be there. Would I have it any other way?"

PART VI

And Now Tomorrow

"Man and woman may only enter Paradise hand in hand.
Together, the myth tells us, they left it
and together must they return"
"De Flagello Myrteo, Preface XV" by Richard Garnett

1

I headed for Marysville in our 1940 Chevrolet, toward Leno's separation center. Our second wedding anniversary had come and gone, but it didn't matter. Our nightmare was over.

After nearly twenty months of waiting, weeping, praying and tolerating, my "Knight In Shining Armor" was returning to rescue me from all of life's problems.

Wearing my sexiest outfit, a chartreuse, too-tight pants suit, I packed the car with my new clothes and a card and gift for Leno for every holiday, birthday and special occasion that we had missed together. My only joy in the passed, dreary months had been preparing for his return.

I arrived in Marysville at dusk to find it packed with returning soldiers; a small, dusty little town seventy-two miles north of Sacramento. My speedometer showed I had traveled four-hundred and twenty-eight miles since leaving Los Angeles, hardly as far as San Francisco.

Marysville, with a population of no more than five thousand, had been named after Mary Murphy Covillaud, a survivor of the tragic Donner party of 1846, the wife of the founder of the town, Charles Covillaud. Primarily agricultural now, growing peaches and pears, Marysville was the center for the processing and packing of the region's produce. The farmers had long since chased out the gold miners, who were filling the rivers with mining debris.

When I arrived in 1946, I was terribly disappointed. It just looked like a typical army town, raucous and unfriendly to an innocent, over-protected twenty-one year-old. All of my independence and courage left quickly as the clerk at the only decent hotel in town said they did not have my reservation.

"We're booked solid here," I heard her say. "Perhaps, I can get you into the California. It's on the next block."

"But my husband is expecting me *here*. I don't know how I can get word to him!" I pleaded, close to tears.

"They can take you at the California," she reported shortly. Then coldly, "That's the best I can do."

My mouth went dry; panic was overtaking me. "Here I am in this awful little town, alone, and Leno won't be able to find me!" As dark descended, I rushed to the California, holding back the tears, but as soon as I was settled in the bleak room, barely large enough for the bed, I threw myself down and cried uncontrollably.

When my tears were spent, I knew I had to do something. I called the separation center. Leno hadn't arrived yet.

"Can you get word to him when he does arrive, that I'm at the California Hotel, here in Marysville?" I asked timidly.

"I'll leave the message," the voice said hurriedly.

I didn't know what to do next. I was afraid to go out of my room to eat dinner. The phone rang. It was Dad. I must have sounded devastated. My voice trembled as I tried not to cry.

"We'll come up there first thing in the morning," he suggested.

"No, I'm all right," I answered bravely. "I'll let you know when I hear from Leno."

I mustered up enough courage to go down to the hotel dining room, such as it was. Most of my dinner stuck in my throat, but was satisfying enough to allow me to sleep.

For the next two days, I read and waited. Fortunately, I had brought Somerset Maugham with me and lost myself in "Of Human Bondage," only leaving my room for nourishment. Finally the phone rang.

"Didn't anyone call you?" I heard Leno asking. "I told them to let you know I had been delayed. This damn army! They goofed everything up right down to the wire!" He sounded hard, bitter.

"When will I see you?" I asked.

"I can come for a little while tonight, I think," he answered anxiously. "But it will take a couple of days to get out of this place permanently. I'll try to get there in time for dinner." And then he was gone again. I felt happily excited but strangely desolate, both at the same time.

After bathing and trying to rearrange my hair, I noticed how awful I looked. My face was pale, and my dark circles were more prominent than usual. No matter how I fussed, I didn't look the way I wanted to for his return.

Then, a soft knock at the door. My heart pounded as I opened it. And there he was—older, thinner, sadder—spent and anxious. I hesitated, then put my arms around him. He held me fiercely, his gentleness gone.

We were strangers.

Technical Sergeant

"I can't believe you're really here," I said at last.

"Well, not for long," he answered quickly.

"You sound as if you can't wait to get back to camp," I blurted defensively.

"How can you think that?" His eyes were sad.

"I'm sorry," I said immediately. "It's just that we've waited so long. I had hoped to have you a little longer."

"That's the army for you, SNAFU," he retorted.

"What does that mean?" I asked. It was the first of the many army "inside jokes" that I was to question in the weeks ahead.

"Situation normal, all fowled up," he responded, laughing for the first time.

"Well, come on in and see all the presents I brought you."

Awkwardly taking his hand, I led him to the elegantly wrapped boxes spread out all over the unattractive bed.

"This is what I did to keep busy while you were gone," I reported, laughing, waiting for his happy approval.

He wasn't interested in gifts and cards, impulsively sweeping them to the floor. He only wanted to hold me close and let all the love agonizingly suppressed for twenty long months express itself in the best way he knew how.

2

TWO days later, we headed for Los Angeles with discharge papers in hand. "I've joined the Army Reserve," Leno announced as we were packing the car.

"In case of another war, I'll have some rank. I never want to have the experience of being a private again," he said when I objected vehemently.

He convinced me that it was the smart thing to do. "After all," I thought, "there isn't going to be another war." I wondered if I really believed my words.

One of his "buddies" from the 524th drove down to L.A. with us, much to my chagrin. "I have gone to all this trouble to have Leno to myself," I thought "and I have to share him with a stranger." I listened to "inside army talk" all the way home.

"These discharged veterans sound like they had one big ball!" I noticed, as they relived their experiences, laughing. "*Now* they can laugh. I wish that *I* could laugh at *my* miserable twenty months. Maybe it was because there was no one to laugh with," I thought.

When we arrived at Oak Terrace I was as disgruntled as I was when I left. All I could think about was "getting away from it all"—taking our long-awaited honeymoon. Of course, Leno's reunion with his family was touching, although Mom and Dad never really showed much emotion. No wonder they couldn't understand me. All I ever did was cry, whether I was happy or sad.

Dad let us know he was anxious for us to get back to work at State Wholesale. "You're needed there, both of you," he said with determination. "Why waste your time vacationing? I would think you'd be anxious to work after being gone so long."

In private, Leno told his father, "Alice needs a vacation. I can't disappoint her," and Dad consented to letting us have three weeks.

We couldn't agree on where to go. I wanted to take a boat to Hawaii, but Leno couldn't stand the thought of getting on a boat again for a long time. He didn't even want to go to Catalina, an island twenty miles off of

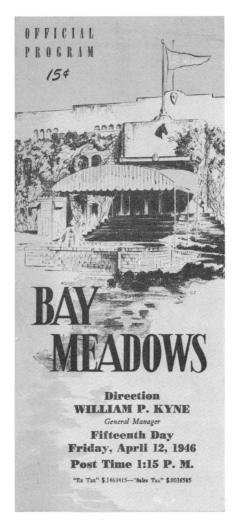

OFFICIAL
PROGRAM
15¢

BAY MEADOWS

Direction
WILLIAM P. KYNE
General Manager

Fifteenth Day
Friday, Aprli 12, 1946
Post Time 1:15 P. M.

"Ex Tax" $.1463415—"Sales Tax" $.0036585

"They're off!"

the California coast. Going to Florida was out—three weeks wouldn't give us enough time. We decided to head for San Francisco and points beyond, as time permitted.

How wonderful it was! We were together, alone, and could stay in bed as long as we wanted to. We went shopping—Leno needed some new civilian clothes, and oh, how he enjoyed that.

We attended the fifteenth day of racing at Bay Meadows Race Track, just south of San Francisco. "Via-Over" won the first race and Leno had picked him. "High Carbon" came in first in the second race, but we were on "Rollaway," who came in third. In the third race, "Forbidden C" was our pick and came in fifth, but Leno picked the winners in the last two out of three races. Our biggest disappointment was "Blue Flag" in the sixth race, who we were sure would win and very nearly did. We came away the happy winners of five dollars.

We both loved the excitement of the race track. If we had been allowed to follow *that* dream, we would probably now be taking our thoroughbreds from track to track. Not so much for the winning, but for the love of the sport and the beauty of the animal. Our day at Bay Meadows was probably the highlight of our trip.

We spent fifty-eight dollars and fifty-five cents for seven days in our room at the Fairmount Hotel on top of Nob Hill. We dined in the Tonga Room and saw most of the shows in town: "Oklahoma", "Voice Of The Turtle", with Hugh Marlowe, K.T. Stevens and Vivian Vance, and "Up In Central Park", produced by Michael Todd. We were disappointed that the movie camera I had bought for Leno's homecoming, developed a problem and we couldn't capture our fun on film. But the memories are still there—vivid and alive and forever imprinted on my mind.

We headed across the Nevada desert from Reno, after spending two nights at a cozy inn at Lake Tahoe on the California border. Visiting Virginia City and then stopping in Winnemucca for the night, we enjoyed whatever movie house was in town—our best form of entertainment. It really didn't matter what was playing.

We found Salt Lake City fascinating, visiting the Mormon Temple and State Capitol Building. There was time for planning. We would get our degrees at the University of Southern California, of course, starting that summer in the College of Commerce. How ambitious one gets when one is on vacation, sleeping till noon.

We went south after four days, visiting Bryce and Zion National Parks, and finally the Grand Canyon. We stayed at the lodge there, getting excited over the little bit of snow on the ground. "We'll come back some day and take the trip by mule down into the canyon," Leno promised.

We stopped in Las Vegas for breakfast on our way home. How Leno enjoyed breakfast out—his favorite meal, I think. There were nickel slots to play, but not much else—just a dusty, little western town.

After three short weeks, we were glad to get back to Oak Terrace and the security it offered. Security and authority. How I loved the security and resented the authority.

3

IN 1946 Los Angeles, no vacant apartment was to be found. When Mother and Joe and brother Bob had returned in the fall of 1945 from Neosho, Missouri, the only place they could find to live was a sleazy motel in East L.A. with a hot plate. The city had changed noticeably during the nearly three years of their absence. The people who had come from outside the state to work in the defense plants and the servicemen who had been stationed in California stayed when the war ended. There wasn't much room left for those Californians who had been sent out of the state to serve.

We had lived next door to the Swansons on Joy Street before the war sent us all in different directions. Mother had kept in touch with them during the war years, as she had with all of her friends. During the war, Dr. Swanson bought every house on Joy Street that came on the market and when Mrs. Swanson heard of Mother's plight in the motel, she proceeded to evict one of her many tenants.

Contacts are everything—it's not what you know, but who you know that counts. For forty-eight hundred dollars, Mother, step-dad Joe, little sister Jane and little brother Bobbie moved into a small, frame, two-bedroom house. They were back on Joy Street again, but not on the alley this time.

Now Leno and I were confronted with the same dilemma, or, at least, I thought we were. As it turned out, we weren't, because we had the apartment behind the garage at Oak Terrace now that Pete and Emma and baby Johnny had moved into the big, beautiful house Dad had built for them in the neighborhood.

I wanted our own place desperately, away from the family. We needed to be alone to get acquainted with each other again. There was nothing available to rent, but we found a beautiful, little house in the Los Feliz foothills, several blocks away from Waverly Drive, for fifteen thousand dollars.

"It's ridiculous to pay an inflated price for a house when we have the

"It's ridiculous to pay an inflated price for a house when we have the apartment here for you," Dad argued.

We didn't have enough money to buy the house without Dad's help, besides we didn't really want to go against his wishes. "I don't see why he doesn't realize how much we want to be on our own," I complained to Leno.

"We'll be busy going to school and working, honey," Leno answered, trying desperately to reason with me. "We won't have much time to be taking care of a big house."

"Now you're beginning to sound like your father. When you were overseas he said you would grow to be more like him as you got older. I guess he was right."

I was furious, but when the summer session started at USC, I became too busy to remember how angry I was at Leno for not taking a stronger stand with his father. Dad was right, as usual. With the long hours of homework and our jobs at State Wholesale, there was little time left for cooking the meals and caring for our little apartment. We resorted to eating with the folks most of the time, and I was thankful for their help.

We registered for ten units that summer, to be completed in ten weeks, attending classes every day from eight till noon. Leno's tuition was paid for by the federal government, under the GI Bill of Rights for returning servicemen, but my classes cost us ten dollars a unit.

After a quick lunch en route, we arrived at State Wholesale to complete eight hours of work in four. Then an hour's drive home to Waverly Drive, a hasty dinner with Mom and Dad and several hours of homework before retiring. The routine was too much for my nervous system and I became difficult to live with and less than loving toward Leno.

We were both in a state of exhaustion and visibly unhappy when Leno announced that his army buddy, Charlie Carlson, was coming to California to go to work for State Wholesale.

He and Leno had become great friends in Vienna and apparently discussed the possibility of Charlie's coming to California when the war was over. They had left Vienna together and returned to the States at the same time, Charlie going home to New York and Leno returning to California. Like so many hundreds of thousands of other veterans, Charlie wanted to come to Los Angeles and the opportunity Leno offered him was too good to turn down.

"That's just what I need now," I thought, "another of Leno's army buddies to take his attention away from me. We have enough problems without my having to put up with more army talk."

The engine of his plane was on fire when it landed at the Burbank airport, which terrified me, but Charlie disembarked with a warm, friendly smile, and I knew immediately why Leno liked him so much. He was tall and blonde, handsome, kind, soft-spoken and full of sophisticated humor. He had no New York accent and was truly "our kind of people."

He almost immediately noticed and seemed to understand the conflict in the family. He and Leno had apparently discussed their problems during those last lonely months in Europe and I learned from Charlie more of what Leno had gone through because of our separation.

"I had to rush him to the hospital after he smashed both of his hands through a window in frustration," he confided to me, "but don't tell Leno I told you. He'd kill me."

Charlie became my support, giving me a smile or a glance of reassurance, when he sensed my hostility toward the arrogance and unfeeling remarks of my in-laws and their derisive laughter directed at Leno, which Leno chose to laugh-off in their presence. Imagined or not, it was comforting to know that Charlie understood.

We set up a blind date for him with Barbara Pierce and had a fun evening at Slapsy Maxie's, a night club in Beverly Hills owned by the former boxer. Ben Blue was the featured entertainer and his "Slowly, I turned" routine had us "rolling in the aisles." We had a great time all evening, laughing and telling jokes, but when I mentioned getting together with Barbara again, Charlie changed the subject. We knew he had a girlfriend back home, but he said he wasn't ready to get married, although he was going to be twenty-five in November. So much for matchmaking!

We showed Charlie the sights of the Southern California we were so proud of—Newport Beach, Laguna Beach and the coastline. We drove down to San Diego where we joined Uncle Hamilton, who was serving in the Navy there.

"Here's the little boy that started Alice and me dating," Leno laughed, introducing Hamilton. We hadn't seen him since before the war. He was the same smiling, happy boy, now a man.

The four of us went "south of the border" to Tijuana and Rosarita Beach. We spent the day swimming in the surf and lunching at the Jai-Alai Cafe. I had been so long without the companionship of men during the war, that I relished every moment of that day. "It's either feast or famine," I thought.

We returned Hamilton to his base that evening—the last time we ever spent a day with my little uncle. The war had done something wonderful for all of us. The long, distant separations brought us closer together.

When everyone was out of the service and home again, we became too busy to enjoy that same kind of reunion, or any reunion, in some cases.

We later introduced Charlie to Castle Rock, north of Malibu, one of our favorite places. The beach was deserted and the air cold, but we braved the surf and Charlie climbed the "rock," beckoning me to join him. We ended the day at Ocean Park, a beach fun-zone on the pier, daring the "Chute-The-Chutes" and eating hot dogs. The boys couldn't get me on the roller coaster, giving me the opportunity to tell the story once again of my experience when I was ten years old on the "Cyclone Racer" at Long Beach. I had been so terrified after that ride, thinking I would never get off alive, that I would forever be frightened of steep, slow inclines.

Our Paillard Bolex movie camera had been repaired and we got some of our good times on film—a grim reminder in much later years of how swiftly time passes and how fleeting the "days of our youth" are.

The three of us signed up for fall classes at USC, Charlie enrolling in two night classes and Leno and I taking a full program of fifteen units during the day. Leno and I worked out our schedules so that we could work at least four hours a day at State Wholesale. After our four weeks of no classes between summer school and the fall, we had trouble getting back into the routine of homework and long hours. But we allowed plenty of time for the football games, always going with Charlie.

In October, Dana returned from Okinawa via the "President Lines" and was also separated from the Army at Marysville, but was smart enough not to sign up for the Army Reserve. We were all there to meet him at the Union Railroad Station—Mother, step-dad Joe, sister Jane and sister Edith and her husband, Mel, brother Bobbie and Leno and me.

The war years had been terrible. We didn't know who would make it back and who wouldn't. The concern was always with us. But the returning! The returning of those we loved without injury was indescribable. With Dana's arrival, we were all home, safely. Now our lives could begin again. Our hopes and dreams could be realized. This would be our reward, we thought, for all the waiting and anxiety. But the end of the war was to be the "beginning of the end" of our dreaming.

It all began when we attended the USC/Stanford football game in Palo Alto, about three hundred and fifty miles north of Los Angeles and just south of San Francisco. Leno, Charlie and I were joined by Dana and his fiancée, Dorothy, who rode all the way in the cramped, back seat of our 1940 Chevrolet.

The three us had a ball in the front, singing almost all the way up and back: "I've Been Workin' On The Railroad", "Fight On For Old SC", "Three Blind Mice", "Row, Row, Row Your Boat" and "Down By The Old

Mill Stream."

Dana and Dorothy were noticeably quiet and when we returned from our week-end fun, they announced that their engagement was off. Dana never did confide in me as to why he and Dorothy couldn't make a go of it; but I remember well, Dorothy's sullen attitude on the trip. She had apparently developed a resentment for the family—starting with our mother. Apart from that, I don't think Dana was ready for marriage. He had yet to finish school, and wanted to go to Michigan to be with an Army buddy who'd talked him into going to Michigan State. Romance and marriage were not a part of his life at that time.

I don't remember Dana ever getting his diamond ring back, which he had saved diligently for while in the service, or who won the football game, probably USC. Dana has never married and Dorothy disappeared from our lives forever.

I was in for another shock when we returned from our big weekend. My doctor informed me that the cyst he had discovered had to be removed as soon as possible. I was terrified. I had never been to a hospital before. "What will I do about school?" I asked Leno, hoping he would make it all go away.

"Your health comes first, honey. School is not that important," he assured me.

Charlie tried to cheer me up, but as I walked into the hospital, I was sure my life was over. I had forgotten for a time, with all the fun we were having with Charlie, how unhappy I really was. Nothing had turned out the way I had hoped it would when Leno returned. "We are caught in the web I have fearfully expected to be caught in," I thought. "Leno's family is running our lives, we'll never be on our own the way I want to be. Now this. Maybe I won't go back to Oak Terrace after the operation."

With that thought in mind, I seemed to have more hope and bravely faced the ordeal. Leno was as scared as I was and was there every minute with his steadfast reassurance and understanding. And Charlie almost always came along on Leno's frequent visits during my five-day stay in the hospital. The experience turned out to be much easier than I expected.

I went to Mother's house on Joy Street to convalesce, knowing that I wasn't going to return to Oak Terrace.

"I'm going to stay here at Mother's, Leno," I told him, hoping he would have the answer to our problem, "I can't go back to Waverly Drive."

"If that's what you want, Alice," he answered, "I won't stand in your way."

"Why doesn't he talk me out of it?" I asked myself. "Why doesn't he tell me he needs me and that I'm making a mistake?"

I quit my job at State Wholesale, went to work for the Sylmar Olive Company in downtown Los Angeles and ended my college career without completing my first semester.

So much for our first set of dreams.

4

"MAYBE Alice will be happier without me," Leno thought as he returned to Oak Terrace alone. "I wonder what it will be like without her? She hasn't been very happy since I came home. I guess she was unhappy a long time before that. I don't know what she wants me to do. I have my folks to consider. Why doesn't she understand that?"

As Leno opened the back door and entered the kitchen, his mother asked, "Why didn't Alice come *here* to recuperate?"

"She wants to be with her mother," was the only answer Leno gave, leaving quickly, to go to his apartment to be alone.

Two weeks later at dinner, Corina asked again, "How is Alice getting along? When will she be home?"

"I don't know," Leno answered quietly.

Anthony spoke up. "Go get her and bring her home where she belongs!"

"Dad, she'll come home when she gets ready," he answered angrily. "I want her to have plenty of time to be sure that she *wants* to be here with us."

"What do you mean?" Dad was outraged. "She's your wife, son. Go get her and bring her home."

"I'm not so sure she's coming back. She told me today she wants to quit her job at State," Leno answered sadly.

"Well, if she wants to stay home and not work, that's all right," Anthony answered.

"No, Dad, it's more than that. She's talking about divorce."

Now Corina was outraged. "Of course, being there with her mother, what could you expect?"

"I don't want to talk about it anymore," Leno snapped, leaving the house and going to his car.

He couldn't explain to his mother and father what the problem was without hurting them. This he didn't want to do. "They don't deserve that," he thought. "Alice knew what she was getting into when we got

297

married. If she doesn't want to be with my folks, then she doesn't want to be with me," he concluded.

He drove to his favorite bowling alley thinking, "Alice was always bored with my bowling." He laughed. "Now I can bowl whenever I feel like it." But tears came to his eyes when he thought of her and how much he loved her. "I'd rather have her than a bowling game any day. But I must give her time to realize what she is doing. She'll come to her senses."

He watched the league that was in progress and spotted Harry, one of his pals from Nightingale that he hadn't seen for years.

"Leno, what are you doing here? I thought you were an old married man."

"A married man needs a night out once in a while," Leno quipped.

"How about joining our team? Joe is leaving. His wife wants him home every night," Harry laughed.

"That sounds great. I'd love to get back on a team. I haven't bowled much since coming back from Europe."

"Let's have a beer," Harry suggested.

"What have you been doing?" he asked when they were relaxed at a table.

"Oh, going to school and working, mostly. You know, the same old thing that I was doing before I went into the Army," Leno answered bitterly.

Getting his mind off of his seemingly unsolvable problem, Leno suddenly felt free. He could do what he wanted to do, for a change. He joined the bowling team and soon his teammates realized that his wife wasn't around.

I thought I needed complete freedom—Leno didn't seem to care. I suggested we see his attorney about getting a divorce. "I think it's better if we make a clean break," I offered, hoping his answer would help me decide. Leno agreed.

"You seem like such nice people," Mr. Spencer admonished. "Are you sure you want this divorce?"

Leno and I both nodded quietly, agreeing that our one asset, our 1940 Chevrolet, should be kept by Leno. After all, his dad had given it to us. We signed some papers and were told we had to wait for a court date, probably a couple of months. That's all there was to it. Just like that. It was easier than getting married and took much less time. That afternoon, I bought a new hat and felt better.

I was back on Joy Street, taking the "W" streetcar to my new job downtown. Charlie visited me frequently and without his knowing it, he helped me stay the independent person I wanted to be. He quit his job at State Wholesale soon after I did to take a position in a firm that was more in his line of work—exporting.

There was no advice from Mother, no discussion about what I should do to straighten out my life. That was my mother—no interference, she was just there, lovingly. In her eyes, I could do no wrong. I would work my way out of any difficulty. Her confidence in me gave me strength—for a while.

But I panicked when New Year's Eve came and went without my hearing from Leno. 1947 found me empty and miserable. I missed the LaBiancas. I missed their strength and stability. I missed their structure and direction. But most of all, I missed their son.

In January, I became deathly ill. I couldn't keep anything down and the pain in my abdomen became unbearable. I longed for a sight of Leno, but he had kept discreetly out of my life.

Later, when the doctor cleared up the infection without surgery, and I knew I was going to live, I had to do something. I wrote to Aunt Pearl and she welcomed me to come and visit her in Palm Springs. I took a leave of absence from the Sylmar Olive Company, telling Margaret Carlson, the head bookkeeper, that I had a spot on my lungs and the doctor had ordered me to spend a few weeks on the desert. The doctor *had* found a spot last fall in my chest X-ray, but it had proved not to be tuberculosis, as originally suspected.

I left for Palm Springs on the Greyhound bus, and wrote to Leno almost as soon as I arrived. "I miss you terribly... I've come to Palm Springs to think things over... Wish you were here..."

Aunt Pearl treated me royally. She introduced me to the important Palm Springs socialites and I attended all the best parties. She knew Leno and I were separated and accepted that, although divorce was something she didn't condone. She wanted me to stay on and get involved in her Palm Springs life, and was disappointed when I told her that I had written to ask Leno to come down.

"Of course, you must try to make your marriage work, but I had hoped you would stay on here with me. You need some coaching in the social graces, of course, but we could have done something about that," she said, in her usual stoic manner. Then, angrily, "You're just like your mother! Every time I thought I could get her to stay down here, she would go back to one of her husbands." Then, thoughtfully, "I guess she has found happiness with Joe now." Her voice trailed and her eyes became distant.

That was the end of the longest conversation we had ever had. Aunt

Pearl was a cold, unfriendly person most of the time, at least with her sister's offspring, who were her only living relatives. To have any conversation with her at all was quite a rarity.

But I was too excited about the possibility of seeing Leno again to care much about her eccentricities. She liked Leno, always preferring the company of men to that of women.

Leno arrived on Saturday afternoon and we had a delightful weekend. Our reunion was a happier one than when he had returned from overseas. Perhaps because I knew he had come back without hesitation. "He really cares about me," I thought, "in spite of my stupidity." Or, perhaps, I realized what my life would be without him. I couldn't face that possibility again.

5

I wasn't ready to go back to Oak Terrace, not yet. Leno and I took a motel room in the Atwater district, a small community between the swank Los Feliz area and Glendale, close to the railroad tracks that went north. I returned to work at the Sylmar Olive Company and Leno went back to State Wholesale.

Our room was gloomy and too small, no place for most of our clothes. There was no Travel Lodge or Holiday Inn in 1947, at least not in the Atwater District. We couldn't have afforded a better room, anyway.

Leno had left USC after his first semester and gone back to LACC to get, at least, an AA degree by June. He was working part-time and my pittance at the Sylmar Olive Company was barely enough to eat on. The room was dark and dingy.

After a week of going downtown on the streetcar from Glendale and eating our dinner in restaurants, I began to feel strange, empty, like I wasn't where I was, at all. I had felt this way only once before during the war, when I went to camp Blue Jay with Toady. I told her then how I felt and she laughed and didn't understand what I was saying. I decided to keep it to myself this time. "It must be the strange surroundings," I thought. "I don't belong anywhere. I can't get along with Leno's folks, Mother's house is too small for both of us and there's no place for us to live except this dingy motel room."

We spent the weekend looking, again, for an apartment, to no avail. I began to cry. "Leno, I want to go back to Mother's. At least I will feel human there."

Leno was angry, at first, becoming impatient with my indecision. But he realized, as I did, that we needed a decent place to live, that we couldn't stay in the dismal motel room any longer. He seemed relieved when he left me on Mother's front porch. I said through tears, "When we can find our own house, honey, maybe we can get together."

There was no more talk of divorce and Leno again went back to Oak Terrace alone. We were both miserable. Is this what we had waited so long for? I became introspective, reading every book I could get my hands on dealing with the mind and how it works—why we do the things we do. Every book on the subject became my constant companion. Nothing seemed to help. Now was the time for a "Unity" thought and for me to "Let go, and Let God" decide our fate, since we weren't doing too well on our own.

My job soon became boring as I settled into its dull routine. Leno was engrossed in another bowling league and Charlie suddenly disappeared from our lives. I missed him and only saw Leno weekends. I signed up for a night class in Radio Production through the extension courses of the University of California at Los Angeles. The class was held downtown in an office building two nights a week. After work, I ate alone at a coffee shop, a greasy spoon, before going to class.

Radio was great fun and I felt that I was, at last, following my dream of being a great actress, if only in a small way. One evening at the fourth meeting of the class, we all had to read from a script that had the word "Monsieur" in it. The instructor sat in a control booth, out of sight, shouting, "Monsieur! Monsieur! Monsieur!" at me. No matter how I pronounced "Monsieur" it didn't please him. He became furious and asked me to go back to my seat. That was the last time I went to the class. I didn't need some frustrated actor taking his wrath out on me!

I had failed again and became determined to find a house where Leno and I could start our lives together. Every weekend we looked. We didn't want to be too far from Leno's work in Vernon and mine in downtown Los Angeles. We decided to try Alhambra, a friendly community southwest of Pasadena and just off the newly-completed San Bernardino freeway. The distance from Oak Terrace also seemed manageable.

We found a little house that was not too attractive on the outside, but had everything we needed inside: two bedrooms, one bath, dining room and kitchen with a service porch, hardwood floors and a fireplace. And a big back yard with trees! Fruit trees—peach, apricot, plum and avocado. A large unfinished room was attached to the back of the detached garage.

Not exactly our dream house, we bought it anyway, without anyone's help, for twelve thousand dollars. Leno applied for a veteran's loan under the GI Bill of Rights, but the Bank of America appraised the property for only ten thousand, four hundred dollars and wouldn't allow us to pay more. The sellers took back a second trust deed, after the escrow closed, for the sixteen hundred dollar difference—our first experience at "creative financing."

We paid two thousand dollars down, which I had saved in War Bonds during the nineteen months Leno was overseas. That means my take-home pay was one hundred and eleven dollars and eleven cents a month which I saved, living on my allotment from the War Department. Of course, I had no rent to pay or groceries to buy. Mom and Dad, in essence, had made our down payment.

Our house payments were seventy-nine dollars a month on the first mortgage and sixteen dollars a month on the second, a total of ninety-five dollars a month, all at an interest rate of four percent. That's how we bought our first house in 1947.

The payment on our new electric Westinghouse range was twenty-nine dollars a month, which didn't leave us much to live on. Leno drove our 1940 Chevrolet to work and dropped me off at the bus that took me downtown to my job at Sylmar. The walk was six blocks to the office and before long I began to feel put out by the whole arrangement.

"My job is getting so boring," I complained to Leno one night after dinner while he was getting dressed to go bowling. "Maybe they could use me at State Wholesale."

"That would be great if you came back to State. I'll ask my dad," Leno responded enthusiastically.

"I don't know." I began to have my doubts. "I haven't seen your dad and mother in such a long time. Your dad is probably disgusted with me."

"They would love to come over, Alice, but are waiting for you to invite them."

"I guess I'm ready to 'face the music.' How about next weekend?" I asked apprehensively.

Although I had been cooking since I was six years old, I couldn't even come close to Mom's superb Italian dishes, and I knew it. "My dinner is awful," I fretted as I was making the final touches. "I hope nobody notices that the potatoes and carrots are dry and under-cooked. I wonder how Mom does it."

Mom and Dad were wonderful, never mentioning our long separation and how stupid it was. We were all a little uncomfortable at first, but before long, it was as if nearly seven long months of not seeing each other, had brought us closer together. At least, that's the way I felt, and Leno's face beamed.

Dad was the community expert on real estate, having had his broker's license for many years. We had bought our house without consulting him—a gross insult to his authority. He inspected the property after dinner, stopping to water a dry area in the back lawn.

"You have a nice yard here. It does need a little work, though. I'll send Roy over to clean it up for you," he offered.

I spoke up quickly. "No, Leno is going to do all of that." I noticed the hurt in Dad's eyes, but it was too late to retract my statement. Leno laughed uncomfortably and Dad dropped the subject. In the months ahead, I was sorry I hadn't taken him up on his offer, as Leno worked such long hours that most of the yard work fell on my shoulders.

When they were gone, I asked Leno what Dad had said about my coming back to State Wholesale.

"He thinks it's better to leave it as it is," he answered.

"Oh, I don't care, anyway," I responded, trying to hide my disappointment. "What I *really* want to do is be an actress."

Leno suggested with a touch of irritation, "Maybe Dana could help you out on *that* one."

Leno always supported me and my ideas, but in his heart he just wanted me to stay home and take care of *him*.

6

DANA was at Michigan State where he majored in Speech, and joined the Delta Sigma Phi fraternity. In the summer of 1947, a group from M.S.C. built their own theatre on Mackinac Island in one of the oldest buildings on the Island—the Trading Post. He starred in the company of players and directed "You Can't Take It With You." At the end of the summer he came back to live in Los Angeles, and I was inspired to get involved in the theatre again.

"How about producing our own play, Leno?" I asked rather unexpectedly one Sunday morning as we lingered in bed. "Dana could direct and I could play one of the roles."

"We don't know anything about producing plays, honey, but I'm willing to give it a try, if it will make you happy. Of course, Dana knows a lot about it." He added excitedly, "I could handle the finances. How much do you think it would take?"

After finding that the Beaux Arts Theatre on West Eighth Street on the outskirts of Hollywood was available, Dana and I estimated that we needed one thousand dollars for advertising, theatre rent and other miscellaneous expenses. "The rent won't start until the play opens," I told Leno enthusiastically.

"You know we don't have anywhere near a thousand dollars, Alice," Leno answered. "Of course, we could bring in four or five others to invest in the play."

We planned a meeting in the dining room around our chrome table, the only furniture we had besides our new stove, the bed Mom had won in a church raffle, and a borrowed ice box. We invited Howard and Ann Bumpass and Edith and her husband, Mel, to participate as investors. After some discussion regarding policy, we each put in two hundred and fifty dollars and called ourselves Zenith Productions. I don't remember where we got our share of the investment—Leno must have borrowed it.

We put the money together, rented the theatre and were on our way to our first production, "You Can't Take It With You." Dana, as the director, held auditions and I was chosen to play "Alice" and Dana's buddy from Okinawa days, Mark Buchoz, was to play "Grandpa." Edith tried out for the part of "Penny" and we were all disappointed that she didn't get the part. Looking back, I think she would have made a wonderful "Penny," better than the one chosen. The rest of the cast came from the actors who arrived from all parts of Hollywood, most of them belonging to "Actors' Equity," their union. We were required to pay them scale wages for not only performances but rehearsals. That was the first crimp in our carefully planned budget.

Rehearsals were scheduled to begin the following day and on my way to work in the morning on the bus, I became ill. I thought I was going to lose my breakfast, so I quickly disembarked. I managed to get to a phone without any mishaps.

"Leno, I'm here on Los Angeles Street. I was too sick to stay on the bus. Can you come pick me up?"

He arrived in ten minutes and proceeded to give me an ultimatum.

"You're going to quit your job *now*. You are just doing too much, Alice."

"I guess I'm really pregnant, honey. I'll go see Dr. Webb this afternoon." I had been suspicious of this possibility for several weeks, but this was the first concrete indication I had of its reality.

"You'll be a mother in about seven and a half months," Dr. Webb announced, giving me my book of instructions and his recommendation for vitamins.

I never went back to the Sylmar Olive Company. I just left—no phone call, no letter of resignation. Seven months later I sent Margaret Carlson a birth announcement, but she didn't acknowledge it.

Rehearsals started and almost immediately Leno began to have misgivings about our financial success and he lost interest altogether when he realized that the script called for me to be kissed by a strange actor at the end of the second act.

Leno was there at every performance during the two weeks of our run, but always left before the kiss. Emma and Stella came with their "Petes" and made matters worse by kidding him about his leaving at that particular moment. When Mom and Dad came to view our venture and saw Leno's embarrassment, they became angry and disgusted with me for having gotten him into such a depraved industry.

I had endured the two weeks of rehearsal and each performance with nagging nausea and wasn't too disappointed when the lack of funds and dwindling audiences necessitated "You Can't Take It With You" being our one and only theatrical production. That was the end of my second attempt at becoming an actress.

Leno couldn't have cared less about losing the money. We came away from this disaster with numerous debts, but he was happy once again, having me home, awaiting our first baby. He was everything in life to me, I knew that, and I let him know it during the next four years, which became the best years of our lives.

7

MOM and Dad were visibly elated at the news of our forthcoming "blessed event" and I became the dutiful, contented, expectant Mother.

"You'll need some furniture now, Alice," Mom suggested. "Dad would like to have you pick out a refrigerator at The Broadway and put it on our account."

Ice men were scarce and fast becoming non-existent. Besides, Mom had a cousin who could use the ice box. We soon had a new Kelvinator with a small, frozen food compartment in our kitchen and were getting used to the idea of having a new refrigerator when Mom called again.

"Would you like to meet Emma and me to pick out a rug for your living room? Also, we can go see Victor Monteleone to order a couch for you."

"Mom, that's too much for you and Dad to do," I answered. "Let me ask Leno what he thinks."

"They want to do it for us, Alice," Leno said at dinner. "You will hurt their feelings if you don't accept."

"They have been so wonderful to me, Leno." I began to cry.

"Now don't start that, honey. They love you like their own daughter."

"I feel like I don't deserve their kindness."

"Alice, call Mom and go shopping with her, please."

I went with Mom and Emma to buy the rug and order the couch. They only made suggestions, were careful not to tell me what to buy. I wish they had guided me a little more. This was my first opportunity at making these large purchases and I'm not sure I made the right decisions.

Victor Monteleone made two green love seats for us, which faced each other in front of the fireplace. That meant we didn't have a long couch, which we later missed. I chose a mahogany coffee table and two tiered end tables on which I placed two matching lamps with decorative shades. The mahogany was difficult to care for, showing every speck of dust, keeping me hopping to avoid rings from cold glasses. Our rug was a swirled wine color with a short nap and I hung crisscross Priscilla curtains at the expanse of windows across the front of the house both in the living and dining rooms. I lived to regret that decision. Their care was tedious and tiring. Why did I always have to be different?

We had a wall left for a piano, and since the folks had paid for all of our furniture, I felt we could afford piano payments. After the purchase of a mahogany spinet we had twenty-six dollars a payday left. This necessitated our having numerous meals at Waverly Drive. Once a week, I drove Leno to State Wholesale and went to Waverly Drive to do my laundry, spending the day with Mom and having dinner in the evening after Dad brought Leno home from work with him. By the time Christmas came, our house was furnished, Leno had a raise, and we all became as happy as any of us had ever been.

In February, Leno's cousin, Jean, came over from Italy to marry Johnny DeSantis, Pete's brother. They had never met, only corresponded, and were required to marry within thirty days after her arrival or she would have to return to Italy. Jean couldn't speak any English and Johnny didn't know much Italian, but somehow they got acquainted. In thirty days, Dad planned a wedding to equal that of his two daughters.

Two days before their wedding was our fourth wedding anniversary—our first to be spent together. Our baby was due in about a month which made dancing at the Wilshire Hotel after dinner nearly impossible. We each had one dry martini and both laughed at my awkwardness. A dozen red roses had arrived earlier in the day, but that depleted Leno's bankroll and my gift would have to wait. I didn't mind. We were together. That was enough for both of us.

In retrospect, Jean and Johnny's wedding was an historical event. The Italian community was well represented and the entire family was in one place and congenial. Jean entered into the festivities, although a little awkwardly; a striking contrast to her arrival just thirty days before.

She had been staying at Oak Terrace and the wedding party met there for the five-mile ride to St. Peter's Italian Church. Dad was giving Jean away as her father was far away in Italy. She came out of the house on his arm preceded by Emma and Stella's two boys, Johnny and Anthony, who were the two ring bearers. The bridesmaids and ushers, mostly cousins of the bride, followed arm in arm and they all marched ceremoniously down the long steep driveway in front of the house to the Buicks and Chevrolets waiting below, while Leno's Paillard Bolex was catching it all on film.

St. Peter's had burned down in 1944 soon after our marriage there, and had been rebuilt, thanks to the donations and fund raisers sponsored by Mom and Dad. It was no longer the quaint, ancient, historical

AA degree from LACC
with Mom
June 1947

Jean and Johnny
DeSantis
with Mom and Dad
March 28, 1948

monument it had been, but was now white, modern stucco, graced by palm trees and a wide, expansive stairway ascending to the interior. The statue of St. Peter was still in place, however, as were St. Anthony and other saints, gracing the walls.

My heart was full of love and great appreciation to be a part of this pervading scene. The wedding was followed by a joyous lunch and reception in the hall adjacent to the church building. Jean and Johnny seemed destined to have a happy life, having been brought together under such odds and at such a great distance.

This was not to be so. They had two children, both boys, one dying with a rare case of pneumonia before he was three months old and the other in a tragic school bus accident at the age of five. These events were too much for the marriage, which ended in divorce and Jean's eventually returning to Italy.

But on that beautiful day in March, 1948, they enjoyed life to its fullest. I waddled around with my one hundred and sixty-five pounds, trying to participate in all the activities. I must have overdone myself, because four days later, my water broke and the next morning, early, I experienced my first labor pain.

8

I felt absolutely no fear at having this baby, although Dr. Webb had told me early in my pregnancy that my blood was RH negative. This was something new to me, but I learned that women who have this problem are likely to lose their babies at birth. I had gone through eight months of planning what I would do if our baby didn't live. Now that it was time, fully three weeks before my due-date, I felt nothing but happy anticipation. My labor pains were coming every ten minutes when Mom called.

"This could take all day, Alice. Why don't you come up here and wait till it's time to go to the hospital."

My bag had been packed for several days and we arrived at Oak Terrace around noon. I hadn't finished my baby clothes so I crocheted all afternoon, while Leno snoozed and Mom busied herself in the kitchen.

"You'd better have a good dinner," she suggested. "It may be a long time before you eat again."

By six o'clock, a delicious meal was on the table. Dad was there to join us and as we ate in the large breakfast room overlooking the fountain, the pains became more intense. They were coming every three or four minutes by the time the fruit was served after the main course.

Leno became visibly nervous and called the doctor. As luck would have it, Dr. Webb, who had been Mother's gynecologist and the one doctor we all trusted, was off for the weekend. His associate, whom I had met, Dr. Buell, was on call, which made me a little apprehensive. I needn't have worried. He proved to be as gentle and kind a doctor as Dr. Webb, leading me through my expected ordeal easily.

"Let's go, honey," Leno said hurriedly. "The doctor said it won't be long now." Mom and Dad stood at the back door and watched as Leno and I drove off in our 1940 Chevrolet.

My second visit to the California Hospital was a much happier occasion. Although it wasn't more than twenty minutes away, getting there seemed to take forever. After being quickly admitted, the nurses

312

prepared me and we were in for a long wait. Leno came in to hold my hand during the worst of it, but after I was given a beautifully relieving shot, he was asked to leave the room.

All I remembered during the night was the nurse coming in once to say, "The first one always takes a little longer. Doctor has ordered another shot."

When I awoke again in what seemed like seconds, a different nurse bounced into the room with a package she began to unwrap. "You have a baby girl," she announced, as she counted her ten fingers and ten toes so I could watch. "The pediatrician has seen her and she's in perfect health."

"What a snap," I thought. I noticed the sun shining through the open window. The baby's arm tag said she was born at two-thirty a.m. and I wondered where Leno was.

"Your husband was here until just a few minutes ago. He was exhausted and I suggested he go downstairs for a cup of coffee," the nurse offered.

As I held this precious baby in my arms, all the love I had ever felt welled up in my heart. Her little face was all I could have hoped for as she struggled to open her eyes and look around. I couldn't keep her long. The nurse snatched her up and was gone from the room. "I hope she doesn't drop her," I thought, observing her seeming carelessness.

As breakfast was being served, Leno walked in, beaming, with roses in one hand and a box of See's candy in the other. "I'm sorry I wasn't here when you woke up. You looked like you were going to sleep for hours. I'm glad it's over, but isn't she a beauty?"

"Did you call Mother?" I asked, remembering how anxious she had been.

"She wanted to come to the hospital last night, but I made her stay home. Yes, honey, she was the first to know."

"And Mom and Dad? Are they disappointed that it wasn't a boy?"

"No, they're just happy that you and the baby are doing o.k. But Dad did have a nice surprise for us."

Dad was going to buy us a new car for the baby and had presented Leno with a Standard Oil credit card to be paid for by the Company. We didn't get our new car for several months, waiting for production to catch up with demand after the war. Dad had put his name in for a Chevrolet, but we gratefully accepted a green 1948 Dodge with Dynaflow (one of the original automatic shift features) by Christmas. It was one of the best cars we ever had.

After five days at the hospital, we went home to Oak Terrace to recuperate. The relatives arrived in a steady stream to see Corina Jane, named after Leno's mother, as was the Italian custom, and my mother, as

313

Paris Inn on Jane's graduation night
June 16, 1948

was my newly-thought-of custom.

Cory, as we decided to call her, was an alert, demanding baby. I tried to nurse her without any luck and her formula was to be given only every four hours with water in between, if necessary, according to the "book."

That poor little dear. No matter how hard she cried, I wouldn't give her the formula until it was time, only water. She became water logged. After a week, we went home to Alhambra and Mother came to stay and help out.

By the time Cory was six weeks old, she was sleeping through the night, just as she was supposed to do. That took a little patience—making her wait and cry herself to sleep. Looking back, I know I did it all wrong, but I believed the "book" had all the answers.

Leno adored her and my days were full of taking care of the two of them. I had the household on a rigid routine and at four months, Cory napped twice a day on schedule. Money was scarce even with Leno's raise and credit card. "I can do some work at home while Cory is sleeping," I thought.

With Leno's approval, I advertised in the local paper: "Bookkeeping done in my home at reasonable rates." The ad was to run for thirty days and when I had no response by the thirtieth day, I was sure it was a bad idea, anyway. At four o'clock in the afternoon, the phone rang.

"Our books haven't been posted for almost a year," Mrs. DiPippo, the wife of the owner of "Our Market," a small grocery store in South Pasadena, announced.

I agreed to take on the task for twenty-five dollars a month. "If that's what you want to do, honey, it's all right with me," Leno said, in a rather irritated tone.

Their books were in a mess, as I found out later all books are. As I struggled with the boring detail, I realized that I didn't like being just a "bookkeeper." The very name seemed to be demeaning. If I was to do this kind of work, I wanted it to be more meaningful—more prestigious. I called the Public Accounting Board in downtown Los Angeles.

"We are not issuing anymore Public Accountant licenses in the state," an unfriendly voice announced. As I began questioning her, she continued, "If you want any more information, call the Board of Certified Public Accountants."

I did and their information was bad news. I would have to become a certified public accountant if I wanted to better my position. To accomplish that I needed a four-year college degree in accounting and two years of experience with a certified public accounting firm. In addition, I had to pass a grueling two-and-a-half day exam. How was I going to do that?

"Anything worth having is worth working for," I remembered Charlie saying, so I proceeded to take the first step.

Leno had received his Associate of Arts degree from Los Angeles City College in June of 1947. He was two years ahead of me. I had to get busy to catch up with him. I signed up for a correspondence course in accounting with the University of California at Berkeley. I could do the work at home and get full college credit.

Between struggling with the DiPippo books and accounting homework, my time for Leno was beginning to dwindle. He kept busy with State Wholesale and bowling leagues during the week and Gateway Markets on Saturdays. The leisure time we *did* have together was spent doting over Cory and watching her every new development. I wouldn't leave her with a baby-sitter, which considerably cramped our social life. The little entertainment we enjoyed was at the local drive-in theatres, where we kept our interest in the movies alive.

When I had completed all the accounting I could get through correspondence, Leno and I decided to take a night class at the University of Southern California. When the 1949 spring semester started, Cory was nearly a year old and Mother offered to take her while we went to class. This was our schedule on one day a week: Cory and I drove Leno to State Wholesale at seven in the morning. After doing our morning chores, we went shopping in Pasadena. At four o'clock, I dropped Cory off at Mother's on Joy Street and met Leno at store number three, where Dad dropped him off on his way home. We had our dinner at the hot dog stand on the corner before going on to class at USC. This we did for three semesters.

We often had Sunday dinner at Oak Terrace with Mom and Dad and the brothers and sisters-in-law and their children. Stella and Pete had added a girl to their family, Angela, named after Pete's mother, as was the Italian custom. Angela was two months older than Cory and the first girl in the family. Emma had a second boy in June of 1947, naming him Anthony, after Emma's father, as was the Italian custom, calling him Tony. Now Dad had two namesakes.

The men talked about the business and the women tried to keep the children out of mischief. I read Cory to sleep quickly so I could join the men. I found men and business much more interesting than domestic issues.

Both Petes worked at Gateway Markets—Pete DeSantis in the produce division and Pete Smaldino as Sam LaBianca's right-hand man. Leno was learning to run the wholesale business under Dad's close supervision.

"Alice is studying to be a certified public accountant," Leno bragged to Dad and the Petes on one such occasion.

Dad was encouraging, Pete DeSantis smiled broadly and Pete Smaldino laughed. "You'll never make it, Alice. Why do you even try?"

"I might as well be doing something in my spare time," I answered seriously, remembering similar long-since-forgotten discussions when Leno wasn't around to back me up.

"I'll tell you what," Pete continued. "If you ever become a certified public accountant, I'll give you a hundred dollars."

"That's a deal," I said, knowing full well that someday I would accomplish just that, although I was never to collect my one hundred dollars.

9

HARRY Truman had made the decision to use the atomic bomb to end World War II—a controversial issue to this day. The 1948 election was a stiff competition between him and our choice, Thomas Dewey. We thought Dewey was great and when he came to the Los Angeles Coliseum to speak to a crowd of over one hundred thousand, we were there to listen and became more enthusiastic than ever. Dewey was overwhelmingly favored to win by the polls and when Truman surprised us all by beating him on election day, we were shocked and disappointed. "Perhaps Dewey's mustache looked too much like Hitler's," I thought.

Nineteen forty-nine was a very good year, full of love and expectations for a brilliant future for Leno and me and our precious little girl. All of the instability and uncertainty of the past were gone. Leno was working long hours now, during the week at State Wholesale and the weekends at Gateway. I wasn't too happy about that, but Cory and I had fun going shopping.

Dad's picture appeared in the March 4, 1949 issue of the Southern California Grocers Journal with the following article:

> A patronage discount of 1.5 percent for the last period of the year ended December 31, 1948, refunded to members of its voluntary retail group, was announced by Mr. A. LaBianca, president of the State Wholesale Grocery Company, Inc. Due to the fine cooperation and support of their members, LaBianca revealed that the State Wholesale Grocery Company enjoyed an increase in volume of more than 35 percent over the year 1947. This increased volume enabled them to turn over their inventory about fifteen times and reduce their operating expense to approximately 2.85 percent. "These factors made it possible to declare this large patronage discount," stated Mr. LaBianca.

"State Wholesale Grocery Company's policy of offering lowest possible prices to its membership, has placed State Grocer members in an ideal position to meet the constant threat of a strictly competitive market. Constantly increasing volume of business through a modern warehouse and efficient methods of handling merchandise within that warehouse, enable State Grocer members to share in the added savings realized."

LaBianca stated that State Wholesale Grocery Company realizes the necessity of keeping its members competitive and has pledged to its membership a policy of maintaining rock-bottom prices and maximum refunds.

In the same issue our picture appeared with Stella, Pete being out of camera range, at the third annual banquet of the Food Employers Council, Inc., held at the Biltmore Hotel in downtown Los Angeles. The article introduced the speakers and outlined their topics of discussion:

Mr. Von der Ahe, personnel director of Von's Grocery Company, in a well delivered address gave a most excellent talk on market operators' problems that contained much food for thought... the cost of operations was continually increasing and market operators are faced with a serious problem in conducting a successful operation, and at the same time furnishing food to consumers at reasonable and attractive prices.

Gilbert G. Rowland, an attorney of Sacramento, California, was the guest speaker of the evening... he outlined the various proposals which have been introduced in the legislature at Sacramento which in one way or another would affect both employers and employees if they were adopted by the legislature.

It was an interesting and worthwhile social and business evening. The officers and management of Food Employers Council, Inc. are to be congratulated.

Our business affairs were progressing nicely, but we had problems on the home front. Dad kept asking us when we were going to baptize Cory. Leno had difficulty accepting the demands of the Catholic religion, but he left the decision to me. I couldn't quite bring myself to tell Mom and Dad that I didn't want to bring up my children as Catholics, that I wanted them to have the right to their own decision when the time came. I simply kept avoiding the issue and Leno supported my position, but with suppressed feelings of guilt.

Norman Abell, Pay Less Markets
M. J. Black, Californian Market
Ray Crawford, Modern Village Stores, Inc.
E. G. de Staute, Spartan Grocers, Ltd.
Arthur Freeman, Freeman Certi-Fresh Foods
Joe Goldstein, The Boys Market, Inc.
Frank I. Hale, Hale's Market
Richard C. Holderness, Certified Grocers of California, Ltd.
J. P. Hughes, Fitzsimmons Stores, Ltd.
W. F. James, National Biscuit Co.
L. O. Lillywhite, Roberts Public Markets, Inc.
R. A. McCarthy, Alpha Beta Food Markets, Inc.
K. E. Meigs, Safeway Stores, Inc.
Benjamin Metrick, Pessin Grocery Co.
C. C. Nigg, Bell Brand Foods, Ltd.
Duncan Shaw, Market Basket
Dan A. West, Haas, Baruch & Company

The possibility of another war had never left our minds as atomic bomb tests were continually being made on the Nevada desert. When World War II ended, the peninsula of Korea, located in the heart of the Far East, was surrendered to the Allies. In accordance with the Potsdam Proclamation between the United States, China and the Soviet Union, Korea was to be given its independence. It was agreed that the Soviet Union would accept the surrender of Korea north of what was to be called the 38th parallel and the United States would accept their surrender south of that line.

The Soviets considered the 38th parallel a political boundary, contrary to the intention of the United States, and Korea became divided into two rigidly separated occupation zones with all communication between the two being severed.

Efforts of the United Nations to establish free elections in what now became North Korea were fruitless. By 1949 the North Korean government, established by the Soviet Union, was making frequent raids below the 38th parallel and on June 25, 1950, the North Korean army launched a carefully planned attack. On June twenty-seventh, President Truman ordered U.S. air and sea forces to go to the aid of the South Koreans.

But before that happened, we had a war of our own, albeit a domestic one. I was allowed to attend the State Wholesale and Gateway Markets shareholders' meeting for the first time in the spring of 1950. The attorney was there to explain cumulative voting to the shareholders, of which I was not one. Apparently, the provision of cumulative voting was in the by-laws of both corporations and had been for some time. It simply meant that a shareholder's number of votes was determined by multiplying his number of shares by the number of board members and he was allowed to divide these votes in any manner he chose. This provision gave Dad the capability of naming a majority of the board of directors himself.

We didn't understand why all this explanation was necessary until Leno was nominated. Dad's brother, Sam LaBianca, owning 19 percent of the voting stock, had been the vice-president of both companies for many years. When Sam objected to Leno's nomination, the attorney explained that he didn't have much to say about it because of the cumulative voting provisions. Sam was furious!

Leno was elected to the board of directors and when the board met after the shareholders' meeting, Leno was elected vice-president of both corporations. What a happy surprise for both Leno and myself—totally unexpected! Emotions ran high. Sam left before the refreshments were served and didn't speak to Dad or Leno for over a year.

Apparently *everyone* was surprised. The two Petes were as gracious as ever, showing no sign of disagreement. Emma congratulated Leno, laughing and joking in her own inimitable way. Stella also seemed pleased, but later we heard that she was quite upset. "If I had been a boy, I would have gotten that job," she laughed bitterly.

Stella hadn't worked for her father since getting married. She seemed totally immersed in her home and family, although I knew that being a mother was frustrating to her. She was such a perfectionist, wanting her home to be spotless at all times. Usually impossible with children around, she seemed to manage somehow. She didn't show much interest in business matters. I suspect she may have wanted Leno's job for her husband, since she was the eldest, but that is pure conjecture on my part.

After dropping this bombshell, unannounced, at the shareholders' meeting, Dad surprised us again. He and Mom were going to Europe and especially Italy, for six months, leaving in May. Ninteen-fifty was proving to be an exciting year, as it also marked their thirtieth wedding anniversary and our announcement of an expected new arrival on Dad's birthday in December.

We planned a gala bon voyage-anniversary celebration to be held at St. Peter's hall. What a night that turned out to be! There was dancing to the best Italian music in town. The food, consisting of antipasto, pasta, olive oil and vinegar salad and meat dishes—bracioles, barbecued chicken, roast—was prepared by the best Italian cooks in the community. The delicious food was topped off with dark red wine and a four-tiered cake, decorated with a bride and groom, but I was too nauseated to really enjoy this fabulous feast.

How I wish we could go back and do it again. Cory was there, but doesn't remember, and the other children have only heard about it through my repeated telling.

There must have been three hundred aunts, uncles, cousins, compadres, godfathers, godmothers, children and "old folks," who just sat there and smiled. Dad and Mom looked wonderful. The evening went too smoothly for Dad not to have had a hand in it. How we depended on him for everything. Such fun, such vying for attention; how spoiled we were and unprepared for what lay ahead.

On the day of their departure for Europe, we planned a send-off picnic at a park in Arcadia. They were driving their new 1950 Buick to New York and taking it on the ship with them, as was Dad's way to travel. We had a picnic lunch and the children played on the swings and slides. We waved goodbye with sadness, wondering how we could

Some of us at the thirtieth anniversary
and bon voyage party for Mom and Dad
April 15, 1950

manage six long months without them.

Leno was a Sergeant First Class in the United States Army Reserve in which he had enlisted on March 1, 1946. In February of 1950, he had applied for a commission as a Second Lieutenant, which still hadn't come through. When Truman ordered troops to go to South Korea in June, all of the non-commissioned Army and Navy Reserves were called to active duty. Leno received his orders to report to Fort MacArthur on July twenty-fifth. I panicked! Our beautiful world was falling apart. I couldn't face the world alone again.

"I wrote to them about that commission months ago. The Army never does anything right," Leno lashed out bitterly. "I won't go back as a flunky for those officers again. I'll leave the country first!"

For several days we talked about what we would do and where we would go if Leno's commission didn't come through in time. Hank Black, our high school chum, had received his orders, too, being in the Navy Reserve after serving four years in the Coast Guard during World War II.

"I think it will be exciting to go over there. I'm looking forward to it," he bragged, as he laughed at Leno's attitude.

Hank and Helen already had two children and a dream house in a suburban community near Alhambra. Helen wasn't too happy at the prospect of Hank's leaving, but laughed and said he would probably get what he asked for.

Miraculously, Leno's commission came through on July eighteenth and he was relieved of having to report to Fort MacArthur. My prayers had been answered again. Later, he resigned his commission, receiving a full, honorable discharge from the U.S. Army on November 14, 1952, and was never called to the service of his country again. We settled down to prepare for our expected December arrival.

Korea
December 8, 1950

Dear LaBiancas,

How is everything in the good old San Gabriel Valley? Leno, if you have to saw your arm off, don't let them get you! This reserve call-up is the biggest SNAFU I have ever seen. The whole war for that matter. For instance, I am now aboard an LST with about thirty other transients being taken to Inchon, Korea, to catch our respective ships. We left at four a.m. Wednesday completely empty! Except for the crew and we thirty transients, this thing is completely hollow. If that isn't a waste of money and manpower, I don't know what is.

I'm having Helen get some letters in order so I can get a hardship discharge. I pray every night it will go through. Don't let anyone ever tell you homesickness is all in the head. When I stop to think of what I gave up to come over here, I get as sharp a pain in the chest as I've ever had.

Well, kids, when I get settled, I'll write you a letter full of complaints; till then, I hope this finds you well, and keep an eye on my family for me.

> With love,
> Hank

10

LENO did his best to translate the two-page letter from the R.M.S. "Queen Elizabeth" and the three-page letter from Adelfia-Canneto, as well as the picture post cards from Paris, Florence, Torina, Pisa, Rome, Bari and Pompeii, all in Italian.

May 19, 1950
Aboard the Queen Elizabeth

Dear Son,

We are in good health and ready to enjoy our trip. We're sorry that we didn't find you when we telephoned from atop the Empire State Building before leaving New York. Alice told us you had gone to school. We hope all goes well.

Write to us at Canneto and let us know what's new; how your wife and also little Cory are doing. We have already been at sea for three days. Only the first day was cold. Now everything is better. Not too cold and not too hot; just comfortable enough. The food is good and so far, we haven't gotten lost, as we did on our first trip over in 1938. There are all the entertainments that there were on the "Rex."

I will continue tomorrow and thus be able to tell you how we spend our days and when we disembark. We send greetings and kisses to everyone.

Sunday, May 21, 1950

The last two days have been a little turbulent, but not enough to make us sick; just a little upset stomach. We disembark tomorrow at 3:04 p.m. Right now we're in the ballroom where music is playing. We're dancing and talking with friends we've made on the trip. Once more, kisses to you and your wife and little Corina.

Mom and Dad

August 15, 1950
Adelfia-Canneto

Dear Son Leno,

I write these few lines to tell you the state of our health. We are feeling well and hope all of you are, too.

In the last letter your mother wrote to your sister, Emma, she asked her to find out if you can buy a Chevrolet sedan and a Coldspot refrigerator like the one we have now. If you don't have enough money, borrow it from State and we'll settle up when we get back.

We are unhappy to hear that Johnny DeSantis was called up for military service. Try to find some way to get a delay in your time to report. If you can't get out of it, I have explained everything to Sammy Bruno and your brother-in-law, Peter DeSantis. I believe you have done well during my long absence, but nothing can be done if you are called to serve your country.

Yesterday Mr. and Mrs. Musacco left by airplane to return to America and I am sure he will give you news about when we will be coming back.

I'm afraid we have some bad news to report. While traveling on one of these narrow roads the other day, I hit a man on his bicycle. He was hurt badly. I wished him "good luck" when they put him in the ambulance to take him to the hospital, which was several miles away. We just had word this morning that he died. We were very saddened and will try to do something for his family. Our car was damaged and will delay our departure from Canneto and our return home.

I have heard that business is going well because goods have become scarce. Take care to keep the best and most faithful customers happy and not to let too much go to those who are only with you because of the shortages.

I close for now sending greetings to everyone. And greetings from Nana [Corina's mother] and all the aunts and uncles. Your mother sends the best to all of you in the family, including your sisters with their husbands and children. Greetings and kisses

327

and, as always, I am your father.

P.S. Keep writing and kiss Cory for us.

Then, on their way home, picture post cards from Venice and Geneva. They returned to Oak Terrace triumphant, with movies of their trip and a newspaper from Adelfia-Canneto:

THE PROVIDENCE MARIA S.S. ORPHANAGE SOLEMNLY INAUGURATED IN ADELFIA-CANNETO BY ACTION OF LOS ANGELES CITIZEN

THE ARCHBISHOP, PREFECT AND ALL TOWN AUTHORITIES PRESENT AT BEAUTIFUL CEREMONY

With the help of the Archbishop, Monsignor Mimmi, the Prefect, Dr. Magris and the honorable mayor, Troisi, the House of Providence Maria S.S. [St. Mary of the Star Poorhouse] was inaugurated August 6, 1950 [Leno's twenty-fifth birthday] in Adelfia-Canneto. Present at the solemn ceremony were Dr. Longo, Major of the C.C. Battalion, Dr. Prezzolini and Colonel Sinisa of the A.P.I. Administration. Mr. Antonio LaBianca, president and founder of the American Canneto Providencial Society in Los Angeles, received the "Star of Solidarity" for his contribution to the philanthropic cause.

The mayor spoke: "Through the generous initiative of Mr. LaBianca, living in Los Angeles, who, not forgetting his place of birth, wished to show his affection and Christian charity for his less fortunate brothers, this orphanage became a reality. Mr. LaBianca's name, along with the names of other contributors, will be forever remembered by posterity, having been consecrated and set in marble. Canneto is endlessly grateful to these noble and generous sons who, with their intelligence and great work, hold high the name of Italy in the land of America."

The Archbishop, Monsignor Mimmi, spoke a few words glorifying the holy work and expressing the wish that this would be an example and a guide to how much the misfortunes of the disinherited can be lessened.

The population visited until late in the evening the places that housed the poor old people of the town.

Oak Terrace
Pete Smaldino, Leno, Pete DeSantis
Stella, Alice, Dad, Mom, Emma
Louis, Angela, Anthony Smaldino, Cory
Johnny and Tony DeSantis

We welcomed Mom and Dad home with great enthusiasm, having missed them more than they realized. They brought beautiful gifts for all of us, including our baby, due in a little more than a month.

During his absence, Dad had left Leno in charge at State Wholesale and Pete Smaldino in charge at Gateway. Leno had done an excellent job while Dad was away, but Dad found fault with his failure to document his actions.

"Why didn't you keep a log of all the events that occurred for me to have when I returned?" he questioned vehemently.

"Why didn't you suggest that before you left?" Leno responded with equal fervor.

"I wanted to see what you would do on your own," he shouted back.

"Were you testing me?" Leno became openly hostile. "I've always done what you wanted me to, with very little thanks from you."

"This is your business. If you don't learn how to do things right now, when will you learn?" Dad ended the confrontation, having the last word.

Early on the morning of December seventh, Pearl Harbor Day, I awakened suddenly. "Was that a labor pain?" I shook Leno. "I think I'm going to have the baby today."

"You're not due for two weeks," was his sleepy reply. "Are you sure?"

"I've been having pains for the last two hours and now they're only five minutes apart," I answered as I dressed myself and Cory quickly. We had to drop her off at Oak Terrace and there was no time to lose.

We arrived at the California Hospital by eight-thirty a.m. and the nurses quickly prepared me. Then, of course, the pains slowed down. I sat in bed with Leno at my side and we both read the Saturday morning newspaper. By ten o'clock, the pains were getting harder as Dr. Webb came into the room.

"It's time for you to have your shot. Are you ready? It won't be long now," he announced with a smile, giving me confidence.

"Your mother wants me to come and get her, I'll go now," Leno said as the nurse told him it was time to leave.

The shot was, indeed, welcome, and in what seemed like a few seconds, I heard Mother's voice faintly, then more distinctly.

"She doesn't know yet that she has a boy," she repeated two or three times before I realized that I wasn't dreaming and Mother was there, smiling, "You have your boy."

I opened my eyes to Mother's beautiful face and shining blue eyes. She was forty-eight years old with not a gray hair in her head. She had recently passed for thirty-five when applying for a filing job which called for a younger woman. What spunk she had! She had never worked in an office before, but wanted to try her hand at it and loved her work and her friends there.

She took the "W" streetcar at seven a.m. to downtown Los Angeles and became an expert file clerk, taking her work seriously and enthusiastically. She had reared all five of us children, virtually alone, with very little financial support. Our father had sent her thirty dollars a month for each of the three of us, all during the depression years when we were growing up. We were lucky we had a father who worked—so many men didn't have work of any kind.

Mother's second and third husbands rarely sent her anything for Jane and Bobbie, but we managed somehow. Mother stayed home to be there when we came in from school, but gave piano lessons to help augment the income and even occasionally took to washing and ironing other people's clothes. She was never depressed—always loving and cheerful under, what seemed to me at times, to be extremely trying circumstances. Often in the afternoon after school, she would play the piano and we would sing the popular songs of the twenties and thirties—the sheet music that was worn from years of use. Mother could play any music, popular or classical, without ever having seen it before. I can still hear "The Twelfth Street Rag", "In a Persian Market", "Chloe", "Come on Down South!" and "Kitten on the Keys." She taught us all to play, but our music never sounded quite like hers.

Mother was an idealist, always seeing the best in everyone, being terribly disappointed when her ideal expectations were shattered. She was emotional at times, usually showing her happiness and sadness with tears, but she was great in a crisis, feeling no fear and showing no panic, taking life on its own terms. Mother was a proud woman, but her pride came from an inner confidence and contentment, rather than from arrogance. She was independent, not only in her attitude, but in her thinking. She was a religious woman, but didn't like going to church, saying, "It always makes me cry. I have my own religion. I don't need to go to church!"

How I loved her and how happy I was to see her, to know she was there, and to know she always would be, no matter what. How lucky I was to have had her all these years.

Later, when the nurse brought the baby in, I couldn't believe that I could feel as great a thrill the second time as I had the first. His ten fingers and toes were all there as he contentedly slept, with a faint smile curling his small mouth. He couldn't stay long and by the time I was fully awake, Mom and Dad were there with Leno looking down on me with great love and pride. Dad was ecstatic, showing more emotion than I had ever seen from him. What happiness it gave me to see them laughing and smiling, openly thrilled.

I knew that Dad would be anxious about the name we had chosen. As soon as they left, Leno and I had a long, serious talk.

"If we name him after Dad, all the kids will call him 'Tony the barber.' He'll be labeled Italian for sure," Leno said emphatically.

"What's so bad about Tony?" I asked. "Leno, we have to name him after Dad. He would never forgive us."

"Sure, let him have his way; whatever he wants, he gets. I've been catering to him all my life," he continued bitterly.

"It's not much to give a man who has been so good to us," I suggested. "You know how much it would mean to him."

"All right, honey, you decide," Leno acquiesced. "Whatever you want is o.k. with me. The main thing is that he's here and healthy."

We decided on Anthony Carl, after Leno's dad, which was the Italian custom; adding my father's name, pleasing both Dads and giving our son some distinction from the other Anthonys already in the family.

11

CORY and Leno had stayed at Oak Terrace while Anthony and I were getting acquainted at the hospital. We joined them there after our five-day visit. Anthony was a contented baby, wanting to sleep most of the time. We decided to call him "Anthony" because Leno didn't want to call him "Tony." Besides, Emma called her second son "Tony." Of course, Stella's second son was called "Anthony," but Anthony Carl was the only LaBianca.

We were still at Oak Terrace when the rest of the family joined us at Christmas time. How Dad doted on his namesake; the only LaBianca that would be left in America when he was no longer here. His eyes revealed feelings that he was too embarrassed to express. Leno had known for a long time what I finally began to realize and understand. Dad was a stern man with a soft heart, who felt that a man who expressed his feelings was not a man at all.

My Christmas card from Leno that year ended with,

"Thanks a million for the real-live wonderful Christmas present, honey." I was thankful in 1950 that Leno didn't take after his father.

Emma and Stella lived in their big, beautiful homes a few blocks away and Stella invited us to a New Year's Eve party that year. Dr. Webb recommended that new Mothers not venture out until, at least, four weeks after giving birth and I wasn't feeling any too strong, but everyone insisted that I go. Mom and Dad stayed with the children and we hadn't far to travel, so I went, reluctantly.

Stella's rumpus room was the "scene of action," in the walk-out basement of their home, a great place for a party. Some basement—as large as any three-room apartment, equipped with a full kitchen and bar and windows across half of its length. Emma's house, which was next door, had the same floor plan, but the exteriors were different; Stella choosing a Spanish architecture and Emma a more modern look, both with heavy tile roofs.

As I indulged in two dry martinis, I wondered if the alcohol would harm my weakened condition. How I wished we had a big house like theirs. Cory and Anthony would have to share a bedroom and the only possibility for a rumpus room was the unfinished area way out behind our garage.

When the new year started, we began to look at houses in San Marino, an upper-class, ostentatious suburb, east of Alhambra, which I felt we were now entitled to. Leno humored me, but was perfectly happy where we were.

We found a large, sprawling ranch house that I thought would be perfect for us and we took Mom and Dad to see it on one of our frequent Sunday afternoon drives with them.

"It's on a corner," Dad said critically. "You never want to buy a house on a corner. You pay more property tax and there is more upkeep."

I spoke up. "But we need a bigger house and I like this one. Besides, they're only asking twenty-two thousand dollars for it."

"It's way over-priced," he concluded and didn't say any more.

Mom was her usual quiet self as we drove back to Oak Terrace for Sunday supper. There was no more talk of that house or any house, except Oak Terrace.

"Our house is yours, Alice," Mom reiterated while seeing us to the car. "This will be your home and we'll move into the apartment in the back when you're ready for it. That's his plan."

"But this is your house," I answered. "I wouldn't feel comfortable with you living in that little apartment."

"That's the way he wants it. Let's just leave it at that."

Leno and I were destined to come back to Oak Terrace, but that Sunday afternoon, we didn't realize how soon.

By now, I had three bookkeeping clients—the DiPippos, Ciccarelli Trucking and Kuus Plating. I was earning the grand total of sixty dollars a month. Leno and I were going to night school two nights a week and it took most of my earnings to pay for my tuition, which had now advanced to twelve dollars a unit.

May 13, 1951

As man and wife and parents
We've shared both sun and rain,
We've known the greatest blessings,
We've had some cares and pain,

But, all in all, our memories
Have just grown dearer still,
That's why we love each other
And why we always will!
Happy Mother's Day, darling

With all my love!

Herlong or Los Angeles, I'll love you always,
Leno

The pressure was on. We were both working hard. Leno had long hours at both companies and I had long hours of accounting homework and another client, a Mormon salesman, who had me write checks each month to various church funds based on his profit.

"You hardly make enough to take care of your wife and four children. How can you afford to make these large donations to the church?" I asked, trying to help.

"I do this now so that if we're ever in need, they will take care of us. That's how we do it—10 percent to God," he answered with conviction.

I admired his faith, but he was giving more like 30 percent, with 10 percent each to tithing, the building fund and the missionary fund. How his family lived on what was left I never understood. I charged him only ten dollars for my several hours of bookkeeping a month. Why I did that I never understood, either.

Now that Cory was three she wouldn't take naps any longer, but Anthony was an easy baby, fitting into our schedule nicely. I was swamped and had to quit going to the bowling alley on Wednesday nights with Leno. The team would often come over afterward for coffee and cookies to keep me happy.

Many Saturday nights were spent with Howard and Ann Bumpass in their little house behind her mother and father on Elm Street, which was next door to where the LaBiancas used to live. Howard had come to work for State Wholesale in the advertising department and he and Leno were still great pals. We played cards and had midnight suppers prepared as only Ann knew how. They didn't have a big house either, which helped ease my thwarted desire for one.

We were busy, pressured, working hard and terribly happy when we decided to take some time off. We headed for a weekend in San

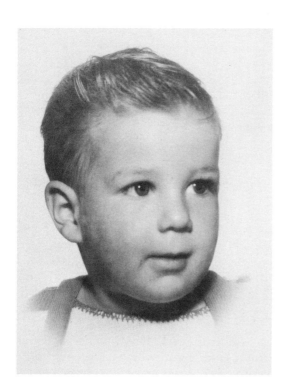

Anthony

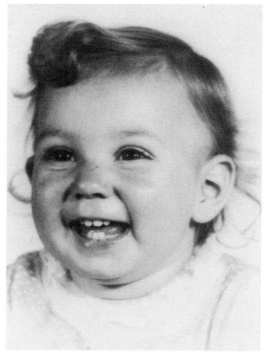

Cory

Francisco with Barbara Pierce, who was now Barbara Lee, married to a sportswriter on the San Francisco Chronicle. We picked an exciting, albeit unbelievable time in history to be in the windy city. Just a few days before, the radios interrupted their normal programming to announce, "President Truman has just removed General MacArthur from his Far Eastern and Korean Commands and from the direction of the occupation of Japan."

We were furious with this hot-tempered, indecisive little man for having the audacity to humiliate so great a General, who had not only master-minded the nearly hopeless situation during the War in the Pacific, but had successfully rebuilt Japan, almost completely destroyed by war. He had been in the foreign service in the Far East for fifteen consecutive years and had been dismissed with the only reason being given that it was doubtful he could "support the policies of the Administration." In MacArthur's own words, "No office boy, no charwoman, no servant of any sort would have been dismissed with such callous disregard for the ordinary decencies."

We sat in the lounge at the "Top of the Mark" watching on television MacArthur's address to a joint session of Congress:

Mr. President, Mr. Speaker, and distinguished Members of the Congress:

I stand on this rostrum with a sense of deep humility and great pride—humility in the wake of those great American architects of our history who have stood here before me, pride in the reflection that this forum of legislative debate represents human liberty in the purest form yet devised. Here are centered the hopes and aspirations and faith of the entire human race.

...The Japanese people since the war have undergone the greatest reformation recorded in modern history. With a commendable will, eagerness to learn, and marked capacity to understand, they have, from the ashes left in war's wake, erected in Japan an edifice dedicated to the primacy of individual liberty and personal dignity, and in the ensuing process there has been created a truly representative government committed to the advance of political morality, freedom of economic enterprise, and social justice...

...While I was not consulted prior to the President's decision to intervene in support of the Republic of Korea, that decision, from a military standpoint, proved a sound one, as we hurled back the invader and decimated his forces. Our victory was complete and our objectives within reach when Red China intervened with numerically superior ground forces...

...I called for reinforcements, but was informed that reinforcements were not available. I made it clear that if not permitted to destroy the enemy buildup bases north of the Yalu; if not permitted to utilize the friendly Chinese force of some six hundred thousand men on Formosa; if not permitted to blockade the China coast to prevent the Chinese Reds from getting succor from without; and if there were to be no hope of major reinforcements, the position of the command from the military standpoint forbade victory... I have constantly called for the new political decisions essential to a solution. Efforts have been made to distort my position. It has been said that I was in effect a war monger. Nothing could be further from the truth. I know war as few other men now living know it, and nothing to me is more revolting.

...But once war is forced upon us, there is no other alternative than to apply every available means to bring it to a swift end. War's very object is victory—not prolonged indecision. In war, indeed, there can be no substitute for victory.

...The magnificence of the courage and fortitude of the Korean people defies description. They have chosen to risk death rather than slavery. Their last words to me were, "Don't scuttle the Pacific."

...The world has turned over many times since I took the oath on the Plain at West Point, and the hopes and dreams have long since vanished. But I still remember the refrain of one of the most popular barrack ballads of that day which proclaimed most proudly that—

"Old soldiers never die, they just fade away."

And like the old soldier of that ballad, I now close my military career and just fade away—an old soldier who tried to do his duty as God gave him the light to see that duty.

Goodbye.

We were moved to tears as we applauded long and loud in that San Francisco bar, not realizing another war was taking shape south of China, with the aid of Red China—a war that would be escalated because of political indecision—a war that became unnecessarily costly in American lives and the beginning of an entirely new way of life for the youth of America. Many Americans listened to what MacArthur said that night in 1951, but were powerless to act to allay the fear they felt in their hearts. MacArthur was our hero and we were all truly thankful that such a man had come along in our devastated generation.

Hank returned from Korea unharmed, after serving one year. I never saw a man appreciate being with his family as much as Hank did when he came home. He had great tales of his adventures, but stayed close to the home fires, as nearly as I could tell.

My little sister, Jane, was getting married in July. She wore my wedding dress and we were a happy group as we all left our house in Alhambra—Jane, Mother, Bobbie and Leno and I with our little family, Cory and Anthony.

She and Harry Gliksman were married at Christ Church, Unity in Los Angeles where Leno and I and the children had been attending. Dr. Wilson married them and they left the church in our 1950 Pontiac. We had traded in our Dodge on the new car when the Korean war broke out in 1950, thinking there would be another shortage of automobiles. There wasn't, and now we were saddled with car payments for the first time—a foolish move we made while Mom and Dad were in Europe.

Jane and Harry headed for sister Edith's house in Westchester, a suburb in west L.A. by the airport. They had planned to serve only cake and punch at the reception, as their budget was limited. Mom and Dad were invited and when Dad discovered the meagre menu, he said he would bring the food. Food? He brought turkey, ham, roast beef, rolls and wine. I decided his mission in life was to make sure that everyone had enough to eat.

When Mom and Dad returned to Oak Terrace that evening, they learned that Zi Zi was in the Glendale Hospital after suffering a stroke. They rushed to her bedside, but she couldn't speak to them—was only able to smile. She was soon given "last rites" by Father Michael and went to sleep quietly for the last time.

Mom and Dad's loss was devastating, happening so suddenly and unexpectedly.

Zi Zi's Rosary was held the night before her funeral, as was the Italian custom. Her body was displayed in an open casket, and after prayers, her friends and relatives viewed her, filing past the immediate family to give their condolences. This was a heart-rending scene, one I had never before witnessed. Leno warned me that the experience wouldn't be easy, but one I needed to encounter, sooner or later.

I felt a deep respect for this tradition, the Rosary and the funeral the following day. These were not morbid rituals to be feared and avoided.

Avoiding them brought the fear and the misinterpretation. This was a coming together of the people who had loved and admired Zi Zi. The funeral is a difficult part of life, but the one time we have the opportunity to share our deep loss with others, others often not seen at any other time.

I had never seen Dad cry, but cry he did at the Rosary, unashamedly, and the whole scene was repeated on the next day at Zi Zi's funeral which Dad had organized and planned. The procession of limousines for the immediate family to Cavalry Cemetery in East Los Angeles, was followed by the rest of us in our Pontiac, Chevrolets and Fords. The graveside service was followed by a veritable feast at Zi Zi's house. We ate and drank and talked about Zi Zi and what a wonderful woman she had been. Dad and Mom talked to the others in Italian, about days past, I imagined, fondly and joyously, but with a trace of sadness.

A card with a dozen roses arrived for me the following week.

8-2-51

Just a little thought — to remind you how much I love all the things you are.

Leno

12

AUGUST sixth was Leno's birthday. Our house was so small, it wasn't feasible to have a party in Alhambra. The family numbered fifteen now with all of the children. I planned a picnic in Santa Barbara, a beautiful beach community, about three hours from Los Angeles, to celebrate Leno's birthday.

We took three cars north, leaving Oak Terrace about eight a.m. and found a beach with grass and picnic tables. The sand beckoned down to the sea beyond and Leno and I enjoyed a leisurely swim in the ocean. Later we all indulged in a lavish lunch, each of us bringing our "specialty," mine being a birthday cake made from "scratch," as my grandmother had taught me to do.

The cousins, Stella's Louis, Anthony and Angela and Emma's Johnny and Tony romped all afternoon with Cory while Anthony Carl slept in his playpen, only awakening long enough to be changed and have his bottle. Dad was quiet and introspective, going for a long walk on the beach by himself.

We returned to Alhambra sunburned and over-fed, exhausted from too much fun, having all agreed that the beach outing was a good way to have a family get-together.

The following Friday afternoon Leno came home from State Wholesale angry and downhearted. "Dad chewed me out again today. Why doesn't he get off my back? I can't please him. No matter what I do, it's wrong in his eyes," he complained.

"What was it about this time?" I asked.

"Oh, nothing very important. He's been impossible since Zi Zi died," he continued. "I made a decision without consulting him and you would think I had committed a crime. He got red in the face and became totally unreasonable. Sometimes I think I should get a job somewhere else," he said sadly.

"Think about the future. Someday you can run the business the way

ALHAMBRA

Cory with
Angela Smaldino

Johnny and Tony
DeSantis

you want to," I suggested.

"I'll be an old man by then. I want to put my ideas into effect now, not when I'm old and gray."

Dad and Leno had had a violent argument, ending with Leno storming out of the office. By the time he got home and related this to me, his anger began to subside and he decided that, perhaps, he had been too hard on Dad.

"I guess I should apologize," he concluded and decided to do just that on Saturday morning at Gateway. Dad usually went around to all the stores then, but the following day he was nowhere to be found.

Saturday night Leno's feelings of guilt were mounting as he hadn't gotten the chance to apologize. "I guess I'm pretty stubborn sometimes. I think I do things my way just to see what Dad will do. I shouldn't be so hard on him. I don't want to call him, though. I'll wait till Monday morning."

Sunday morning we headed for Laguna Beach with the children, Mother, brother Bob and sister, Jane. Harry had to work almost every Sunday, so we tried to include Jane in our outings. We loved the beach. At every opportunity, we headed for Balboa or Laguna, about fifty miles from Alhambra. There were no freeways in that direction, so it was nearly a two-hour drive. Cory and Anthony loved to get messy in the sand and Leno and I loved swimming in the surf.

We returned home late that evening, tired and sunburned, but relaxed. The phone rang and it was Emma. Dad had gone to the hospital.

"He began having pains in his left arm and Dr. Curtis suggested he take two aspirin and meet him at the hospital. We don't think it's too serious, but it could be a mild heart attack. We'll keep in touch."

Monday afternoon Leno came home from work early and we took the children to Ann Bumpass' on the way to the hospital. By the time we arrived, Dad was unconscious and in severe pain—something we hadn't expected. He had been put in a room with another man on Sunday night, but Mom had him moved to a private room so she could stay overnight with him. As Dad was wheeled out of his semi-private room, his roommate called out, "Good luck!"

"I hope I don't have the same 'good luck' that I wished to the bicycle rider in Italy," he joked.

He had gotten steadily worse after being moved Sunday night. Mom's cot was next to his bed where she was going to stay until Dad came home with her. Leno paced nervously as I sat in a chair and prayed silently; the only thing I knew to do.

"Dear God, don't take him away from us now. We need him. I

promise to have the children baptized as Catholics, if you will only make him well." I made a promise to God, trying to strike a bargain, feeling deep remorse at not having granted this small request when made, by a man who had given so much of himself to me.

As we reluctantly left on Monday night, we could hear Dad with each agonizing breath he took, all the way to the elevator. We went to see him every night, although he didn't know we were there. Mom never left his side, having her food brought in. Thursday, she called Father Michael, and Dad received his "last rites." He awoke momentarily, looked around, and spoke, "Why is he here? Aren't you rushing this a bit?"

"Just in case," Mom laughed, relieved to hear his voice.

He lingered for several days, not knowing any of us were there, then seemed to be improving. He awoke and tried to speak. I leaned over to kiss him and looked deep into his anguished eyes. There are no words to describe what I saw or how I felt. His eyes were full of love and compassion as he struggled to express his feelings. I knew that those years of disagreement had been his way of teaching us, and learn we did, although we didn't realize it for many years to come.

He fell back into a coma and regained consciousness only one more time. He didn't open his eyes, rather spoke as if in a dream, saying matter-of-factly, "Now the Petes have their jobs and Leno has his... " and his voice trailed off.

Stella called early the following day. "Come right away if you want to see him. The doctor says there's not much hope." As we walked down the hospital corridor toward Dad's room, Stella came out, calmly shaking her head and gesturing with her hands, "It's all over."

"His heart improved," the specialist said, "but his kidneys had been too badly damaged. There was nothing we could do about the kidneys. If he had recovered, he would have been a vegetable, as too much oxygen was lost to the brain."

He lay there white and still. His face had relaxed and showed no signs of stress. I wanted to awaken him and tell him how much I loved him, how sorry I was for causing him so much pain. But it was too late, the opportunity was gone. I have never used the words "good luck" since that day.

The August twenty-second issue of the Los Angeles Evening Herald & Express reported:

Anthony LaBianca, president of Gateway Food Stores, Inc. and State Wholesale Grocery Company, Inc. and prominent in Italo-American and Catholic affairs, died suddenly today in a Glendale hospital from a heart ailment. He was fifty-six and resided at 3301

Waverly Drive.

Born near Bari, Italy, he came to Los Angeles when sixteen. He immediately started himself in a little meat store at Cypress Avenue and Elm Street. Thirty years ago he formed the Gateway Corporation which now owns six markets in various parts of the city.

A member of St. Peter's Catholic Church, he was active in its construction, and also led a campaign to provide a home for aged victims of the last war at his native Bari, Italy.

He leaves one son, Leno LaBianca; two daughters, Mrs. Stella Smaldino and Mrs. Emma DeSantis; a brother, Saverio, and a sister, Carmella Marisi.

A Rosary will be recited in St. Peter's Catholic Church at eight p.m. Friday evening and a requiem Mass celebrated at the church at nine-thirty a.m. Saturday.

Somewhat inaccurately reported, nevertheless, the sum total of a great man's life.

PART VII

Beyond Tomorrow's Dream

"There's a divinity that shapes our ends
Rough hue them how we will"
"Hamlet" by William Shakespeare

1

WE left the hospital and returned to Oak Terrace with Mom, and stayed.

"I have lost my company," she said sadly as she unlocked the back door and we walked in with dread. The house was cold and silent. The task of going through Dad's clothes and personal belongings was Mom's, alone, to do. The telephoning to all those who hadn't heard the news fell on Emma's shoulders. I called Ann Bumpass, who had the children, and my mother, who took the news tearfully and with great sadness.

Facing the Rosary and funeral in a few days brought the next painful experience. We wore black and were in for a spectacle to behold. Several hundred people, many of whom we had seen just a few short weeks before, gathered to extend condolences. A large, representative group came from the business and political community to show their deep respect for this man who had been their friend. Dad was buried in the mausoleum at Calvary Cemetery and Mom purchased a place beside him.

Leno plunged headlong into the overwhelming tasks ahead, and I submitted, willingly, to all that was expected of me. I wore nothing but black for the next six months, along with Mom and Stella and Emma. We sold our little house in Alhambra, the last vestige of our independence, and moved into Oak Terrace. The property belonged to Leno now.

I only ventured out to do my marketing, and was there with Mom to visit with her many friends that continued to call, expressing their sorrow at her loss. The loss was ours as well. The house was no longer alive with stimulating conversation or competitive motivation, but was quiet, as the laughter and noise of a three-year-old and the demands of an eight-month-old gradually took over.

Mom moved into the little apartment behind the garage. She wanted it that way, but I felt uncomfortable having her live in such a small space,

OAK TERRACE

Anthony's second
birthday party

Anthony's third
birthday party
with Howard, Jr.,
Tony and Pat DeSantis
December 7, 1953

which we had occupied so grudgingly just a few short years before.

Wanting to bring my own individuality into the house, I soon began to make changes. And what I did over the next few years! The small, French windows in the living room became two large picture windows. I replaced the ornate, brocade drapes with modern nylon and removed the Italian marble around the fireplace, installing Palos Verdes stone, popular in the fifties.

We took the statuesque fountain away that was in the lush, fenced patio behind the den, and the exotic plants and flowers, to make room for a play yard for Cory and Anthony. The ornate shrubs were uprooted from the stone planters to house a pile of sand for their myriad of games and make-believe.

The one improvement I wanted to make and didn't was the installation of a security system. The house was isolated, being two hundred feet from the house on the east and separated from the house on the west by a twenty-foot concrete wall. I decided I was being paranoid. No one had security systems in 1951 except gangsters and the extremely wealthy.

Mom watched attentively to my "improvements" without a word of disapproval. How she must have agonized over the changes taking place to her home. When Anthony was two years old, we put him in the beautiful panelled den with the polished parquet floors to play. He threw the pieces of numerous jigsaw puzzles around the room, where they would stay for days while he put them together again. How brilliant we thought he was to do this feat at such an early age. And how quickly he destroyed the polished floor.

Anthony had his first birthday party in the breakfast room overlooking the fountain with all his cousins, aunts, uncles and grandmothers. Cory had birthday parties there, too, and later their parties were held under the huge mulberry tree on the terrace below, while the men stood around in their suits and ties, discussing their business problems. The manicured rose garden that separated us from the house on the east, became Anthony's favorite place to fly through in his superman suit.

Yes, Oak Terrace became a happy place, once again, as we learned, slowly, to live without Dad's direction and to enjoy what he had worked so hard to attain.

When the escrow on our Alhambra house closed, we received five thousand dollars and put it as a down payment on a bayfront house at Beacon Bay in Newport Beach at a purchase price of thirty-two thousand, five hundred dollars. This was a dream come true for me, as I had loved the area since spending time on Balboa at the age of two with Aunt Pearl and Mother, my very earliest memory of life.

We had some difficulty in getting the house, however. We were required to get references from several sources; and we suspected this requirement had something to do with our Italian name—LaBianca. Beacon Bay was, after all, rather "exclusive" and restricted—although, certainly not in writing. Dana, at the time, came through for us. Fortunately, he had settled down momentarily from drifting from east coast to west coast and had a job as shipping manager for California Electric Service in Los Angeles. He wrote a glowing reference!

To afford the payments and upkeep on our furnished, three bedroom house, we had to rent it out to others. From September fifteenth till June fifteenth, we received three hundred dollars a month and during ten weeks of the summer, we received three hundred dollars a week. That's the way it was done at the beach. I loved it at any time of the year, especially the fog that rolled in on a moment's notice. We only got to enjoy it for two weeks in June, however, spending our time cleaning and scrubbing, getting the place ready for the next tenants. But it would be all paid for and ours in twenty years, our escape from Oak Terrace.

2

THE stock of the two corporations, State Wholesale and Gateway Markets, was left in such a way that each of Anthony's three children owned one-third of half of Anthony's interest; the other half being left to the born and unborn grandchildren. Mom owned the remaining half and the controlling interest.

Leno was left no more nor less than his sisters, but he was given the full responsibility, as president of both companies, to guide the businesses through the highly competitive period that was upon them. As the only son, this was his legacy—his obligation.

Leno was barely twenty-six years old when his father died so suddenly. He hadn't completed his college education which was a high priority to him. The new demands on his time weighed heavily on his shoulders almost from the beginning. He threw himself into the task of filling his father's shoes with complete devotion and total frustration. Our relationship began to suffer and deteriorate under the burden, as Leno took on the role that his father had bequeathed him.

I encouraged him to continue to attend night school with me, as I wanted to get my degree and certified public accounting certificate someday, hoping to be of some help to him professionally. Night school kept us together for three semesters at USC, while Mom took care of Cory and Anthony.

Just before Cory was four years old, in the spring of 1952, I enrolled her in Toyland, a pre-school off of Franklin Avenue, a couple of miles from Oak Terrace. She thrived on the social life and her new friends, having no one to play with in our neighborhood except her little brother. Anthony kept himself occupied, being contented to play alone, enjoying the freedom from his older sister. Once a week, he and I waited in the car outside Cory's piano teacher's studio for thirty minutes, while she learned to play "Swaying Silver Birches."

I had missed the chance to help Thomas Dewey in 1948 and I wasn't going to miss the chance to help nominate and elect Dwight D. Eisenhower, "Ike", in 1952. I called the "Young Republican" office in our area and offered my services. I soon became an "area chairman," which meant I had to go door-to-door to make sure that all Republicans were registered. As the chairman, I had to solicit the help of others to assist me. This was a time consuming effort which we sandwiched in between our other numerous activities. Many Saturday nights we spent with Howard and Ann, folding and stapling flyers to be mailed and passed out in my territory. We had great fun, now having something to do on Saturday night other than waiting in long lines at the movie theatres.

Our efforts were not in vain and once we got "Ike" nominated, we worked harder than ever to get him and Nixon elected. The Glendale train depot was the scene of a planned rally for Nixon's arrival and we were there, getting pushed and shoved and ignored. We continued to mail and pass out flyers, but that was our last attempt at attending any "Young Republican" affairs.

We had a party at Oak Terrace on election night, setting up a chalkboard to record the latest results. We were victorious, of course, and felt we had done our part to put into office one of the best Presidents we thought we were ever going to have. I have a certificate of appreciation, signed by "Ike" and "Tricky Dick," a nickname given to Richard M. Nixon, Ike's new Vice President.

Opportunity abounded in Newport Beach in 1953, we thought, but was premature for most to recognize, even the Irvine Company, who controlled most of the land. Across the street from the bridge going to Balboa Island and adjacent to Beacon Bay was a large parcel of vacant land—sand really. We thought it a perfect place for a supermarket and on one of our frequent Saturday evenings with Howard and Ann, we all got quite excited about the idea.

"I can never talk Gateway into a market so far from L.A.," Leno reasoned. "If I can figure out a way to finance it, Howard, maybe you could manage and operate it."

"I've wanted to get out on my own, Leno. This may be the opportunity I've been waiting for."

The rest of the evening was spent working out a plan to present to the Irvine Company and laying out the store. Leno contacted our real estate representative on Balboa Island, Mrs. Maroon, and gave her the offer. We waited impatiently for the answer by telephone.

"The Irvine Company doesn't think the area is ready for a plan like yours, Mr. LaBianca," Mrs. Maroon reported two days later.

That decision had an impact of some magnitude on all four of our lives. Leno's disappointment at not having a market that belonged to him, without the family, went deep, and became a dream forever thwarted. Howard was now discontented at having to work for someone else at State Wholesale and left to open his own store with his brother-in-law, Johnny Bruno, in Torrance. That separated us, Flash and Bumpy now going their separate ways, never again to be the friends they had once been. Twenty years passed before the Irvine Company developed the site with a Safeway supermarket, an extensive row of shops and later a bank.

By the summer of 1953, I had completed all of the classes I could take at night school. The decision had to be made to either go on with my education in earnest, or stay home and be a full-time mother and wife. Anthony would soon be old enough for pre-school, having been ready mentally for several months. That meant the children would be gone all day. I had added Victor Monteleone's upholstery shop and Johnny Smaldino's fish market to my list of illustrious clients and was more determined than ever to be something more than a "bookkeeper." Leno was struggling with the changing situation in the grocery business and the increasing dissension between himself and his brothers-in-law, keeping him away from the house for longer periods. What would my life be as a housewife? I registered to take twelve units in the fall at USC.

After getting the Beacon Bay house ready for the summer tenants in June, we joined Mom and the children on a two-week vacation, stopping first in Las Vegas, going up through Utah to Yellowstone, through Montana, Idaho and Washington to Victoria, British Columbia. State Wholesale received a post card from Yellowstone.

7-22-53

Hello everyone,

Enjoying the beautiful scenery around this place, but there isn't much to do. The kids are getting a kick out of seeing the bears and deer, etc. We had one bear stand up against the side of our car when we were stopped. The kids were scared, but I wasn't—??

Plan to leave for home this afternoon via the coast route. Should be home before long.

Leno L.B.

Returning home after such a relaxing, renewing trip, I began to have second thoughts about going to college on a full-time basis. I would get far ahead of Leno and wouldn't have much time to give to him or our children.

"Maybe I shouldn't try taking all these units," I suggested to Leno when I finally got the children to bed.

"You want to get your degree, honey. If you don't do it now, you'll probably be sorry later. I know it will be hard on us, but if it's what you want, I think you should do it."

3

THE decision to commit myself to getting a college degree changed our lives drastically. The beginning of classes necessitated an exacting and rigid schedule. Our one and only full bathroom became a frantic scene; Leno shaving and planning his day, the children running in and out and I, trying to put myself together to face the young, college crowd. The many veterans returning from the Korean war, continuing their educations, raised some of the age group.

My first class was at nine a.m. and the house was left in a shambles as we all raced out to be on time. Leno went his way, down Rowena to Riverside Drive, through east Los Angeles to the Central Manufacturing District. USC was down Hoover Avenue, almost a straight line to the crowded parking lot, about a half an hour away. Dropping the children off at Toyland was somewhat of a detour, but I managed to arrive on time. To find a parking space behind Bridge Hall took some doing, but we students got so we stopped anywhere, parking space or not. The trick was to find a way to get out when classes were over. The parking lot became a wild scene of frustration as we maneuvered our way through, pushing cars onto the street that impeded our departure.

Most of my classes were in accounting and I was the only woman among boys and men of all description. I became the center of attention, being considered somewhat of a novelty by the students and instructors. I loved it, because as the semester wore on, there was increasingly very little attention being given to me at home.

When classes were over, the USC library was the best place for me to do my homework. And there was plenty of it! After completing a full year, which was not without its nightmarish cramming and memorizing, the frustration and challenges left me drained.

Leno was in another world. His problems were mounting with the business, as he struggled to expand to keep up with the competition. He was under increasing stress on the job and seemed to be growing totally discontented at home.

I picked the children up from Toyland at three-thirty in the afternoon, rushing home to straighten the house and prepare dinner. Leno found fault with the hurriedly prepared meals and flew into a rage if we didn't have soup, or his favorite ice cream was not in the refrigerator. When the children were finally in bed, usually by eight-thirty, there was studying to do and bookkeeping for the three clients I had kept to help pay my tuition.

Leno became bored and restless, watching television by himself. He had stopped taking classes at night when I started on a full-time basis and joined another bowling league, first one night a week, then two. On other nights, he left to go to the movies, he said. He became so involved without me that when I did have a free evening, he had made other plans.

He seemed totally confused as to what he wanted from me. He continued to encourage me to keep on with my studies, but he now made it clear that he didn't want me to ever work for him.

I never knew why he was so against my becoming a part of his business world. As my knowledge increased, I know I could have been a support which he probably needed. But for some unknown reason, he chose to shut me out.

There were no more endearing cards and flowers, only tenderness when it suited his purpose. We had our "moments," but they were few and far between. Had I been older and wiser and less sensitive, I might have understood what he was going through. But I was deeply hurt by his attitude and turned away from him, consumed with the idea of having my own career.

The certified public accounting exam seemed impossible to attain. Professor Devine of USC said, "It can be had. It can be had," as if it were some distant, exalted goal that only a few could reach, and women almost never.

With determination to take the exam and pass, I signed up for the one to be given in November of 1954. Staying away from classes for two weeks, I studied the questions and answers from previous exams, working problems that were likely to appear this time. One of my best friends at college, Howard Smith, was also sitting for the exam and we studied together, via the telephone.

On Wednesday afternoon, the day for the first leg of the exam, I met Howard for a martini, which we thought would calm us down for the ordeal ahead.

"I'm probably the oldest person to sit for this exam, Howard. Today is my birthday and I'm thirty years old. What a way to spend a birthday."

Handball Champions
Circa 1955

"You sure don't look thirty, Alice. Besides, there are a lot of guys a lot older than that, coming back for the third or fourth time," he answered encouragingly.

We walked two blocks to the Pasadena Civic Auditorium, where the exam was being held. Walking onto the large dance floor, now set up with tables and chairs, brought a pang of sadness and very nearly tears, as I remembered the happy times I had had there with Leno "What am I doing here without Leno? What has happened to us? When did I lose him?" I asked myself as I settled down to try to think and write.

The next morning, at eight a.m., which started a full eight hours of concentration, there were no martinis, only total devotion to the challenge. Then, on Friday, another full eight hour day of law and accounting theory. As suddenly as it started, it was over and Howard and I had another martini to celebrate its conclusion. We were relaxed and happy that we had completed the task. Two months would pass before we knew the results.

Leno seemed proud of me and bragged to Howard and Ann how smart I was, on one of our infrequent Saturday night get-togethers.

"Well, I haven't passed yet," I responded, humbly. "If I don't pass, I think I'll give up the whole idea and settle down to being a better mother and a devoted wife," I laughed, looking at Leno for a sign that he still cared. For the first time in months, he looked at me with tenderness. I felt good again, happy and contented.

We were planning our usual Christmas buffet and invited Aunt Pearl and Uncle Austin of Palm Springs fame to come to Oak Terrace. My mother's brother, Jack, had also invited them for Christmas dinner, but they chose to come to our house. This infuriated Uncle Jack and we became the envy of the entire family!

Uncle Austin's health had failed miserably since I had seen him last. Aunt Pearl had to feed him and help him walk, leading him everywhere. He didn't talk at all, only smiled. Aunt Pearl was her usual self, arrogant and domineering. When they were ready to leave and her driver hadn't returned from his visit with friends in south central Los Angeles, she was on the telephone to the police.

"This is Pearl McManus of Palm Springs," she announced in her own incomparable way. This meant nothing to the officer on the other end, but that didn't bother her. She knew who she was and thought everyone else in the world knew who she was, too.

We had a short time of anxiety about her car and driver, but he finally arrived in one piece, and sober. Off they went, after Aunt Pearl gave her usual, gracious words of appreciation for the hospitality we had shown her in our beautiful home. She was impressed.

We never saw Uncle Austin again. His health continued to fail, and later we heard that he was seen wandering aimlessly down Palm Canyon Drive in Palm Springs, when he could get away from Aunt Pearl's watchful eye, handing out one-hundred dollar bills to passers-by. He died quietly in the spring of 1955, leaving Aunt Pearl alone.

Throughout the month of December, Leno and I had a short-lived happiness that faded in and out intermittently. We had moments of ecstatic passion and hours of wild disagreements. He was home only long enough to eat and sleep and find fault. I couldn't go on like this, but I didn't know what to do. I turned to Unity and God for guidance. The answer came, totally out of my control, it seemed—it all just happened.

Living at Oak Terrace had become a nightmare for me, as Leno's absences became more frequent. The house frightened me, especially at night. I don't know why. I had lived here all during Leno's absence in the war, not ever concerned if the doors were locked, and felt no fear. Since moving in after Dad's death, I had sat up in the chair in the living room many times after Leno and the children were asleep, afraid to close my eyes, jumping at every noise. On one such occasion, it suddenly came to me... "We must leave this house. But how can I tell Mom that I'm afraid to live here? How can I tell her that her son seems terribly unhappy here?"

Pete Smaldino, for all of his capricious behavior, seemed to understand about the house. He had asked Mom why she insisted that we live there. Her views hadn't changed. "This is our home. Anthony wanted it that way. This was our plan."

I decided to discuss my problem with her after confronting Leno, who reacted differently than I expected.

"I feel a foreboding about this place, Leno. I want to take the children and leave."

"I'll find you an apartment," he answered without an argument. "I don't want to stay here without you. I'll find one for myself, too. I need some time alone."

"I don't understand what has happened to Leno," I told Mom when I announced my decision to move. "Sometimes he acts like he hates me, and he's so critical. I just can't take it anymore."

"His father was like that a lot, Alice," she confided. "But I never thought of leaving him. Are you sure that's what you have to do?"

"We're both miserable and it's hard on the children. Besides, Leno wants his own apartment and you can have your house to live in again."

"I understand. Maybe, if you're separated awhile, you'll look at it differently." Mom didn't try to talk me out of it, either, as I thought she would. Perhaps, Pete's interference had made her realize how I felt.

In January, we left Oak Terrace, which was more difficult than I had anticipated. Mom looked sad and down-hearted as the children and I drove away, although she did nothing to try to stop us. I hated leaving her there alone.

We moved to a two-bedroom apartment on Talmadge Avenue, only a few blocks from Oak Terrace, off of Franklin Avenue. Leno's apartment was close by on Los Feliz Boulevard and he seemed relieved. Our apartment was big enough to include Leno, but he stayed with us only on occasion, preferring his newly-found freedom.

Unpacking was a tiresome chore and I wasn't feeling any too peppy when Leno called to give me the news.

"Your notice came from the Board of Accountancy. Shall I open it?" he asked with a laugh.

"Leno, if I didn't pass, that's it. I'm not going to go back to USC until you can go with me. Now, please, read what it says!"

"Auditing... B. Commercial Law... B. Theory... B," he started, then hesitated. "Are you ready? Practice... B. Alice, you made it!" he concluded excitedly.

"I actually passed. I can't believe it!" I exclaimed and, half to myself, "I guess it was meant to be."

Then I dropped the bombshell. "Leno, I think we may have another problem here. Or, at least, I have a problem. I'm not sure, but I think I'm pregnant."

4

"PERHAPS this will bring you back together again," Mom told Leno when she heard the news. Leno was upset. He had enough stress in his life without adding this additional responsibility.

By June, I would be six units away from getting my degree in accounting. If being pregnant didn't bring Leno back to us "all the way," I knew it was more important than ever that I go on with my career. When I faced that reality, I hated what I was doing. Having a choice was one thing, but now that it seemed a necessity, getting my degree lost most of its appeal.

I swallowed my pride and suggested to Leno that he move back in with us, that I still loved him and needed him with the new life that was active within me.

"Alice, you're a wonderful Mother," he began, "but a terrible wife. I can't give up what I have now for these children. Someday, they'll have their own lives, and I must have mine!"

He was cold and unfeeling and I felt lost and alone, not understanding what I had done to alienate him so.

The ensuing months were busy ones, passing quickly. Rather than wear typical maternity clothes, I purchased larger sizes and my college friends just thought I was eating too much. I completed the semester discreetly.

Leno provided our every financial need, always taking me out to dinner on Saturday night, sometimes with Howard and Ann. I was busy in the evenings during the week with my homework, having given up all of my bookkeeping clients. I had finally gotten beyond that demeaning task and was close to becoming the professional person I had planned to be. The children were having fun at school and seeing Leno on the weekends, not noticing that our lives were any different, which was the way we wanted it.

The "big eight" accounting firms signed up their recruits well in advance of graduation. I had met all of the top personnel people at the annual meetings of Beta Alpha Psi, the accounting fraternity which I had joined at USC. In the fall of 1954, before I took the exam, they were all on campus to pick the "cream of the crop" graduating in the summer of 1955.

Jack Larsen, a friend in Beta Alpha Psi, had graduated in 1954 with a 4.0 grade point average, passing the exam in the spring. He had gone to work for Arthur Young & Company, the best of the "big eight," according to Jack. Don Gamble and Charlie Gillette were their representatives on campus in the fall and, like everyone else, I had an interview with them. They were friendly and likeable, with a keen sense of humor, I thought. It would be great working for a firm that wasn't stodgy or stuffy, the typical accountant profile. Jack had praised me so highly to them that they were anxious to meet me.

"Yes, we hire women. In fact a woman with your grades in accounting comes highly recommended," Charlie announced cheerfully.

"The other advantage to our hiring you is that you are mature and have already had your family," chimed in Don.

They made two offers of employment, Howard Smith and myself, offering us each a starting salary of three hundred and twenty-five dollars a month. I was delighted with my offer, but Howard decided to go with Arthur Andersen, another of the "big eight," because they offered him twenty-five dollars a month more than Arthur Young had. Arthur Andersen didn't hire women for the audit staff, and in my interview with them, they asked me if I could type. I answered emphatically, "No!"

In March I went on my tour of the Arthur Young offices in the General Petroleum Building at Sixth and Flower Streets in downtown Los Angeles. I was in the most difficult period of my pregnancy, feeling that at any moment I would lose my breakfast. But I got through the tour and the luncheon at the men-only Jonathan Club without an accident and agreed to join their staff on October first. I also got through the day without anyone knowing I was three months pregnant.

I went along with all these preliminaries, secretly hoping that when my promised starting date of October first rolled around, I would somehow get out of the commitment. Since I was the only student from USC that passed all four parts of the exam in the fall, I was in demand, I thought, and could write my own ticket.

When school was out in June, I headed for Beacon Bay to perform my usual chores and enjoy the beach with the children. I was feeling wonderful and eagerly awaiting our new arrival in September. Leno joined us on the two weekends we had down there, and what wonderful weekends they turned out to be. He relaxed and became, for a while, the man I loved so much, once again.

We had dinner at The Castaways, a rustic steak and lobster house on the hill overlooking the bay, with Hank and Toady, who now lived on Balboa Island. Very soon after, The Castaways burned down and has never been replaced.

Howard and Ann came down that June, too, and brother Dana and our good friend, David Woehrle. He was our favorite artist and many of his oils and watercolors had graced our home on Waverly Drive and now my apartment on Talmadge.

In between swims in the bay, we scrubbed and cleaned the house, getting it ready for the summer tenants. We headed back to our estranged life in the city, not knowing that was to be our last visit to Beacon Bay together.

Leno changed when we came back and I seldom saw him. He stopped taking me out to dinner on Saturday nights and became more involved in his bowling. Visibly pressured under the burden of conflicting interests in the businesses, he rarely told me what was actually going on or the problems he was having, but when I did see him, he seemed stressed almost beyond endurance. I loved him more deeply than ever and was pained and unhappy that he didn't confide in me. But I was as independent as my mother had been, and my pride made me arrogant and stubborn.

The summer was long and hot. That September was the hottest on record and I was still wearing my high heels, swollen ankles and all. For a while, the doctor thought I would have twins, but determined I was only going to have one, big baby, probably a boy.

On September twentieth, the baby became impatient, although it had another week to go, according to the doctor. Leno had a crucial game to bowl that evening, but consented to drive me to the California Hospital, for the fourth time. But on this occasion, he didn't stay.

Having babies must have been my reason for being here, because whether it was due to the efficiency of Dr. Webb or my natural instincts, it was my happiest time of life. This most precious, contented, happy baby arrived during the night as I slept and Leno bowled.

Having fulfilled our duties toward the grandparents for names, we were free to name our beautiful little girl a name of our choosing. I wanted a name that started with "L" and chose Louise, giving her the middle name of the grandmother I had never known, May McCallum.

Leno called in the morning to see how I was feeling and came to visit

BEACON BAY

With Leno,
David Woehrle,
Anthony and Cory

Ann, Howard,
Leno, Howard, Jr.,
Cory, Anthony

us in between other engagements. He dutifully arrived to take us back to our apartment at the appointed time, but seemed troubled and uncomfortable. He avoided giving us much attention.

"Isn't she precious, Leno?" I asked as he was getting ready to leave us in the capable hands of the nurse, Miss Clark, who had taken care of Cory and Anthony and was now going to take care of all of us.

"I don't plan to get attached to her," he answered quickly.

"We really should have another one in a couple of years to make it an even four," I chided.

"You can find another stud for that," he snapped, not amused at my suggestion.

5

LOUISE had arrived one week early, the twenty-first of September, which gave me nine days to prepare myself for my new job at Arthur Young. I called A.Y. (as Arthur Young is known to all accountants) and asked for Bob Safford, who was now their personnel director, since Don Gamble had moved into a higher position.

"This is Alice LaBianca," I started. "I was scheduled to start work on the first of October."

"Yes, Alice, I've heard all about you," Bob answered with the same feeling of camaraderie I had felt with Charlie Gillette and Don Gamble.

"Would it be all right if I didn't start until December first? We're planning to move and I need more time to get settled," I lied.

"That will be just fine, Alice. We probably wouldn't have much work for you until then, anyway," he answered agreeably.

Leno made an honest woman out of me by finding a house in Burbank for us. He had decided the apartment was not the proper place for a mother with three children. Burbank was a suburb in the hot, hot San Fernando Valley, about ten miles from Oak Terrace. The house was cute, but small and had three units beyond the driveway in the rear, which left us very little yard. The arrangement was good from a financial standpoint, but gave me the added responsibility of keeping the apartments rented. If I had no vacancies, my mortgage payments would be met.

Leno had paid thirty-two thousand, five hundred dollars for it, but I had to agree to sell our house in Beacon Bay.

"We can't handle that responsibility anymore with you going to work full-time. The land lease has only seventeen years to go and we can always buy a better house at the beach later, if you want to."

Leno's argument was convincing. The city of Newport Beach had given a Mr. Beek a forty-year lease to develop the some fifty acres of waterfront sand and we had been concerned when we bought the house as to whether the lease would be extended in 1972. Besides, I did have

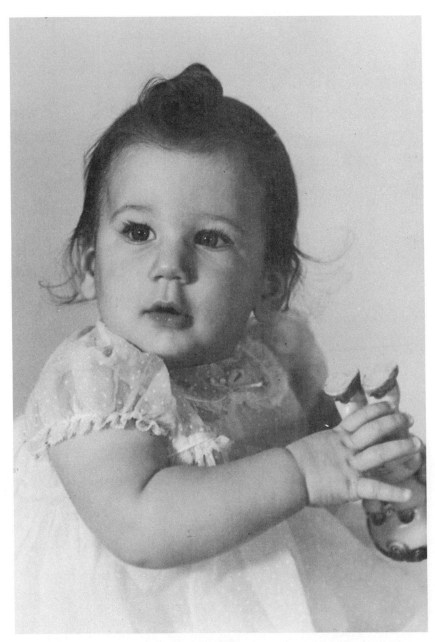

Louise

the next two years cut out for me and didn't need any more to do.

We sold our bayfront home sitting on the sandy beach with the bay window, fireplace, three bedrooms and garage apartment, with an expansive view of the myriad of boats of all sizes cruising by and envying our position, for thirty-seven thousand, five hundred dollars. When the escrow closed, we received fifteen thousand dollars in cash which Leno gave to me to invest, my first venture into the stock market.

I had six more units to take at USC before I could get my accounting degree. I planned to take three in the fall and three in the spring, getting my diploma in June of 1956—twelve years after graduating from Franklin. I enrolled in the insurance class three weeks late, and when I told the instructor my baby was only four weeks old, he was somewhat shocked but made a concerted effort to help me catch up with the rest of the class.

Nothing was interfering with my starting date at A.Y. and the thought of going to work in an environment so sophisticated scared me. The idea of leaving my new baby with Miss Clark, although she had been with us since Louise's birth, left me terrified. But off I went when Louise was barely two months old.

Don Gamble grinned when my insurance papers revealed that I had three children instead of the two he thought I had.

"When did you find time to do that?" he asked good-naturedly.

"I thought I'd fit that one in before getting started on my career," I laughed.

"You sure put that one over on us," he retorted.

I soon settled in to the routine of the staff room. Coffee breaks were precisely at nine a.m. and three p.m. in the large coffee room on the third floor of the General Petroleum Building. A variety of personalities was represented throughout the staff of men, but they were all, almost without exception, comedians. Bob Newhart, who had been an accountant, was just beginning to make a name for himself, but he didn't have anything on these characters. They were all friendly and kept me laughing most of my first day. My fear of a sophisticated atmosphere soon disappeared.

I was the only female on the audit staff, which they came to ignore on the professional level, but their jokes concerning my gender never stopped as they ran in and out of the staff room, being called by the seniors and managers into their offices for instructions. The second day Bob Safford informed me that I had been assigned to the Pacific Finance semi-annual audit. Their offices were located on the next block and that's where I spent the next two months.

My paycheck was just enough to pay Miss Clark and was all taxable, since there were no child-care tax credits in 1955. Leno provided private school educations for Cory and Anthony and their school busses picked them up each morning in front of the house and delivered them; Cory's to the Isabelle Buckley School in the San Fernando Valley and Anthony's to the Black-Foxe Military Academy in Hollywood.

Almost immediately, I was put on a sixty-hour week, working until ten, three nights a week, and all day Saturday. The children's clothes were lined up in the living room before I went to bed each night and I left before their busses arrived in the morning to make it to Pacific Finance by eight a.m. Louise had to stay home with a parade of nurses, as Miss Clark soon became tired of her extended schedule, but Louise grew happily and was a joy to greet at the end of a long day.

Leno was there if we needed him and usually spent the weekends with us. The A.Y. Christmas party was coming up and I asked him to go with me. The party was gala and the evening fun as I introduced him to most of the new crop of "juniors" that I worked with, as well as my favorite "senior," Ed Lamb. He was the illustrious senior on the Pacific Finance audit who had become a certified public accountant by an act of Congress. He had gone to USC and was a brilliant student—his reputation preceding him on the job. He was all business when instructing us "knuckleheads" on audit procedures, but as soon as he led his four or five juniors off of the tenth floor of the Pacific Finance Building and down the elevator, he became a veritable comic, allowing us to poke fun at him, returning our witticisms with humorous rebuttals. His wife, Vaughn, was an equal delight, joining in the jokes and laughter as if one of us, telling a few of her own.

Bill Findley, a junior I had met only casually at staff meetings, stood out as the life of the party and insisted on buying drinks for Leno and me when the party was otherwise over. We joined him, and he and Leno liked each other immediately, although they had clearly opposite personalties. Leno was quiet, serious and reserved while Bill was affable, loose and noisy. Very few who met Bill Findley were unable to succumb to his Irish charm and our evening ended in a festive spirit.

Leno had been negotiating to sell the wholesale grocery business. The retail markets needed to expand if they were going to keep abreast of the changing grocery picture. The wholesale business was becoming increasingly competitive and the net margin was dwindling. Leno decided to sell the operation to A.M. Lewis and keep the building in Vernon, leasing it to an egg producer. He took me on a tour of the new facility, the "candling" of the eggs and the grading, which took place on a moving belt running through most of the warehouse. Leno seemed happy with his new arrangement, feeling he could now concentrate on the retail stores.

He reiterated that he didn't want to become too attached to Louise, but he had difficulty when she smiled at him and ran to greet him when he visited. Several attempts were made at a reconciliation as we double dated with some of Leno's new-found friends. I felt left out as they talked and joked about events I knew nothing of. My pride and my independence were getting in the way as I strived to feel close once again to this man I had loved so intensely. But I had found a new life with new goals and new friends. I was a different person, no longer content to live in the shadow of a man and his dreams.

We might have worked it all out, somehow, but our little house in Burbank was too small. We looked for a larger one, knowing we couldn't go back to Oak Terrace and we thought we had found our dream house on the top of a hill in North Hollywood. We made an offer, but Robert Wagner and Natalie Wood had just put a deposit on it, the real estate agent said. Our house-hunting ended as Leno became engrossed in expansion and I became a "heavy" junior.

My next assignment was a manufacturer in a dingy building in west Los Angeles. Pulling files to verify signatures and dates, with no help and no colleagues to have fun with, was not my idea of progressing. I hated it! Why was I doing this? After a miserable week, seeing no end in sight, I feigned sickness and called Leno.

"Can you meet me for lunch?" I started, then couldn't go on.

"What's wrong, Alice?" There was concern in his voice.

"Oh, Leno, I'm so sick of this job. Couldn't we make a go of it if I quit?"

We had lunch together and Leno seemed happy that I needed him again. "I'll give my notice next week," I promised.

"I've decided to go ahead with the hernia operation I've been needing," he then announced. "But as soon as that's behind me, we'll find a bigger house. I'm tired of being alone, and I miss you and the children. We can make a go of it, Alice, if we really work at it."

Leno moved out of his apartment and into Oak Terrace with his mother after getting through the operation without too much difficulty. He was recuperating when I joined them for dinner one night on my way home from work.

"I've decided to go to staff school before I quit my job at A.Y.," I announced. "It's required of all first year juniors," I began to explain, noticing the hurt in Leno's eyes. "That way, I will have completed the first phase of my apprenticeship if I want to get back into it later. I've come this far, I think I can stand two more weeks," I laughed.

"Yes, that sounds like a good idea," Leno agreed reluctantly, while Mom looked on with quiet sadness.

As I left to go home, Leno and Mom came to the back doorstep to wave goodbye. What a terrified, ominous feeling I had, all of a sudden, as they stood there. I was frightened at the thought of their isolation, and I knew I could never live in this house again. I don't know why, but I had a feeling of doom as I drove down the steep driveway.

6

THE first session of staff school at A.Y. in June promised to be fun, as well as technically rewarding. Most of the other students had completed their first year, but, of course, I had gotten a late start. We ranged in age from twenty-two to thirty-one, I being the oldest and the only female, but I held my own with the rest of them as I had throughout my first six months. The sessions were stimulating, the lunches were riotous and the time passed quickly, in spite of the grueling homework.

Mike Donahue, a "heavy senior" of some stature, was our instructor during most of the sessions, but the partner in charge of our office, Alan Petch, made an appearance as well as Charlie Gillette, who was quickly moving up in the firm. Alan Petch was a charming, distinguished gentleman who had put me at ease since our first meeting at my Beta Alpha Psi initiation at USC. These men were an inspiration to all of us, who were still involved in the demeaning tasks that are the junior accountant's burden.

"You men and lady," Alan Petch started, smiling in my direction, "have come through the most difficult time you will encounter in the profession. You are now ready to embark on a rewarding and lucrative career. You will be required to take new, additional responsibilities as 'semi-seniors' and on some assignments, as 'seniors.' You are the 'cream of the crop' in the accounting profession, having 'graduated' from your first staff school with an excellent performance. I want to wish the best of luck to all of you as you now start your careers in earnest."

We were being treated to lunch at the Jonathan Club. On my first visit here over a year ago, I had to eat in the ladies' dining room, but, on this occasion, I was smuggled quickly up the back stairway and into the men's dining room and seated next to Bill Findley.

Bill was six feet two with blue eyes, a boyish face and blonde, somewhat unruly hair. He was called "Wild Bill" by the audit staff and he tried hard to live up to his reputation. I found him fun to be with, as did most everyone, his presence making staff school an exciting and

Bill Findley

happy place to be. When caught off guard, Bill showed a serious and introspective side that I found intriguing. He had showered me with attention almost from the beginning, making me feel important and special. The fact that I was the only female in the group to flirt with, didn't enter my mind.

"We're having our picture taken after lunch," I reminded him, as he seemed preoccupied.

"I can't make it," he said quickly. "I'm leaving on vacation."

I stood with twelve of the "graduates" and Mike Donahue to smile for the camera, but Bill couldn't delay his vacation one hour to be in the picture. I was disappointed. The picture just didn't seem complete without Bill Findley.

Staff school renewed my ambition to become what I had set out to become—a certified public accountant.

"After all, Leno," I started, knowing my decision wouldn't make him too happy, "the worst is over and my work should get more interesting now. In a year and a half, I'll have my certificate."

"You're different, Alice," Leno observed. "What happened to you in the past two weeks? I don't think you need me anymore."

"Yes, I do. It's just that all my work seems wasted if I don't finish. If I don't do it now, I never will."

The children and I stayed on in Burbank, Leno moved out of Oak Terrace into another apartment, close to where he had been before, and I went back to A.Y. with a new determination.

Monthly A.Y. staff meetings were held in the evening at the Los Angeles Athletic Club where, following the technical session, we had an open bar for an hour. The "happy hour" was in full swing at the July meeting when, suddenly, Bill came bounding up to the bar with enthusiasm. He found his way to my side and when we were called to dinner, he led me to a table. Bob Safford's task before eating was to go around the room of some seventy men and me and attempt to remember and pronounce each person's name. This was usually a spirited event and one we all looked forward to. Bob managed to complete this feat without error, and the kibitzing from the audience, as he searched his memory in hesitation, was more hilarious than any television comedy. A speaker followed dinner and Bill walked me to my car, parked some five blocks from the office and we talked.

"Did you have a nice vacation?" I asked.

"Yes," he answered, thoughtfully.

"How about a night cap?" I asked, suddenly, not wanting to end the evening so abruptly.

"You're married, aren't you?" he asked.

"Leno and I have been separated for over a year," I answered, honestly.

"He seems like such a great guy, Alice. I don't want to get in the way."

"I'm getting a divorce," I answered quickly.

At that, he ushered me to his rather dilapidated 1950 Plymouth and we were on our way, heading we knew not where. He took my hand and his introspective mood came upon him. The conversation was sparse, but the sparks were flying. "What am I getting myself into?" I thought, as we silently continued down Wilshire Boulevard, past the Wilshire Hotel and Dr. Webb's office.

Bill Findley came into my life with a suddenness, out of nowhere, really. His obvious interest in me went straight to my heart. I must have been terribly vulnerable. I had loved Leno with an unexplainable intensity since I was fourteen years old, through good times and bad. In the weeks that followed, I fell in love with a man five years my junior, whose only common ground with mine was that he was also an accountant. Being a UCLA graduate, his thinking was more liberal and was to become a serious point of disagreement between us.

I found myself, almost automatically, applying for our often-delayed divorce. I received my interlocutory decree from Leno in November and set about to win Bill's heart completely.

It wasn't easy. He enjoyed his bachelorhood with enthusiasm and wasn't about to commit himself to a divorcee with three children. He had joined the staff at A.Y. at the same time as I, after serving two years in Germany in the Army. His big ambition, which had been realized, was to be assigned to the Guam audit, and he was scheduled to go in June of 1957 for a two-month stay. That's all he talked about on our frequent Saturday night dates after my divorce from Leno, which, of course, took one year to be final under California law.

"Leno wants to buy us a bigger house," I told Bill one Saturday night. "He hasn't been able to find anything here in the valley. The prices are a little out of reach for the kind of house he wants us to have."

"*I've* always wanted to live in La Canada," Bill answered. "When I was in high school in Glendale, some of my best friends lived there, and I thought it was really beautiful."

The next day, I suggested to Leno that he try looking in La Canada. Not more than a week later he called to say he had found a big house there for forty-two thousand, five hundred dollars.

"It's on an acre of land," he said enthusiastically. "It only has two bedrooms and maid's quarters, but we can add on another bedroom and enlarge the family room. It will be perfect for you and the children, Alice, and there's plenty of room for me, if you ever want it that way."

We went to see it together and talked about how it could be expanded. Nestled in the foothills of the Angeles Crest Mountains, the view was beautiful and an acre of land afforded several possibilities. Descanso Drive was one of the most prestigious streets in the area, rural but sophisticated. Leno engaged a contractor before the escrow closed to start the remodeling and placed the first mortgage to exist on Oak Terrace to make the down payment and pay for the remodeling. I was to start making the monthly payments when I moved in, which would be in about six months, the time it would take to complete the improvements.

When the remodeling was well underway, I took Bill to see the house. "This will be a real nice place for you and the children," he said thoughtfully. "Maybe when your children are grown up, *we* can get together."

The Pacific Finance audit was in full swing in January of 1957 when a new junior arrived on the scene, Chuck Van Arman. Chuck was tall, dark and handsome, and being unattached, became an interesting prospect, since Bill was being so "hard to get." Chuck was quiet and thoughtful, with expressive, penetrating eyes that caught mine on more than one occasion. He joined into the camaraderie on the job almost immediately.

The following staff meeting became more interesting when Chuck's attentiveness went unnoticed by Bill, who was playing the "bon vivant," and showing his independence by going off with friends after dinner, excluding me. I quickly tagged along with Chuck and others to our favorite spot, the Cask and Cleaver.

"My car's in the garage, who can give me a lift home?" Chuck asked when we were getting ready to leave. I offered quickly, grasping the opportunity to get better acquainted.

That started a series of Friday night dates with Chuck, who took me anywhere and everywhere I wanted to go, always being the perfect gentleman—a real-live Cary Grant.

My weekends became rather hectic—Friday night with Chuck, Saturday night with Bill and Sundays with Leno and the children. Bill continued to talk excitedly about Guam, and many Saturday nights were spent at the airport, looking at the huge airplanes that took passengers to far away places where Bill longed to travel one day.

By April I was concerned how it would all end. I knew I couldn't keep this deception up much longer. Bill didn't know I was seeing Chuck, Chuck didn't know I was seeing Bill and A.Y. didn't know I was seeing anyone. I became confused, not really knowing what I wanted.

Fate stepped in again. The "happy hour" at our April staff meeting was just about over when dinner was announced. Chuck came toward me, put his arm over my shoulder, and led me into the dining room and the chair next to his. We had fun with Bob Safford's trying to name all the members of the staff, which had increased in difficulty since the merger with Marty Samuelson's firm. After the usual speaker boredom, we broke up and headed for the Cask and Cleaver, Chuck and Bill both being in the entourage. Bill lost out to Chuck in the seating arrangement, and as we drank and talked, Bill kept trying to get my attention. When Chuck had to step out for a minute, Bill came anxiously over and said he had to see me afterwards.

We took both cars to Burbank and when we were alone in his car in front of my house he said, "Alice, I want you to marry me."

"This is rather sudden, isn't it?" asking the obvious question.

"When I saw you with Chuck tonight, I thought I was going to lose you," he explained. "I've just come to my senses."

"What about Guam and all of your dreams of traveling?" I asked.

"I don't care about that. I only care about you. I love your children and I love you."

I found myself trying to talk him out of it. I was having fun just as it was and didn't want to make any decisions. But Bill had made up his mind and his persistence settled the matter.

"I have a date with Chuck on Friday night. What shall I do about that?" I asked, ready to turn everything over to Bill.

"You'll have to get yourself out of that one," he laughed.

I called Chuck the next morning and reluctantly cancelled our upcoming Friday night date, not giving him any explanation.

As our planned wedding day approached, I began to question my decision. Howard Smith and I had stayed close friends and had lunch together frequently.

"Maybe I've made a mistake, Howard. Bill seems so independent, I wonder if he really needs me. Chuck was so attentive and more conservative, like Leno was."

Howard laughed. "You weren't too happy with a conservative man. I think you need a change. Bill is really a great guy, Alice."

With this succinct advice, I threw "caution to the winds" and on June fifteenth in Reno, Nevada, Bill and I were married by a Justice of The Peace, with strangers as witnesses. He had "swept me off my feet" before I had time to realize what was happening.

Leno's mother agreed to take care of the children for me—Cory, nine, Anthony, six and Louise, two. As soon as we were married and on our way to Lake Louise in the Canadian Rockies, I missed the children so much I wanted to turn back. "Why didn't Leno talk me out of this?" I wondered.

7

THE Korean war had come to an end in 1953. President Eisenhower fulfilled his campaign promise by ending the war with terms which reflected his belief that "unlimited war in the nuclear age was unimaginable, and limited war unwinnable." But U.N. Commander General Mark W. Clark, appointed in April 1952, signed the armistice with a heavy heart. He, like MacArthur, believed that the war should have been carried to the Chinese mainland, eliminating Beijing as a permanent threat to U.S. interests in Asia—the price of a draw in Korea would be trouble in the future. He admonished, "I have grave misgivings that some day my countrymen will be forced to pay a far higher price in blood than it would have cost if the decision had been made to defeat the Communists in Korea."

But we were glad to have the war ended. Our men were being sacrificed for a cause the politicians refused to support with an all-out effort. If we couldn't exert sufficient pressure on China to win the war, we wanted our boys to come home. And those who survived did come home, beginning a decade that history would later prove to be one of the most resilient and bountiful in the twentieth century.

By 1955 the Salk polio vaccine put our minds at rest concerning this most dreaded disease. Mortgage interest rates were in the 5 percent range and homes were being built in sufficient numbers so that young couples could afford to buy them without mothers having to leave home to work. The average family could afford a new automobile every two or three years and enjoy a vacation in it at an uncrowded resort.

Of course, Khrushchev promised to "bury the United States" and there were the usual war clouds in the Mideast; the threat of atomic warfare seemed a real possibility and Ike had to enforce school desegregation by the use of U.S. troops—events that were in the background of our fruitful existence.

Leno's decision to sell the wholesale grocery business was a wise one. The advent of the supermarket in the grocery industry greatly increased competition for the smaller stores that were State Wholesale's lifeline. The margin of profit to the wholesaler was so small that he depended heavily on ever-increasing volume. The demands of the retail business were great as Gateway sought to compete by remodeling and expanding. The local newspaper reported the following:

GATEWAY MARKETS OPEN NEW STORE NEXT MONTH

From a humble beginning in a little thirty foot grocery store at 1527 Cypress Avenue, Los Angeles, Gateway Markets have grown in thirty-seven years to an expanding food chain with modern supermarkets in the San Gabriel Valley area, Monterey Park and the Los Angeles metropolitan area; with a new store to be opened in La Habra in August.

A. LaBianca and his wife, Corina, ran their little Cypress Avenue store from 1922 to 1930. As they prospered each year, plans for other stores developed in their minds. Since expansion would require capital and more people to operate the growing business, Mr. and Mrs. LaBianca took in Sam LaBianca, Sam Bruno, Ray Natale and Vito Luizzi as partners. These were the original stockholders in the corporation formed in 1930.

Today the Gateway Markets are headed by Leno LaBianca, son of the founder. The executive staff also includes Peter R. Smaldino, vice-president and general sales manager; Peter J. De Santis, secretary and personnel director; Joseph M. Cimarusti, produce buyer; Joseph C. Arnone, liquor and delicatessen supervisor; Joseph P. Renna, advertising and warehouse manager; James V. Sciarra, meat buyer and supervisor; Ray Norwood, office manager and Ray Natale, produce supervisor. Sam LaBianca, one of the original stockholders, is now honorary president.

Success of the markets should be attributed in large part to the philosophy of the founder, according to president Leno LaBianca. "My father's idea was always to give good value, good service and satisfaction," LaBianca declares.

"Today, more than ever, we know that this is a good philosophy for any business, and certainly not the least of the contributions made by my father and mother throughout the years. They always concentrated on giving more quality for less money, and giving it in a friendly atmosphere. We keep these ideals before us, and want Gateway Markets always to mean service, friendliness, satisfaction and value to our customers. Our

ARTHUR YOUNG AND COMPANY
1956 Staff School
Sans Bill Findley

Another Gateway Market
Top Row, second from left: Uncle Sam LaBianca;
on right, Pete Smaldino

Maurine

sincerest thanks to all our wonderful customers in Los Angeles, Monterey Park and the San Gabriel Valley for making our rapid expansion possible; and our continuing pledge to give the same good service to our new customers in La Habra."

The rapid expansion of Gateway Markets brought additional problems for Leno. He needed some help in the management services area and I recommended A.Y., of course.

Don Gamble was now a partner in the firm and I told him of Leno's requirements. Since the days at USC, Don had been one of my favorite people. Gateway became a large client for A.Y., but I never received more than a thank you from Don. I also heard that when he found out that Bill and I were married, six months after the event, he laughed and said, "So, that's who she hooked." So much for favorite people.

Bill and I kept our marriage a secret at A.Y. My two year apprenticeship was to be completed in December 1957 and I was afraid they wouldn't let me stay on as Bill's wife. On December second, I called Bob Safford.

"Will you be sending my experience record to the Board of Accountancy now, Bob? I think my two years is up. I don't know how I made it, but I did."

"Yes, Alice, everything is cleared. You haven't been on many inventory observations, but we feel that the one in November will qualify you. Congratulations."

"It's only taken me fifteen years," I laughed. "One more thing, Bob. I guess I should have my correct name on the certificate. I'm Alice Findley, now. Bill and I were married last June and I'm expecting a baby in May."

"You're just full of surprises, aren't you? Does that mean you'll be staying home now?"

"Oh, no, I'm going on with my career. I've worked too long to get this far, to quit now," I answered emphatically.

My certified public accounting certificate is dated December 2, 1957. In January of 1958, Leno got his Bachelor of Science degree from USC in finance and in May, I had my fourth child, Maurine Ann Findley.

When I returned to A.Y. to pursue my career, six weeks after Maurine was born, Bob Safford asked me if I wanted to go into the tax department.

"Our clients haven't objected to you on most jobs, Alice, but you will advance more quickly and be a greater asset to the firm if you specialize in taxes."

That sounded convincing and I found myself in a new environment, staying in the office rather than going out in the field. We weren't too busy in the fall and my time was spent studying the tax laws and researching tax problems that I wasn't totally privy to. I missed my friends on the audit staff, rarely saw Bill, and my work became boring. Bill and I were only intermittently happy and when the annual Christmas party came around in November, I made a fool of myself, drinking too much. Bob Safford called me in again.

"Alice, I've been asked to speak to you about your drinking," he started.

"I know, Bob, I overdid myself the other night. I hadn't had any lunch and it went right to my head," I apologized.

"This is just a friendly chat, Alice. I'm not reprimanding you. Don Burns asked me to speak to you about it," he concluded.

Don Burns was my new boss, being the tax partner in the office. I was furious! None of the men had ever been called in for drinking too much and, believe me, their behavior on occasion was far worse than mine had been. "It was Don Burn's wife," I thought. "I noticed her glances and annoyance at my camaraderie with the staff."

Bill defended me, telling Bob, "Alice is her own worst critic. She has been a lot harder on herself than you have been."

After fretting all weekend on the matter, on Monday morning, I decided not to go back to A.Y. Charlie Gillette called to apologize and ask me to reconsider.

"I resented being singled out, Charlie. I'd rather stay home with the children, anyway."

"If you ever change your mind and want to come back, Alice, please call me."

I received a complimentary, appreciative letter from Alan Petch. His glowing recommendations paved the way for me for the next fifteen years, but I left the best time of my career behind forever.

In 1959 Castro seized power in Cuba, there were new war rumors, a steel strike started, Alaska and Hawaii became states and the new flag had fifty stars. The government announced that cigarettes might cause cancer and Leno met and fell in love with Rosemary Struthers.

8

"WHY do I always go for women who want careers?" Leno asked on one of his frequent trips to pick up the children for the weekend.

"Maybe that's the only type that are interesting to you," I suggested. "What does she do?"

"Well, she's a waitress right now, but she wants to own a dress shop," he confided.

"Maybe she'd really like to be a model. Is she a real beauty?" I asked, feeling the pain.

"She's more sophisticated than you, but I do like the way your eyes look, Alice. That's what men go for." His gaze held mine for a moment, which I dismissed quickly as the children joined us.

Leno was referring to my eye shadow, which I had learned how to apply properly at the Loretta Young School of Beauty where I had been going for a few weeks. I was trying to impress Bill Findley, who seemed to care only for his work. He was advancing rapidly at A.Y., where all of his energies were directed.

Our marriage had been blessed with a beautiful, baby girl, but not even her happy, loving ways could hold us together and our tumultuous marriage soon found its way to the divorce courts. Perhaps Bill didn't love me enough or I loved him too much, or, perhaps in the end, in 1968, a house in La Canada won his heart again.

My marriage to Bill was over and my feeling of failure as a wife intensified. "I guess I'm just not meant to be married," I thought. I missed my friends at A.Y., all Bill's friends now. Chuck Van Arman had gone to work for Addressograph-Multigraph and then I.B.M. and I received an announcement of his marriage on the day I sent my signed final divorce papers to the Glendale court. I had a beautiful home and four terrific children, but I felt so friendless. I decided to attend the alumni dinner meeting of Beta Alpha Psi at USC, hoping to see old friends.

"Leno has been alone for nearly four years. I think I'll call him for lunch tomorrow. Maybe he still cares," I thought, as I drove toward the campus. With that in mind, I felt better as I walked into the Town and Gown dining room. Don Gamble came toward me with his usual smile.

"Well, I guess they did it," he laughed.

Not knowing what he was talking about, I returned his remark with a questioning look.

"I understand Leno and Rosemary went to Las Vegas this weekend to tie the knot," he continued.

"Oh, that's right," I answered, laughing lightheartedly, as my heart sank and I wanted to run from the room. "Now I am destined to be alone forever," I thought.

Cory and Anthony were excited about their father's marriage, having met Rosemary and her two children, Sue and Frankie, both close to their age. How my heart broke and how good the bourbon tasted when they left on Friday nights for long weekends with their new family.

I hadn't felt this desolate since Leno was overseas. At least, I had the hope of his returning. Now I had no hope at all. "I must get busy with something," I thought.

I did. I enrolled at the Pasadena Playhouse, a renowned theatrical school close to home, where several famous actors had graduated. I sold more stock to pay for my tuition and put Louise and Maurine in the hands of a nearby mother with two children who needed someone to play with.

I entered into the six-hour day with boundless enthusiasm. I found that I excelled at being a comedienne, turning all my improvisations into hilarious comedy, no matter what the subject. And I thought I was a tragedienne! The trials and tribulations of living had brought laughter to my being.

But my rekindled ambition only lasted ten weeks. Again, I had been living in a dream world. The bills and the work were piling up at home and I had to quit and return to what I could make the most money doing—accounting.

Another of the "big eight" beckoned me—Touche, Ross, Bailey & Smart. They became an interesting challenge to my dull routine. But they weren't A.Y., and any attempt at making the kind of friends I had had there was futile. I soon advanced to administrative assistant to one of the partners, Frank Daft, whom I had met some years before at USC. Staffing the many jobs in the office was one of my numerous duties and I met a young, inspired visionary, Rod Thomson. Rod was a "junior" returning from his two-year service in the Army Reserves and he became the friend I needed. As almost all of the juniors did, Rod cajoled and flattered me to get the best assignments. Before long he knew all about me, my problems and goals, and I knew his.

Rod had an inner spiritual quality that seemed to inspire my creative imagination. I told him my innermost dreams and he had me convinced that I could realize them. I became awed in his presence and receptive to his every suggestion. He arranged a meeting with one of the V.I.P.s at the Irvine Company in Orange County to discuss the possibility of leasing land on which to build homes. Our meeting was interesting, but the usual outcome prevailed—we were premature. By the end of the meeting, Rod knew another of my dreams was to live in Newport Beach one day and he didn't rest until he helped me make that dream a reality.

9

THE piano bar at Chef's Inn on Foothill Boulevard in La Canada had become my place to go alone on Friday nights, where I could listen to my favorite music. Bill joined me on occasion, making sure I behaved myself. But I was unhappy and drinking too much. Leaving my two little girls in the hands of baby-sitters, was not what I wanted for my life or theirs.

Rod convinced me that a change for the better was possible and with his prompting, I took a day off and drove to Newport Beach, looking for an office and a place to live. "A small town could give me a new beginning," I thought. "I'd be far away from the unhappiness that had befallen me in the big city."

At the entrance to Lido Isle, the most swank neighborhood in the area, was a quaint, two-story building which had a real estate office and art gallery on the street side and apartments on the bay. "I might as well start at the top," I thought and strolled into "Eileen Richardson, Real Estate."

Sitting at the front desk was a tall, blonde woman, a little older than I, who became ecstatic over the possibilities for me and my family. Virginia Nash, to become one of my closest friends and confidant, found an office for me, overlooking the bay, and a home on Lido Isle.

"The barber below this office is June Allyson's new husband," she pointed out as she unlocked the door and led me up the stairway to the office which I immediately fell in love with. The large window afforded an expansive view of Newport Bay and the yachts anchored below and across the bay.

"You have Berkshire's Restaurant next door to have lunch and you can watch the boats come and go as you work," she announced enthusiastically.

Virginia was a most gregarious, glamorous lady and later became my constant companion. "I admit I'm a snob," she said often. She enjoyed going places where she could "see and be seen by the moneyed people of

Maurine and Louise

Louise, Anthony, Cory

Newport Beach," but was at the same time a barrel of laughs. She was more riotous than anyone I had known for a long time, saying, "Who has more fun than we do?" and meaning it. She had been divorced for several years, having two grown children, which she was careful not to mention when she met an eligible man on the prowl.

"This house is brand new. The couple just finished building it, when the husband died suddenly with a heart attack," she reported, opening the wrought iron gate that led to the three thousand square foot home at 117 Via Nice.

In Newport Beach in 1963, a divorcee, such as myself, with somewhat limited funds, could buy a new house on Lido Isle for one thousand dollars down and three hundred and sixty-five dollars a month; albeit under tragic circumstances. The yard was only a patio that backed up to a strada, but after having an acre of ground in La Cañada to nurture for six years, it looked pretty inviting.

Lido Isle was threaded with stradas (walkways) that went from one end of the island to the other in both directions. The island was surrounded by boat docks and sandy beaches. A clubhouse was available for parties and performances of the Lido Isle Players. The only way in and out was over a bridge that led to elegant shops and Richard's Gourmet Market with red carpeting and live organ music.

I returned to La Canada, elated over my good fortune at accomplishing so much in one day, and was sure Rod's advice had been truly inspirational. I put our house up for sale, packed the household belongings and the children and moved to the beach, amid Cory's crying protests that she would never speak to me again for taking her away from her school chums and the chance to be in the first class in the new La Canada High School.

I lost Cory for a while when Rosemary came into her family. Rosemary picked out her clothes, showed her new ways to wear her hair, spent time doing things with her that I didn't have time for and convinced her that Westridge School for Girls was a weird place to go to school. She was probably right on all counts, but the painful truth was that this was a bitter pill for me to swallow.

But on Lido Isle, everything would be different, as soon as Cory learned to appreciate our new way of life. Moving away from my family and the few good friends I had in L.A. to all new territory was quite a daring act for one as untraveled as myself. I would never have done it but for Rod's prodding and I would never have stayed but for Virginia's friendship. She introduced me to everyone in town worth meeting.

Commuting to L.A. became impossible, making it necessary for me to give up my good job and to sever relationships with my friends. Although they visited me occasionally, I lost track of all of them over the next few years, with the exception of Rod. He took a little longer.

But I was busy making new friends and struggling to make my office a financial success. My first love was real estate, but I turned to accounting and tax work to make ends meet. A close friend of Virginia's and her employer, Eileen Richardson, inaugurated my next project.

Eileen, who had lived in Newport Beach since the twenties and had two real estate offices and a yacht anchorage on Bayside Drive, introduced me to a designer, one Richard Jay Smith, who, together with his wife, Sylvia, became my dearest friends for the next six years.

Dick had plans for redeveloping a twenty-six acre parcel of land owned by nearly one hundred individuals and needed a feasibility study. Of course, he couldn't pay for it, but I could share the project with him equally.

The land was triangular in shape, located adjacent to the Newport Beach City Hall, fronting on Lafayette Avenue on the south and Newport Boulevard on the north. Dick called it "Lafayette Square."

The project was European in design with four five-story buildings, which would house shops on the first floors and apartments above, an eight-story office tower and eight-story hotel. Subterranean parking surrounded the buildings with a live theatre and restaurant centered in the landscaped mall.

This was another dream come true for me and for the next two years we put our heart and soul into signing up the property owners, meeting with the Planning Commission, laying out the plans with the utility companies and designing traffic patterns. We had commitments from 95 percent of the property owners, the City Council, prospective lessees and were arranging the first aspects of the financing, when in July of 1966, Aunt Pearl died suddenly.

But that happened after Leno was confronted with a crisis at Gateway Markets.

E SQUARE'
For Newport
, MAYNARD

nucleus around which to plan, the 'Sacred Cow,' so to speak. It was decided that the theatre should form a hub for night time activity with three additional restaurants.

"It is hoped that the theatre will become a center for music and the performing arts of an intimate size of 800 seats. A projection booth would be included for film showings.

"A 138-room hotel faces the 28th Street entrance to the project. The lower floor will contain the lobby, travel agency, men and women's health studios and barber shop and beauty salon. In the sunken court will be a pool and coffee shop. The top floor will serve as night club for dining and dancing with luxurious penthouse suites at the very top of the building.

"PARKING, A MOST VITAL element of the plan, is kept from intruding into the pedestrian malls by being on the perimeter. This design functions well in serving the shops with apartments above. To minimize ground coverage, two levels were provided with ramps to the lower level, three to four feet below existing grade.

"This level serves as covered parking for residents with convenient entrances to elevators to apartments and also as storage, mechanical and stock room space. Ramps up five feet to the upper or main level provide open air parking for shoppers. Material excavated from lower parking and basement areas will be used for filling the interior mall areas.

"Lafayette Square will contain two well known quality retailers and as many as seventy small specialty shops. The variety of services and merchandise will rival what one would expect to find in a complete village and arranged in logical sequence starting with hardware, household goods, furniture, decorative arts, wallpapers and paints, antiques, decorator's studios and art galleries adjacent to the theatre-restaurant complex, then gourmet foods, delicatessen, liquors, drugs, candy and bakery and gifts, stationery, photography and art supplies, cleaning and shoe repair, toys and books, all facing the parking for the one stop shopper. Clothing and shoes and other specialties will be found on the mall side for the more leisurely shopper.

"The office tower, being the tallest structure, is placed on the most prominent corner of 32nd and Newport Boulevard and separated from the residential and shopping area by its self-contained parking and resultant low level open space. The parking is adjacent to and would supplement the nighttime requirements of the theatre-restaurant complex.

Richard Jay Smith
...It's His Plan

THE MAN WHO created the master plan for "Lafayette Square" is Richard Jay Smith, who lives on Lido Isle and has maintained his own office in Newport Beach for five years, and has designed homes in Laguna Niguel, Irvine Cove, Cameo Shores, Lido Isle, Huntington Harbor and Dover Shores . . . plus commercial buildings in the Lido Shopping Center and in other areas of Southern California.

A graduate of Ohio University, with degree BFA PAA Major in Architectural Design, he enlisted in the Army Air Corps in 1942 after completing his schooling, and began his experience in architecture following his discharge in November, 1945.

He has worked on a variety of major projects in the offices of Rowland H. Crawford, Douglas Honnold, Victor Gruen & Associates, Barondon Corporation, Raphael Soriano, A. Quincy Jones, Pereira & Luckman and Philmer J. Ellerbroek.

Major projects have included such as Romanoff's Restaurant, Rancho Santa Anita Shopping Center, Milliron's Westchester, Mach's Kansas City, Donovan & Seaman's Jewelry, Master Plan for Edwards AFB in Palmdale, CBS TV City, Urban Redevelopment in National City, Camp Pendleton Marine Barracks, Newport Elementary School, and residences for such prominent people as Leonard K. Firestone, Ray Milland, Milton Bren, Jody Hutchinson, Bob Waterfield.

Mr. Smith's work has been published in Arts & Architecture, Interiors, Sunset, Building Design and other magazines and publications.

TYPICAL "LAFAYETTE SQUARE" townhouse apartments, with retail shops at first level. There are seven buildings planned for the 15-acre mid-Newport development, similar to this sketch with varying elevations. Underground parking is provided for residents as well as surface parking.

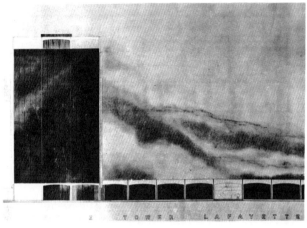

ELEVATION OF OFFICE TOWER BUILDING facing Newport Boulevard.

THE AREA...AS IT IS

..AFAYETTE SQUARE"

'LAFAYETT

... A New Look

BY PAU

BY PAU

NEWPORT BEACH MAY BE on the threshold of a
new concept in redevelopment through private enterprise, perhaps providing our own answer to ever-
increasing pressures of relying on federal government

It is the result of a plan for redeveloping a large
area in the heart of Newport Beach — approximately
15 acres bounded by Newport Boulevard, 32nd Street,
Lafayette Avenue and 28th Street. Due to the strategic
location, the acquisition will rank it with the highest
cost land area in Southern California, exceeding the
cost-per-acre of Century City and Bunker Hill in Los
Angeles.

The area that has been under intensive study for
the past 19 months has been named "Lafayette Square"
by Richard Jay Smith /Associates, who have prepared
the comprehensive master plan and architectural design. Alice Findley, resident manager of the Newport
Beach office of Lyons, Bandel & Bryant, certified
public accountants, has prepared cost studies and
income projections for the development.

The entire plan will be presented to the approximately 81 property owners (representing 129 parcels
of land, mostly 30x90 feet) at a meeting to be held at
the Newport Beach City Hall on Tuesday evening, May
25, at 7:30. Miss Findley and Mr. Smith have prepared
a 26-page presentation which has been distributed to
the property owners and potential investors, and they
told THE NEWPORTER that property owners controlling a majority of the 129 parcels involved have signed
letters of approval of the plan. They will present per-
tinent financial data at the May 25 meeting.

ASKED WHAT PROMPTED the ambitious undertak-
ing — certainly the most comprehensive and exciting
concept of urban improvement of Newport Beach in
many years — Smith, a building designer who lives on
Lido Isle, told THE NEWPORTER:

"It's like the mountain climber's answer...'because
it's there'."

He then outlined the sweeping plan in considerable
detail for THE NEWPORTER:

"We began our studies along modest lines of cleaning up the area block by block with row type town-
houses. In early consultations with the Newport Beach
Planning Commission we were told that rezoning in the
area would require grouping of lots under single own-
ership, perhaps in whole blocks. An answer was needed
as to how this could be accomplished. Bringing in outside land developers seemed obvious but perhaps a
new concept would be more successful. Forming a
development corporation of existing owners, supple-
mented where necessary by local investors.

"The high cost of acquisition shaped our thinking
of land use and as each succeeding plan was evolved,
it became more apparent that a total concept for the
area was needed calling for abandonment of existing
streets and alleys, and creating a new pattern to provide maximum land use and consequently maximum
financial return to the owners. A townhouse apartment
or a typical one level shopping center use became
questionable due to land costs.

"It was out of this analysis that the unique ap-
proach to Lafayette Square was born — a combination
of commercial and residential uses in a compatible
relation. We studied the factors that made American
and European urban centers charming, attractive and
stimulating both for shopping and living. The goal was
to create this atmosphere with a theatre, restaurants,
exclusive shops surrounding landscaped malls, in
short to distill the best lessons of the past improved
with the latest land use thinking.

"As the seven buildings containing shops with four
floors of apartments are similar in plan, a decision was
made not to treat them as contemporary blocks with
continuous rigid lines of balconies, but as groups of
vertical buildings such as one would find in a village.
The facades are ever changing with varying treatments
of windows, balconies, shutters, rooflines and construction materials.

"The shop fronts would likewise be treated individually and the whole concept scaled to satisfy the
the human element, to fascinate and delight the pedestrian. Paving, awnings and landscaping would not be
dogmatic interpretations of the past but stylized ver-
sions to recall the atmosphere found in Paris, Rome,
Madrid and New York.

"As Karam's Restaurant is perhaps one of the most
attractive buildings in the existing area, it became the

PERSPECTIVE OF "LAFAYETTE SQUARE"...looking north from 28th Street
and Newport Boulevard to the Bay. Numbered identification of area landmarks:
(1) Newport Boulevard; (2) Newport Beach City Hall; (3) Richard's Market; (4)
Newport Balboa Savings & Loan; (5) entrance to Lido Isle; (6) Lafayette Street;
(7) 28th Street; (8) Karam's Restaurant Building; (9) THE NEWPORTER
PUBLISHING COMPANY office building.

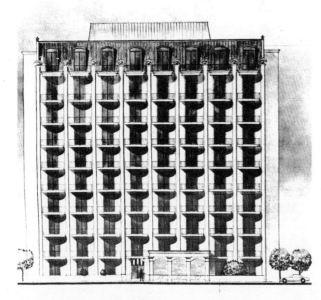

ELEVATION OF THE 10-STORY, 138-room hotel, site of which is the corner of
Newport Boulevard and 28th Street, with plans calling for extensive underground
parking, plus sweeping views of ocean, bay and coastline.

LAND USE PLAN OF

THE NEWPORTER

WEEKLY NEWS MAGAZINE • NEWPORT BEACH. CALIFORNIA • FIFTEEN CENTS
VOL. VI • NUMBER 312 • WEEK ENDING MAY 28, 1965

MEN BUILDING ORANGE COUNTY

As one property owner aptly put it: "Let's consider our alternative. No one else
will ever devote as much time and money to this as Mr. Smith has done, If we
reject the project, we face the prospect of continuing to live with some rather
expensive slums."

10

THE whole world had begun to change in 1961.

John F. Kennedy (JFK) became our next President, the Russians put a man into orbit and built a wall separating east and west Berlin. North Vietnam invaded South Vietnam and JFK started an arms buildup in South Vietnam with U.S. "instructors." John Glenn orbited the earth and a crisis loomed in Cuba as Russia placed missiles there. Kennedy made Russia withdraw the missiles, but Russian troops remained. JFK had the same dilemma in the Far East as had plagued the United States since 1949—what to do about the Communists in Asia. Kennedy chose to do virtually nothing and later it would be said that the difficult years that ensued might have been avoided if the U.S. had made a hard commitment on the ground in 1961.

In 1963 Cuban refugees were swarming into Florida and computers were hailed as a business "miracle." In November, the day we were moving into our new Lido Isle home, President Kennedy was assassinated and Lyndon B. Johnson inherited his problems. By 1964, business was booming as the Dow Jones Industrial average reached eight hundred and was expected to go higher. That was good news if one owned stock, but by this time, I had sold all of mine to keep us going. But Goldwater was defeated, losing to Lyndon Johnson for the Presidency, an event I considered to be disastrous to the country.

North Vietnam attacked two U.S. warships in the Tonkin Gulf and in 1965 the riots started; black riots, mostly, but campus riots, too. Everyone seemed to be protesting everything. Didn't they know how lucky they were to be in America? Why had they lost respect for the authority that had controlled our lives for as long as I could remember?

Johnson had run as the "peace candidate" in 1964 and refused to retaliate against aggression toward the U.S. by the North Vietnamese until after his election was secure. And in 1965 troops and planes started going to Vietnam and draft calls were doubled.

We were headed toward another aimless war—MacArthur's words in

1951 came to mind:

> ...There are some who for varying reasons would appease Red
> China. They are blind to history's clear lesson. For history teaches
> with unmistakable emphasis that appeasement but begets new
> and bloodier war... "Why," my soldiers asked of me, "surrender
> military advantages to an enemy in the field?" I could not answer.
> Some may say to avoid spread of the conflict into all-out war with
> China; others to avoid Soviet intervention. Neither explanation
> seems valid. For China is already engaging with the maximum
> power it can commit and the Soviet will not necessarily mesh its
> actions with our moves. Like a cobra, any new enemy will more
> likely strike, whenever it feels that the relativity in military or
> other potential is in its favor on a world-wide basis. ...

The cobra was striking again in Vietnam and the politicians were still
indecisive. History had taught us nothing, it seemed.

Leno had a cobra of his own in the demand of one Peter R. Smaldino,
who wanted out of the family business.

"I just don't agree with your policies, Leno. You're expanding too fast
and borrowing too much money. We're spread too thin! I want to get my
money out," he argued, "before you lose it all!"

"Our only hope of surviving in this business is to expand," Leno
fought back bitterly. "You know we don't have enough cash to buy you
out now. And your asking book value is totally out of the question. It
will cripple our operations. Why, you wouldn't have a nickel if my father
hadn't been so generous with you!"

"Yes, and if Stella had been a boy, you wouldn't be running this
business. I've taken a second position to you as long as I'm going to. I
want to run things my way. I want out!" he shouted vehemently.

Leno didn't need this kind of aggravation. His hands were full with
pleasing his wife and taking care of his step-children. He went to
Howard Alphson, his attorney and friend, to see how the problem could
be solved.

"Give him 25 percent in cash and let him take a note for the rest,"
Howard suggested.

"He wants out and if I don't pay him in cash, he'll remain on the
board, breathing down my neck," Leno replied angrily. "Howard, he has
given me nothing but trouble since Dad died. I've had to acquiesce to
many of his ideas which went against my better judgment. Dad didn't
leave me enough control to run the business properly. Maybe with Pete
out of the way, I'll have a freer hand."

"I advise you to get your emotions out of this, Leno. Don't give him all cash," Howard insisted.

"I'll have to talk it over with my mother," Leno added sadly. "In the end, she has the final say."

"Maybe you have grown too fast, Leno," Corina admonished. "Pete and Stella are unhappy with the way you have managed things. We should sell some of the stores and give them their money. That's the only way to bring peace to the family."

Knowing he was beaten again, Leno acquiesced and decided to sell the newer, bigger stores in Monterey Park and La Habra and the San Gabriel Valley. "They are the most profitable and will bring the most money," he told Pete and Emma. "But this will create a real hardship on our cash flow, Pete. We'll have to take a cut in salary and fringe benefits."

Pete and Stella received their cash and immediately purchased liquor stores in the San Gabriel Valley. That was the beginning of the end for Gateway Markets.

11

LENO'S problems were unknown to me at the time and I had my hands full with my own. Aunt Pearl's health began to fail and I visited her in Palm Springs as time permitted. She was bedridden and I was only allowed to see her when Joan McManus, who was caring for her, said I could. On one of my visits, Aunt Pearl was obviously upset.

"Alice, I want you to get an attorney and bring him down here," she pleaded. "I don't like what's going on. There won't be anything left for the family by the time they get through with it."

"What do you mean?" I asked, confused by her statements.

Joan walked in with a Scotch and soda and insisted Aunt Pearl drink it. "The doctor has ordered her to have a highball every afternoon."

"I don't want this drink. You know I don't drink, Alice. Joan, I want you to call Mr. Dillon and tell him I want to see him this afternoon while Alice is here."

Joan left the room and Aunt Pearl continued, "They don't call the doctor when I ask them to and the trunk I had with all of my papers is gone. I've asked my attorney to change my will and he refuses to."

"I'll do anything I can, Aunt Pearl, but you mustn't get so upset," trying to reassure her. Using a straw, she took a long sip from her highball. Joan came back into the room.

"Mr. Dillon is out on the golf course this afternoon and can't be reached," she reported.

"See if you can reach Leon. He's probably in La Jolla, but we can talk to him on the phone," she instructed her and Joan left the room again.

"That's what she always tells me when I want to talk to the attorney. He's never in when I call. Alice, don't you know an attorney you could bring down here to talk to me?"

By this time, she had finished her drink and her words became incoherent. When Joan returned, Aunt Pearl was sound asleep.

"Leon wasn't in his office either, Alice. You better go now so she can get some rest."

I left in a state of confusion. I didn't know what to do. When I got back to the beach, I called Rod and told him my story.

"Alice, I wouldn't get involved in that situation. Your aunt probably didn't know what she was saying," he advised.

I trusted Rod's opinion, but I wanted to know the truth and felt uncertain as to what that was. When I called Leno a week later, he suggested that I talk to Howard Alphson about it. Before I had a chance to call him, Mother phoned.

"Aunt Pearl died this morning. She insisted that the nurse give her a tub bath every day and as soon as they took her out of the tub this morning, she collapsed."

Aunt Pearl's death brought about my inability to continue to work on "Lafayette Square" almost immediately. She left all of our precious Palm Springs land to charity and in the hands of trustees who cared nothing about the family's heritage. I had to try to do something about it, especially because of my last conversation with her. The land belonged to the family, having been purchased by my great-grandfather in 1884. Aunt Pearl, who had no relatives but her sister's children and grandchildren, of which I was one, was holding the land in trust for us during her lifetime, I contended. I called Howard Alphson.

Howard's sister-in-law, Mimi, was prominent in Palm Springs and Howard knew people there who told him there seemed to be some truth to my story. For whatever reason, Howard agreed to take the case.

"We'll claim one-half of the estate as belonging to your grandmother's offspring and charge fraud and coercion in the signing of her will, giving Pearl the benefit of the doubt. I'll take 25 percent of what we recover on a contingency basis. In other words, if we don't collect anything, I won't get anything."

"That sounds fair to me, Howard. When do we start?" I knew we had a strong case and agreed to do all of the research and pay for the court costs. To save money for process servers, we had to personally serve over twenty people and institutions that were named in Aunt Pearl's will, mostly in Palm Springs. I couldn't do it myself, as the complainant, so Dick and Sylvia offered to help. The three of us spent the next two months tracking all of these people down. It wasn't easy, but we had a great time, trying to outwit those who were going to great lengths to escape us.

The research took me to San Diego, Los Angeles, Riverside and San Bernardino counties and was long and arduous. The court costs of one thousand dollars to get started might as well have been ten thousand. I called Leno.

"I'll loan you a thousand dollars, Alice," he answered quickly. "She should have left that property to you. If we had stayed together, she probably would have named *me* a trustee," he laughed, somewhat seriously.

The thought had already entered my mind. She had liked Leno from the beginning, confiding in him considerably more than she had ever confided in me. I couldn't think about it. I thanked him for helping me out, not knowing what problems he had had with Peter R. Smaldino.

12

I met Rosemary for the first time at Cory's graduation from Newport Harbor High School in June of 1966. She was an attractive woman, more sophisticated than I had ever been. She wore a large, black floppy hat and a designer dress to the graduation and reception afterward at the Balboa Bay Club. Leno agreed to pay for the gourmet dinner and champagne and we invited everyone: Mother, step-father Joe, my father and Alice Ruth, Edith and Mel and their two children, Jeanne and Dennis, Jane and her seven children, Leno's mother and Cory's friends and current beau, Wayne Smith, Anthony, Louise, Maurine and my grandfather, Pop, who was now ninety-six years old.

I thought of Nana as Pop walked in, alert, slightly bent but proud. She had passed away in 1959 at the age of eighty-four which left a deep sadness in my heart for her life of struggle and unfulfilled dreams. Until the very last, I tried to help ease the pain of her poverty, her degradation. Nana was a proud woman from an illustrious background who was sent to the Los Angeles County Hospital, when she couldn't be cared for at home. When I visited her there, her situation was appalling. She hadn't been bathed since arriving and her lunch tray still stood next to her bed. She had had a mild stroke and was unable to feed herself and the nurses were too busy to help her. I immediately made arrangements to have her moved to the private hospital closest to her home in west L.A. and rode with her in the ambulance, down the Harbor freeway, past USC, and onto Century Boulevard to Inglewood. She was well cared for there, but didn't improve and couldn't go home, where her life had become a nightmare with Uncle Stuart's wife and three children having taken over the small, deteriorating house. I was making arrangements for her to be moved to a rest home, as the doctor said there was nothing more he could do, when her lungs suddenly filled with water and she was gone.

My thoughts were interrupted and I was brought back to the reception—this most happy, albeit divergent, gathering as Bill bounded into the bayfront room with the long, decorated table in time for dinner,

402

having flown down from San Francisco where he was working on an audit.

"I'm glad he made it," I thought. "Tension will be somewhat eased with his presence." He looked handsome and dashing as he greeted everyone reassuringly. "I'm not alone, at least for tonight," I comforted myself.

My father and mother talked freely as Dad, putting his arm around Mother, announced, "This is my blushing bride," and everyone laughed, even Alice Ruth and Joe. Dad had a way of saying almost anything without rancor or bitterness and we loved his sense of humor.

Leno joined in the fun, reservedly, and Rosemary smiled quietly. That must have been a difficult evening for her, especially with Leno's mother showing such affection toward me and my children. Rosemary's fondness for Cory was evident as she took part cheerfully in the celebration.

Rosemary had tried her hand in the business world by converting an old Gateway truck, a 1957 Ford, into a dress shop on wheels; painting it pink and labeling it the "Boutique Carriage." Later she opened a dress shop in Beverly Hills, taking in a partner. She was developing into quite a business woman as Leno struggled with his problem of fewer stores, making competition more keen. He had purchased the old Walt Disney home in the Los Feliz hills for his new family and now found the maintenance and repairs to be a drain on his resources.

Aunt Pearl had died soon after Cory's graduation and shortly thereafter, sister Edith's husband, Mel, was taken ill suddenly one Friday afternoon and died in the Veteran's Hospital that night—a terrible shock for all of us and especially Edith and her two children, both teenagers. Edith came down to the beach to stay with us for awhile and assisted me as I was plummeted headlong into my lawsuit with the Bank of America on a grand scale. I found other members of the family, my mother's sisters, Aunt Katherine and Aunt Marjorie, as well as Uncle Jack's daughter, to be unsupportive and in turn, bringing legal action against me. For a year and a half, Howard and I were in and out of the court room as diversionary tactics used by the opposition were keeping us from moving forward.

In the spring of 1968, two months after Bill married Elloree, a divorcee with three children and a house in La Canada, I settled out of court for five hundred and fifty thousand dollars, to be divided among thirty-nine heirs. I had totally dedicated myself to this endeavor for two years, giving up my stake in "Lafayette Square."

Leno wasn't doing much better. He was discouraged with the downhill trend of the grocery business and was trying to work his way out, once and for all. His mother and Peter DeSantis were now the only other stockholders in Gateway Markets, besides Louis Smaldino, Pete's eldest son, who kept a nominal share of stock when his father was paid off. Leno owned 26.5 percent, as did Pete and Emma. Mom owned 44 percent and Louis 1 percent. None of them were interested in buying Leno's share.

I received a phone call from Leno in May.

"Thanks for repaying me the thousand dollars, Alice," he started quietly. "I'm glad you got something out of it."

"It wasn't much when you consider the property was appraised at eight million dollars and is probably worth a lot more than that," I answered, more the vanquished than the victor.

"I want to get out of the grocery business for good, Alice," he continued. "But no one is interested in buying a minority interest. If I had the money to buy Pete's shares, I would have controlling interest, which I could sell. I was hoping you could loan me the money temporarily."

I wanted desperately to help him. How many times he had pulled me out of the quicksand in the past.

"I don't have that kind of money, Leno. The most I could scrape up is about twenty thousand dollars."

"That isn't enough. That wouldn't help. Thanks anyway," and he was gone.

Anthony graduated from Newport Harbor High School and Louise from Carden Hall, an exclusive private school in Newport Beach, in June. Leno, Rosemary and Mom came down for the graduations. Rosemary didn't talk to me, only smiled slightly, "To be polite," I thought. "She's as attractive as ever, but holds on to Leno as if he's trying to get away." I laughed to myself. "That's just my wishful thinking."

Since coming to Newport Beach, I had become more and more casual, loving the relaxed, unsophisticated life, but I felt plain and unattractive next to Rosemary.

"She thinks I still love you," Leno had told me several times in the past. I let it go at that.

I had planned a small dinner for Anthony's graduation at Berkshire's, next to my office on the bay, where the ambiance was open to the water and the sky and the boats. A romantic place—beautiful, elegant and casual.

The conversation was stilted, although after a few drinks, became more relaxed. Leno, sitting with his arm loosely around Rosemary's shoulders, looked in my direction. Our eyes met. For a fleeting moment, we were back in Miss Fraser's English class—he was at his table at the back of the room. He lowered his gaze quickly and was gone from me forever.

That summer, a few blocks away, by the Newport pier, a group was emerging, strangely dressed and with weird behavior—a group I didn't understand and one that seemed totally foreign to my code of ethics and sense of values. They were kept at a minimum by the efficient Newport Beach police, but, nevertheless, appeared frequently and I found them frightening.

I started going to Newport Unity Church in July and Leno went back to live at Oak Terrace, this time with Rosemary and Sue and Frankie. The house had been vacated when Mom moved into Stella's house, buying it from her when she wanted to move to San Marino. Leno sold the big, ostentatious Disney house and planned to live at Oak Terrace only long enough to realize his goal of owning a horse ranch as far as possible from L.A. He wanted to increase his stable of thoroughbred horses, which he had been racing and breeding for some time, sharing this enthusiasm with his life-long friend, Roxie Lucarelli.

L.A. was fast developing an undesirable element. Griffith Park was a beautiful recreation area of several hundred acres, in the hills across Los Feliz Boulevard, only a few blocks away and partially visible from Oak Terrace. The park was being frequented more and more by hoards of transients, "flower children" or "hippies," mostly from San Francisco. Their gathering in the hills was difficult to prevent as they could wander from one location to another, undetected. They were beginning to appear in the Los Feliz neighborhood, taking over some of the houses with their "free love" and "pot" parties, appearing next door to Oak Terrace on more than one occasion.

1968 had seen increasing black riots and war protests. A 10 percent surcharge was added to our tax burden to pay for the expanding government and expanding Vietnam War and Richard Nixon became our next President. Martin Luther King was assassinated in Memphis, Robert Kennedy was slain in L.A. and twenty miles from Beverly Hills, a plush, swank city of the rich and famous, the Spahn Movie Ranch became the home of one Charles Manson, along with some thirty devout followers.

13

WE had lived on Lido Isle for nearly six years. They had been busy, happy years, but the children were growing up too fast. Maurine, the youngest, was my pal. When she wasn't riding and caring for horses at the Orange County Fairgrounds, she was with me and my friends. She was a beautiful, but serious girl, beset with a discordant environment almost from the beginning of her life. She was loving and agreeable, entering into the activities of her older brother and sisters obediently. She received straight "A"s at Carden Hall, the private school she had attended since the fifth grade, receiving the best possible education. Bill took care of the tuition before the infamous "law suit" was settled, and the education trust that Aunt Pearl had set up for her sister's descendants paid for it after that. She loved all animals, especially horses. Starting at the tender age of eight, she spent seven days a week learning to ride and care for them. Under the watchful eye of her trainer, Katrina Lantz, Maurine became an accomplished rider, winning numerous ribbons and trophies.

Louise was also afforded a Carden Hall education, being a little older when she started. Of course, Louise had been attending private school since kindergarten at Chandler School in La Canada. All the children had private school educations until high school. We had gotten them off to a good start, we thought—the one thing the three of us had done right. It paid off.

All of the children were bright and wholesome—never giving us any serious trouble. Oh, they were independent and fought to keep that independence. They had definite opinions of their own and couldn't be led or swayed by any of us or by anyone outside the sphere of family influence. None of them were ever involved in drugs or alcohol. So much for the myth of "problem" children from "broken homes."

After graduating from Newport Harbor High in 1966, Cory had tried her wings in the business world and spent some time at Orange Coast Junior College, receiving her AA degree in 1969. She began dating a boy

With June, Mother, Bob
Mother's ocean front home
Summer 1969

she had met in high school, John LaMontagne, after a skiing trip. They were going steady, off and on, and generally having a good time, when they both began to get serious about their educations. They wanted to go away, far away, out-of-state. John was looking for a good aeronautical engineering school and found the one he liked at Utah State University (USU) in Logan, Utah. Cory liked the school too, because it was located in the foothills close to skiing and the quality of the environment with four distinct seasons appealed to her. Off they went together in the spring quarter of 1969 to USU, much to the dismay of all sets of parents.

Cory had been somewhat trying, during her teen years, although she did eventually get over being devastated by our move to Newport Beach. There was never a dull moment when Cory was around, and oh, how we missed her when she went so far away.

Anthony had left home, too, by 1969, having moved into his fraternity house on the campus of Long Beach State. Our home on Lido Isle, that had once been so full of noisy teenagers, became comparatively quiet with Louise, Maurine, Pauline, our housekeeper from England, and myself.

Louise loved the beach and her numerous friends on Lido, which was a paradise for children and parents, as most of their activities were right on the island.

I became happily involved at Newport Unity Church as the treasurer and a member of the church board and even had a couple of dates with our divorced minister, Loren Flickinger.

Loren had a unique singing voice and I wanted to record it. I expressed my desire to my little brother, Bobbie, now a mature big brother, married to June, with three boys and a promising career in the "sound business." He arrived at the Sunday morning service with his sophisticated recording equipment and although he claimed to be an agnostic, dutifully sat through the sermon and Loren's solos. After several sessions on Sunday in addition to the Wednesday night "Singspiration" meetings, we were ready to invest more time and money into the producing of inspirational albums.

Cory would be twenty-one in April and the thought was overwhelming. Only yesterday she was learning to walk and talk, having long conversations with her imaginary friend before Anthony was born.

"Can you come home for your birthday?" I asked on one of my frequent telephone calls to Logan.

"I can if you will pay for my ticket," she answered. "I hate to ask Dad for the money."

"You have to be here for your twenty-first," I insisted. "I'll raise the money somehow." I flew both Cory and John home and we were celebrating her birthday with champagne when the call came from Leno.

"Can you come up to see us?" he asked Cory.

"We won't have time, Dad," Cory answered.

"Of course, you won't have time. What was I thinking? I'll come down there tomorrow, but I won't be able to stay long and I'll have to come alone," he answered quickly. Cory noticed an anxiety and tenseness in his voice. "I wonder what's wrong at Oak Terrace?" she thought.

The next morning Leno rushed in, obviously in a great hurry. He brought his usual lavish presents and a birthday card with a personal note:

My little girl is now a full grown woman—and I can't believe it. You'll never know how much your love has meant to me, or how much I pray for your future happiness.

I love you, Cory

Dad

"I wonder what's wrong with your father," I asked Cory after he had gone. "He seemed so preoccupied and upset. I haven't seen him like that in years."

"I noticed it, too," she said.

April 9, 1969

Dear Cory,

It was sure wonderful seeing you for your birthday. (John, too) The only thing wrong is that I hate having you leave California again. But then I suppose all good things take some sacrifice and it will be worth it in the long run.

I hope you had a pleasant trip back and are safe and sound up there—I worry about you. I sure hope you are getting to like the people better—it can't be much fun if you don't.

Not much happening here. No new burglaries, thank goodness! No new clues, either. There has been a plain clothes detective hanging around here occasionally, but I'm beginning to doubt as to whether the "culprits" will ever be caught.

I'll bring you up to date on our horses. (I'm sure you are interested!) The only one that has been racing is The Kildare Lady (a three-year old filly). She raced seven times at Santa Anita this winter (January through March), and placed third three times, fifth once, and eighth twice. Not too good—last year she won once. Last week she was entered in a race, and was in the gate ready to run, when another horse in the next gate fell over and started kicking and thrashing around. In the process, The Kildare Lady was kicked in the leg and was scratched (withdrawn) from the race. She seems o.k. now and should be racing at Hollywood Park in a couple of weeks.

We have a two-year old colt in training at Santa Anita which should be running in a month or two at Hollywood Park, also. He is named Never Digress after his dam (mother) whose name is Digress.

The first colt we ever bought (You remember, named Traveling Gent and nicknamed Bern Boy) cannot run fast enough and we will probably have to sell him. He is three years old now—part of the disappointment of raising horses, I'm told.

Our nine-year old mare, Fra Mar Belle, a full sister of The Kildare Lady, is in foal (pregnant) and should foal (give birth) any time now. In fact, she is overdue a couple of days.

Our other two mares, Hill Bride and Viva Pueblo, are in Riverside and San Clemente, respectively, being bred to two stallions, Have Tux and Poona II. It takes about eleven months for a mare to give birth to a foal.

Our other horse is the filly (female) foal of Fra Mar Belle, which was born last year—you might remember. She is unnamed as yet—we can't come up with a name for her. Her sire (father) is called Nigret. She is beginning to look real fine—I saw her a few weeks ago.

Now you have a blow-by-blow description of our livestock! As you can guess, I sure would like to get a ranch of our own soon. L.A. is getting to be a pretty scary place. There are a group of hippies that have taken over Griffith Park and two "pot parties" have been broken up by the police just next door. That's a little too close for comfort. I have a place picked out in Escondido, and as soon as I can get my affairs straightened out, we will be able to buy it and move from this house.

I'm not much of a letter writer—I hope you are not quite as homesick, honey. We're looking forward to seeing you or hearing from you about May second.

Rose and Frank send their best.

Love, Dad

P.S. I'll try to write more often.

14

Dear Cory,

GUESS what? We finally made it to the Salton Sea last weekend. What a trip! We left here at six Saturday evening and discovered that the lights on the trailer wouldn't work. We were in the service station until ten-thirty and finally made it to Indio about one-thirty. We pulled into an all night station to leave the boat battery for an overnight charge. The next morning we went to pick the battery up and the man hadn't charged it. So, we had to wait two *more* hours.

We finally got out to the lake about one in the afternoon, got the boat in the water and it wouldn't start. I guess sitting idle all those months caused a problem. It took over an hour to get it started. Frank skied for a few rounds, we drove across the lake and then it was time to go back.

We were so stupid! We took Shadow in the boat with us (couldn't find anyone to take care of her). The first thing she did was jump overboard and drink a lot of the salt water. She got sick, poor thing, and just lay in the boat like a limp rag the whole time we were out.

I was too chicken to even try to ski this time. I still don't know whether we were on the best side of the lake. We were in Desert Shores, but from what we could see of the other side, it looked a little nicer. I guess we'll go again in a couple of weeks. Your dad didn't object to it too much, like I thought he would.

We haven't had any more robberies, but every time I come home I expect to either find someone in the house or something missing. I think the police have stopped working on the case and we haven't heard anything from the insurance company.

We're looking forward to seeing you when the quarter ends. Hope you're still planning on staying here. Say "hello" to John and take care of yourself.

Love and kisses,
Rose

Leno had Howard Alphson draw up a contract between himself, his mother and Peter DeSantis. He was to remain at Gateway as a consultant, if needed, and Pete would buy Leno's shares over a period of ten years. Leno would use the contract as collateral to purchase the ranch he wanted in Escondido.

"This arrangement shouldn't work a hardship on the Company," Leno told Pete and Emma.

"I don't know, Leno," Pete began. "We'll have to talk it over with Mom."

"I've got to get out of this town, Pete, and can't unless I can sell my shares," Leno tried to explain. "It's a matter of life and death. I'm asking for my life, Pete!" His voice was near panic now as he strained to make Pete understand the importance of what he was asking.

Pete was noncommittal and Leno went to see his mother. He tried to explain how he felt, but it fell on deaf ears.

"Mom, we can't live in that house any longer. We can't sleep and never know when it will be ransacked again. You're the only one who can help me," he pleaded.

"We kept this business going through much more difficult times than these," she started. "No, Leno, we can't jeopardize the future of the business to help you leave town. You must work this out some other way," she admonished with a heavy heart.

Leno's situation seemed hopeless. "My father did it all for me," he laughed to himself. "I'll be forty-four tomorrow and I'm still doing what my father wants."

He drove up the long, steep driveway slowly, watching for anything unusual. Rosemary hadn't come home yet. He parked the car and entered the service porch, unlocked the back door and stepped into the kitchen. Everything seemed to be in place. The phone was ringing.

"Leno, this is Pete. We just finished talking your situation over with Mom and we think we can work something out. I wanted to let you know. It's a birthday present," he laughed.

Leno didn't have time to assimilate the good news before the phone rang again. This time it was Cory.

"Dad, we want to come up this weekend to celebrate your birthday," she said.

"I don't want any of you to come up to this house," he answered emphatically. "Sue and Frankie are at Lake Isabella and we have to go bring the boat back. We probably won't get back until Sunday and I'll call you then. We'll come down there to see you."

Cory was disappointed. Her dad's birthday was special to her, and the one time, more than any other, when she wanted to be with him.

"I guess you'll have to wait till Sunday for your birthday present, then," she answered sadly.

EPILOGUE

I was startled back to reality as the phone's ring seemed to shriek in my ears. The light was beginning to fill my bedroom; I had been awake all night, reading my letters, looking at my scrapbook and waiting.

"Alice, this is Roxie. They're both gone, murdered. I just came from the house. Alice, it was horrible," his voice cracked.

Disbelieving, holding back the panic, I asked, "What happened? Who did it?"

"We don't know. It was the work of someone crazed. If there's anything I can do, please let me know."

Roxie had been on the L.A. police force since getting out of the Navy in 1945 and received word of the tragedy while on duty. I hadn't seen Roxie for several years, but knew that he and Leno were still close friends.

I was stunned. The children had heard the phone ring and stood in the doorway of my room with questioning panic. I couldn't hold back the tears now. I could barely speak.

"They've been murdered. Dad and Rosemary have both been murdered. Roxie just called," I said quietly.

Anthony left quickly, Cory threw her arms around me, sobbing, while Louise and Maurine looked on in horror.

Later, the phone rang again. This time it was Bill.

"Alice, I just heard the news. I'm so sorry. You'd better not let the children see the newspaper this morning. I don't want Maurine to go to the funeral. Why don't you bring Louise and Maurine up here for a few days?" Then he was gone.

The next phone call was from the Los Angeles Police Department.

"This is Sergeant Patchett of homicide," he started, matter-of-factly. "Do you think you and the children could come up to L.A? We need to have some questions answered. We'd like to have you come tomorrow."

"Yes, we'll be there in the morning," I heard myself saying.

Who told the police about us, I never knew, but early the next

415

morning we were all on our way. We had to divert to the airport to pick up Dana who was arriving from New York for our father's funeral to be held on Thursday.

The shock of losing my father so quietly in his sleep had paled in comparison to Leno's death at almost the exact, same time. It was eleven a.m. and our Dad's birthday, August twelfth, when Dana came down the moving sidewalk at the American Airlines terminal, somber-faced. None of us were very good company and soon we were on the Pasadena freeway to La Canada where we dropped Louise and Maurine off at Bill's.

In an advanced state of shock, we got back on the Pasadena freeway, headed for downtown and Parker Center. I had rarely made the trip to L.A. since moving to the beach and had never been to Parker Center. The ride continued to be its usual frustrating one, with too many cars and too many drivers who didn't know how to drive. But we arrived safely in the big city at Temple and First streets.

The Parker Center was huge with long, white corridors leading to a myriad of rooms and my head swayed and I became disoriented, as Dana and I followed Anthony and Cory.

Sergeant Patchett greeted us as we finally found his department. Except for Dana, who waited for us in the ante-room, we were ushered separately into different places, after having our fingerprints taken, "as a matter of course," we were told.

"Do you mind if we record our conversation?" I was asked.

"Not at all," I answered, suddenly feeling vulnerable to the cold gaze of the interrogator.

"At this point in time, we have no idea who committed these crimes," he began. "Perhaps you can help by telling us as much as you know about Leno and Rosemary's activities."

I knew very little, except to tell him what a fine man Leno was and that I was sure Rosemary was just as fine a woman.

"Why did you divorce him?" I heard him asking.

"I don't know. We just drifted apart, but he has always been there for me and the children, whenever we needed him."

I listened to his incredulous accusations concerning Leno's lifestyle and habits, denying that there could be any truth to them.

"Leno loved his horses and must have spent a lot of time at the track, probably gambling," I admitted, "but that did not make him an addictive gambler. As far as being involved in drug dealing or with the Mafia, there is no way this man could have been guilty on that score. No, you have the wrong slant on what might have happened on the tenth of August. Whatever it was, it had nothing to do with Leno's character or credibility." Anger must have been evident in my voice. I *was* angry, although I knew this man was only doing his job. I hoped I had set the record straight.

"You still love him very much, don't you?" he asked.

Tears filled my eyes as I answered, "Yes, I guess I do." I couldn't help thinking, "Whatever our souls were made of, Leno's and mine were the same."

I imagined that the children's answers were similar to mine, as we joined Dana again, and gathered together in the lobby. Two days later we all tearfully attended Dad's funeral, but still somewhat in a state of shock, we were unable to face Dad in his coffin.

Edith attended Dad's funeral with her fiance, Randall Pycha. Randy had never met Dad. Edith had invited him and Alice Ruth over for Sunday dinner to celebrate Dad's birthday and to announce her engagement to Randy. Dad died early that morning.

But before Dad's funeral, we had to face arrangements for Leno's funeral. Sue, Rosemary's daughter, had insisted that Rosemary wanted to be cremated, but Leno's mother and I wanted to have a Catholic funeral for Leno, interring him at Calvary Cemetery, close to where his father was. The children acquiesced.

We had a joint Catholic Rosary for Leno and Rosemary on Friday night and the chapel filled to overflowing with many outside who couldn't get in. Dana had to return to New York, but I joined Leno's family, along with the children, as if I had always been a part of them, had never left to wander in a foreign land.

I thought I had shed all the tears that were in me Friday night, but Saturday morning with the service in the mausoleum, I was devastated. The children sat with Leno's family and I was left alone behind them. How I managed to make it walking alone, down the long stairway to the crypt which was outside in a separate building, I'll never know. I sat next to the children as friends and relatives streamed by to give their condolences, and when Bill came along with Elloree and attempted to kiss me, I instinctively pushed him away.

Remembering "Wuthering Heights" again, I silently pleaded to the lifeless body that lay in the closed casket. "Do not leave me in this world of darkness without you. I cannot live without my life, I cannot die without my soul."

The black limousines took us back to Emma's house, where seeing all my friends from so long ago and feasting on the scrumptious Italian buffet and indulging in several bourbon and sevens, relaxed me and I slowly began to accept the tragedy that had befallen us.

Back on Lido Isle, we faced a nightmare for over three months, jumping each time the phone rang.

Cory refused to sleep in our house and stayed with John's family until she returned to the fall quarter at USU. We all slept with baseball bats and hammers next to our beds.

One evening, several days after the funeral, Anthony answered the phone, and without saying a word, his face turned white. He dropped the phone and ran for the front door, calling to all of us: "Let's get out of this house!"

We all ran after him, getting into the car parked at the curb.

"Who was it, Anthony?" I asked. "What did they say?"

"I don't know," he answered in panic. "I couldn't understand what was being said, but it was crazy and wild and incoherent."

"Let's report this to the police," I suggested as we headed off of the island frantically. The Newport Beach police station was just over the bridge, behind the market, and we all jumped out of the car, probably looking a little wild ourselves. The officer took our report in a disarmingly calm manner and we left.

Edith and Randy were married in September and I don't know if they have ever understood why we couldn't attend their wedding.

We didn't go back to our house on Lido after that phone call, or ever, except to move out. I had purchased a one bedroom apartment a year before in an eight story security building on Newport Bay as an investment. It was vacant now and that's where we went to live. We felt safer and were still there on December second, the birthday of Laura Evans, one of my dearest and closest friends. I was joining her for cocktails at Reubens on the bay, where Mark Davidson was at the piano. He started playing "MacArthur Park" when he saw me come in, knowing it was my favorite.

As I walked toward Laura's table in the bar, she asked nervously: "Have you heard the news?"

"No, what?" I questioned as I sat down, almost afraid to ask.

"They found them. They've been arrested."

I ordered my usual, Harper and Seven, as she talked on, giving me all the details. Mark continued playing and my head began to swim; I felt a knot in my throat and my stomach was nauseous. I couldn't sit there any longer without crying.

"Would you mind if I didn't stay, Laura? I don't feel very good and I'd like to get home to the children."

In September, Oak Terrace had been visited once again when the police department took down the barricade that sealed off the house. Cory and Louise were too afraid to go, but Leno's mother, Anthony and I returned; Mom to clean and gather Leno's clothes to be sent to Italy, Anthony to investigate, and myself to sort out what I wanted to keep for the children.

The house was sold, almost immediately, as if selling would ease the pain and erase the burden of having to care for such a monster, which it had now become.

Then there were the painful legal matters.

"Leno never signed his will, Alice," Howard Alphson reported when I turned to him for advice. "Here it is. He left everything to the children in trust, naming you as trustee, but he hadn't gotten around to signing it. He kept saying he wanted to think it over. The court will have to appoint an administrator."

"I guess Cory would be the logical one," I suggested. "She's twenty-one. Of course, I can help her with the details."

Leno's 26.5 percent of the Company had no appraised value because it was a minority interest, but when the balance of the inventory was assembled and appraised and the creditors' claims all in, the liabilities far outweighed the assets. Everything would have to be sold.

We went to see the horses. Roxie took us to watch "The Kildare Lady" race at Del Mar, a famous seaside race track just north of San Diego. All who knew Leno at the track seemed genuinely fond of him and were saddened and shocked at his tragic death. His horse didn't place in the race, but her trainer, Lou Glauberg, had one who came in first and he invited Cory, Anthony, Louise and Maurine to join him in the winner's circle to be photographed.

"Never Digress" was too feisty at the track and had to be gelded; then was too slow to be a good runner. He was at Lynn Boice's ranch in Corona, along with the brood mares and the unnamed filly, which Maurine and I later named "Leno's Lady."

We all loved the horses and didn't want to part with any of them. Although Maurine was only eleven years old, she helped us make decisions, knowing more than any of us about their care and breeding.

We had to sell all of them that first year, but I purchased "Leno's Lady" and "Never Digress," my favorites. "Leno's Lady" showed promise and we took her to Hemacinto to be trained when she was two. She was so fast that her rider ran her too hard and her two front legs bowed, making it impossible to ever run her in a race. We decided to breed her, which turned out disastrously. She lost her first foal, and I was unable to pay the board bill and stud fee for her second foal, at Springvale, and we

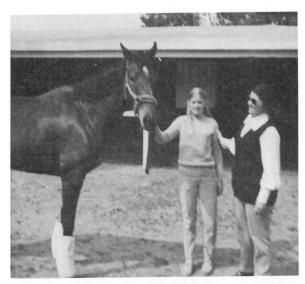

Leno's Lady
at Hollywood Park
with Maurine and me

Maurine on Never Digress

had to sell them both.

Maurine took "Never Digress" to the Orange County Fairgrounds and her trainer, having the horse she had always wanted for her horse shows. As the settling of the estate dragged on for nearly six years, in the end, we had to sell "Never Digress," too.

All that was left to dispose of now was the 26.5 percent interest Leno had in Gateway Markets. No one wanted to buy a minority interest in a business where the chief financial officer and president for eighteen years was gone. The stock would be sold to the highest bidder, ruled the judge.

"The stock is worth considerably more than ten thousand dollars," I spoke up in the courtroom. "We need some time before we can accept the bid."

"Do you want to buy the stock?" the judge asked.

"I might," I heard myself saying. "I'll need time to examine the value more closely."

"I'll give you thirty days to meet the offer made," decided the judge.

I wanted to buy the stock if there was any way to help save the Company and called Pete to suggest we have a meeting; Cory, Anthony and myself with him, Mom and Emma.

"You will have no place on the board," started Pete in an authoritative manner. "There won't be any dividends; there never have been. I don't see any way right now that we can even save the Company."

"If you let the creditors buy the stock, Pete, your position will be weakened. There will be no way you can pull it out," I suggested.

"I wanted to sell right after Leno died," Pete continued, "but Mom wanted to hold on. Now we *have* to hold on, we have no choice."

"I can't put ten thousand dollars into this and not have anything to say about decisions," I insisted.

"That's up to you, Alice," Pete concluded, with a nod from both Mom and Emma.

The issue was closed and the stock was sold in court to one of Leno's creditors for ten thousand dollars, well under the book value of the Company, let alone the appraised value. The proceeds went to pay the attorney and court costs.

I would have had nothing to say as a stockholder, but the creditors had plenty to say and a year later State Wholesale and Gateway Markets were no more.

On a morning, soon after, Corina awoke with tears that wouldn't stop. "My husband and son are both gone. Now the business is lost." She arose and started to dress. Her head was spinning and she fell to the floor, never to regain consciousness.

We followed her to Calvary Cemetery as we had followed Leno, exactly six years before, placing her next to Anthony in the mausoleum.

Cory joined John at the altar.

"Who gives this woman in wedlock?" the minister was asking.

"I do," Anthony answered, then stepped back and sat beside me where Leno should have been.

The preliminaries and vows were audibly distinguishable, but the words were lost in their profound meaning. "Love, honor and cherish, till death do us part," I heard myself repeating, knowing what being faithful to those words meant.

I hadn't been able to keep that promise, but I certainly did love, honor and cherish the *memory* of all of my loves. Rod had said, "You can love someone deeply and not be happy living with them." How true those words were for me. But I have the children now to love and cherish. "Can we expect more from these few short years we journey here?" I wondered. "Love is a powerful, invisible force," I thought.

The wedding was as beautiful as I expected it to be and the reception would be remembered by everyone for a long time. All of Leno's family and friends that had been invited came, and the reception line went on almost all evening with hugs and kisses—sharing memories of all the good days that had gone before.

Loren sang "Love Is A Many Splendored Thing" and I danced with Bill, while his wife slept in the car with a headache. There was plenty of champagne and John's cousin, on crutches from a diving accident, knocked over the wedding cake.

The party didn't break up until the neighbors called the security guard. That was the last party allowed at the clubhouse in the Bluffs in Newport Beach.

But in the end, I went home alone. Louise and Maurine didn't last as long as I did, and had long since gone to bed.

I undressed slowly, stood to look at the moonlight on the back bay, then crawled into bed alone as the tears started—from joy, or, perhaps, from sadness. I knew not which.

"We'll have a great time tonight," I had said to someone in the endless line of well-wishers, "but I'll probably declare bankruptcy next week."

I cried myself to sleep—a fitful sleep. I dreamed of Oak Terrace, as I had many times before.

We four were there again, just as if all those years hadn't happened. It was a Sunday afternoon and the wonderful aroma of spaghetti sauce was in the air. I was setting the table and Dad was watering and cultivating the fruit orchard which sloped down the back of the property

to Los Feliz Boulevard.

Leno suddenly appeared at the back door and for some reason, Mom and I were surprised to see him. He seemed to be returning from a long absence and appeared to be in perfect health, which also surprised us. He smiled as he came toward us and said not to worry, that it didn't hurt anymore. He lifted his shirt to show us that his wounds had healed.

Dad came up the stairs and I wondered how he could be back with us again, but without questions we all sat down to our Sunday dinner and were soon engaged in a typical argument about how the office should be run and why we didn't open more markets.

Suddenly, it all began to fade and Leno said he couldn't stay. After all, we were divorced, and although there was no one else in his life, he had to give more thought to our being married again.

That horrible feeling of emptiness came back and I awoke, as I had often done, sobbing with feelings of regret for all the wasted years without Leno.

My room seemed misty, I thought. Perhaps the fog had rolled in through the open window. Then I heard Italian singing coming from what sounded like a radio in the other room. I remembered how aggravated I used to get on Sunday mornings at Oak Terrace when Leno was overseas and the radio would wake me up with Italian singing. Puzzled, I stumbled out of bed, but didn't feel my usual aches and pains. I walked without difficulty, much to my surprise. "My prayers must have helped," I thought.

As I looked around the room, I realized I was in my old bedroom on Oak Terrace that I had occupied while Leno was in Germany. I decided I must still be dreaming. I looked in the mirror and discovered that I was young and thin again.

But it couldn't be a dream. I felt more alive than I had in years! I quietly opened the door, not knowing what to expect. The house was quiet, except for the Italian singing. I looked into the front bedroom. The bed was made and, except for the broken lamp in the corner, it all looked exactly as I remembered it. I opened the bathroom door. The shower was running but no one was there. I turned off the water. By this time, my eyes were beginning to well up and I was trembling.

I walked into the living room expecting to see it as I remembered it last. But there was no blood on the floor and no vulgar markings on the walls. The red couches were gone, replaced by the furniture of Leno's mother and father. The china closet with the ornate glass door was there as before in the dining room with all of Mom's dishes.

I heard conversation coming from the breakfast room. Mom and Dad were speaking Italian, so I didn't know what they were saying. I was afraid to go in, fearing it would all disappear. Tears were now streaming down my face. I had missed these people and this house for so long that I didn't dare hope they were really here. I opened the door and stepped in.

Dad spoke up in his usual harsh tone at my display of emotion. "What's the matter with you? Pull yourself together!"

"You're here. I can't believe you're really here," I sobbed uncontrollably.

"Of course, we're here. You're the one who's going. I thought you were leaving for Marysville at six this morning." Dad was visibly annoyed.

"You mean I haven't left to go meet Leno in Marysville yet?" I asked in wonder and disbelief.

"No, honey, you were going to leave this morning so you would be there by the time he arrived tonight. It's a fourteen hour drive." Mom spoke with kindness.

"I don't know what's wrong," I stammered. "I must have had a bad dream, but it lasted so long and was so real."

"Well, it's nine o'clock," Dad said abruptly. "You'd better get ready to go."

"Dad, I wanted to go alone, but," the tears were coming again, "will you and Mom go with me? Let's all go meet Leno together."

"We're all ready to go," spoke up Mom. "We knew you wouldn't leave without us."

Dad didn't say a word. He picked up his coat, went out the back door, backed his 1941 Buick out of the garage and came back into the house to get our luggage.

I was ready in no time, and as Mom locked the back door and came toward the car, I felt a peace and contentment that I had never known.

We were all together and on our way to see Leno after his absence of nearly twenty months. As we drove down the steep driveway, the fog began to lift and was gone by the time we reached the road.